D0262528

WINNING THEIR SPURS

WINNING THEIR SPURS

The Tottenham Hotspur Dream Team

JEREMY NOVICK

EDINBURGH AND LONDON

For Gilly, Elly, Maxwell C. Wolf, Lily-belle and
Joshua-Louis who came and went
but will come back soon.

First published in Great Britain in 1996 by
MAINSTREAM PUBLISHING COMPANY (EDINBURGH) LTD
7 Albany Street
Edinburgh EH1 3UG

ISBN 1 85158 873 6

A catalogue record for this book is available from the British Library

Typeset in New Century Schoolbook by Bibliocraft, Dundee

Printed and bound in Great Britain
by Butler & Tanner Ltd, Frome, Somerset

CONTENTS

ACKNOWLEDGEMENTS

In a fancy hotel just outside Belfast, the members of the German national team are getting themselves together in preparation for Euro 96. A press conference is called for the German media and the assembled journalists, sportswriters and TV crews gather to ask team captain Jürgen Klinsmann how it's all going. The questions fly around (in German), cameras flash, other cameras roll and Jürgen deals with them all with his customary grace. The air is full of laughter and confident cheer when a young English voice pipes up: 'Excuse me. Jürgen, what was the greatest game you played for Spurs?'

I'd like to thank Cliff Jones, Ron Henry, Pat Jennings, Gary Lineker and Keith Burkinshaw who all asked me round for tea and ended up giving me coffee; Bill Nicholson, who turned out to be the sweetest man; Glenn Hoddle, who saw me even though he must have had other things on his mind (it was the day before his new job was announced); Gary Mabbutt, Ralph Coates and John Duncan who all let me into their worlds; Garth Crooks, Dave Mackay and Steve Perryman who all made my phone bill a wonder to behold; and Jürgen Klinsmann who smiled back and said, 'Sure'.

Thanks also to club historian Andy Porter, a man who almost knows more about Spurs than there is to know; Jacqui Crawley; Peter Martin, who would have seen more matches if he could have brought himself to watch; Martin and Katie for supplying the good news; Rob for being Rob; Davies . . . We could go on all day. Then there are the good folk of Mainstream – Judy Diamond, Bill . . . And British Midland . . .

Meanwhile, back in the real world . . . Elly for making life perfect;

Maxwell C. Wolf, still the ultimate embodiment of 'being'; my mum and dad, sister, her family . . . and Gilly. Gilly, without whom it wouldn't have been possible . . . Transcribing tapes, understanding the double team, finding me becoming increasingly reliant on the word 'obviously', listening to theories on the significance of Ralph Coates, chasing round looking for Alan Gilzean . . . Poor, long-suffering Gilly.

'I'm going out with Maxwell and Elly. You coming?' she says.

'Sorry, love. I'm half-way through Gary Mabbutt.'

Still, by the time you read this, I'll obviously have thanked her properly.

PROLOGUE

Picture this for a moment. We're approaching the climax of the football season and things are tight. It looks as though it could go to a photo finish, and Manchester United are the team nearest the camera. After a few years of rebuilding and consolidating, Alex Ferguson has moulded his team, nipping and tucking and now they are near. He is near. All the pieces of the jigsaw are there, it's just a question of finding the knob that turns the volume up to twelve. No one doubts that they'll win the League, it's 'when' rather than 'if'. There are four matches left to play; three home matches against low or middle of the table opposition and one crunch game – away to title rivals Wolves, who are going for a unique FA Cup and League double.

It's Easter Saturday. The sun is shining, the birds are singing and the crowd is well up for it. The ground is full, bursting with song and anticipation. The atmosphere is celebratory and today's visitors, let's say West Ham, are merely guests at the party. Bring a bottle, join in the fun. Why not? They're safe from relegation, have no chance of winning anything and are just playing out time.

The game gets off to a cracking start, with the pitch resembling a one-way street. Even West Ham, it seems, are attacking their own end. The three points are there; no ifs, no buts. Half-time's approaching and, even though there's no score, there's no concern either. Then, just as the oranges are being peeled, Giggs is brought down in the box. Penalty. There's probably time for the kick – the goal – the celebration and nothing else. What a perfect way to end the half. The air is filled with that curious mix of silent anticipation and deafening tension. Up steps the mercurial Eric Cantona to take the kick. Cantona the wizard, the crowd favourite, the club's talisman – it had to be him. In the split second between Cantona's foot making contact with the ball and the ball being propelled on its way, the silence breaks. The roar that was always there becomes audible. Extraordinary. The kick is saved and silence again descends – a raw, unreal silence; a mass grave of silence. Almost in slow motion, the ball rebounds off the goalkeeper. As ever, Cantona is the quickest to react. The ball flies into the net and Old Trafford erupts. Cantona – cool, sharp, Cantona – looks like ice, but inside feels like a man on Death Row who's been given a 13th-hour reprieve. The referee points to the centre of the pitch and, after the kissy celebrations, the teams go to reconvene for the kick-off. But the referee isn't walking to the centre spot. He's walking off the pitch. Okay, it's half-time. There isn't even time to re-start the game.

But something's happened. Something's not quite right. Slowly and silently word gets out and the truth starts to dawn.

You're following the story so far? Remember all this is happening in the space of a few minutes and in an atmosphere that, if it weren't such a cliché, we'd call electric.

As the players walk off the pitch, Alex Ferguson goes to meet them. He looks calm and thoughtful, a touch serious, but that's the nature of the man. The eye conversation, the body language of the players and the crowd's disbelieving silence confirms what has happened. The goal has been disallowed. In the nano-second between the ball rebounding off the goalkeeper and Cantona striking it into the net, the referee had blown for half-time. By the time the ball had crossed the line, the half was over. The ball hit the net in half-time. The 'goal' is disallowed. The score is 0–0.

During the half-time team talk, the players are a bit down, but Ferguson's having none of it.

'That's the rules of the game. The rules are the rules and that's that. If you can't accept that then you shouldn't be playing.' The players know he's right and decide to get on with it. They'll still win.

But this is a story and not all stories have happy endings. As the game progresses and time starts to run out, United get edgy. They throw more players forward in search of that goal, in search of those vital points. Gaps appear at the back and, during one of West Ham's rare counter-attacks, they score: 0–1. That's it. Manchester United lose.

After the game, Ferguson appears and tells the press: 'That's the rules of the game. The rules are the rules and that's that. If you can't accept that then you shouldn't be playing.'

As if to compound the grief, a few days later United beat Wolves 3–1 at Molineux, but it's not enough. They lose the championship by three points, the three West Ham points, that penalty, that nano-second, that decision.

It's a nonsense story, of course. Elly, my nine-month-old daughter, would yawn at the fantasy. A much more likely scenario is this:

The referee blows his whistle and signals half-time. Cantona stares coldly at him, walks over and breaks his spine with a jujitsu kick. As the players gather around, pandemonium breaks out. Alex Ferguson rushes on to the pitch screaming that the goalie had moved before the kick had been taken, that there were players encroaching on the penalty area, the kick must be retaken the kick must be retaken the kick must be retaken the goal stands the kick must be retaken mother mother the kick must be retaken . . . Eventually Ferguson, froth dribbling down his chin, grabs the ball and the whistle out of the prostrate referee's mouth and, after kicking the ball into the net, blowing his whistle and running around the pitch in triumph, falls over and dies of a heart attack. Now Elly's laughing with delight. You can't beat a good story.

The curious thing about this story is that it's true – the first version, that is, the unbelievable version. It actually happened in the 1959–60 season, but it wasn't Manchester United, it was Spurs. And it wasn't West Ham, it was Manchester City. And it wasn't Eric Cantona, it was Cliff Jones. And it wasn't Alex Ferguson, it was Bill Nicholson. Everything else, though, is true – the situation, the penalty, the whistle, the decision, the result. Everything, right down to the 3–1 win at Wolves, is true.

Nicholson said: 'That's the rules of the game. The rules are the rules and that's that. If you can't accept that then you shouldn't be playing.'

> If you can get today right, it makes yesterday a pleasant memory and tomorrow a vision of hope.
>
> Danny Blanchflower

Telling that story like this isn't meant disrespectfully to either Ferguson or Cantona, or to make a snide comment about the Old Trafford notion of sportsmanship. Hell, no. You see, times were different then. Jones had only been out of national service for two years, Nicholson's hair was still in the army. Possibly the reason that Nicholson, Jones and the rest of the Spurs team behaved more like menschen than like a bunch of spoilt brats was that they knew what they had. What they had was the finest club team the world had ever seen. Maybe the finest club team the world would ever see.

But the story's more than that. It's not just a 'times were different then' story. It's a Spurs story. Maybe it's time to drag up Danny Blanchflower's oft-repeated dictum: 'The game is about glory. It is about doing things in style, with a flourish, about going out and beating the other lot, not waiting for them to die of boredom.'

Trying to articulate an intangible quality like an institution's personality is a near-impossibility, but Tottenham Hotspur Football Club defines itself with a crystal clarity that cannot be denied. It's something that non-football fans will never – can never – understand, how teams have definite, recognisable personalities that exist in themselves, irrespective of the particular personnel at the club at any given time. Take a match played on 19 November 1887, the first-ever match between Spurs and the Arsenal. Legend has it that the Arsenal turned up late, scored an early goal, defended resolutely for the rest of the match against a vibrant attacking Spurs team before losing 2–1. It could be 1987 and it will probably be 2087. That's the Arsenal and that's Spurs.

Spurs play with a flourish, with a dash. They will entertain, dazzle, infuriate, dismay. Spurs, in their classic all-white strip, will play like Di Stefano's Real Madrid in some glory-filled European competition, then lose at home to Southampton. Spurs will win the FA Cup, but never the League Championship. And, somehow, the fans wouldn't have it any other way. Time and again, you'll hear Spurs fans bemoan their inconsistency whilst saying – in a completely up-front way – that they just wouldn't tolerate a team that specialised in grinding out grim 1–0 victories.

Irving Scholar saying 'Arsenal will spend one million pounds on a solid, safe defender while we will spend one and a half million on an exciting, erratic attacker' can be dismissed partly as PR and partly because Scholar was, at heart, a fan. But what about a player's perspective on these notional ideas; the image, the face, the clichés.

Gary Lineker: 'I don't think they're clichés. Probably watching Spurs and the Arsenal proves the point, even though there are spells where that is not the case. I mean, you look at this season, 1995–96, and Spurs haven't exactly been flamboyant. They've been very solid, well organised, well disciplined up front, and Arsenal, although they haven't been particularly expressive, they've got the likes of Bergkamp, Wright – people who've got real flair. So I suppose there's not that much truth in it, but it would be a shame to think otherwise, wouldn't it?'

Garth Crooks: 'It's absolutely correct to say that the personality of a club exists above and beyond anything else. It grows with the history of the club. Entertainment has always been an important feature of the Spurs game and it's been something which the fans have always demanded. It's a continental philosophy and they can never get away from that. If they did, it would bring down the management. In any given situation you've got to define what your goals are and, for example, Arsenal's goal wasn't to entertain; it was to win. When you go into White Hart Lane, you're always likely to hear the clinking of champagne glasses, but if you go across the road to Finsbury Park and Highbury, you see sharp Windsor knots and stiff collars. When you go to the core of the clubs, that's what you find. I think that the core with Spurs is a club that wants to entertain, that wants to bring a smile to people's faces. You go to Arsenal and the first and foremost thing is that they're professional and they want to win – and if a smile comes thereafter, so be it. It's something I've always sensed.'

For anyone watching Spurs in the mid to late 1960s – or anyone watching football, come to think of it – it was the double team that held the allure. Maybe they attained their glow because they were gone, but I don't think so. More probably it was because they represented an excellence, a purity and – possibly this is an important one – a time when Spurs were winning everything in sight. It was a magical time, extraordinary in a way that no other time can be; freeze-dried between monochrome and colour, between Presley and the Beatles. I bet, if pushed, your average Arsenal fan could name the double team. Curiously, and I swear that this isn't prejudice, I couldn't name the Arsenal's double-winning team. I'm a football fan, but I can't. Really, you'd fall asleep before you got to the goalkeeper.

Cliff Jones: 'The special thing about the double is that we did it with style. I'm not taking anything away from the Arsenal, but when we did it, we did it with flair. We entertained while we got the results. And you look at the number of people who came to see us that season – two million people. Two million people. And that was just in the League. About 400,000 watched us in the Cup run. You'd never get that today because of the grounds. We put bums on seats. They'd get value for money. That was Bill's criteria. Winning wasn't enough, it all had to be done with style and flair. We were very effective. Bill had it spot on. Yup – lovely days, they were. It was a pleasure and a privilege, and we got paid for it. Can't be bad.'

The double team came at a perfect time, an era on the cusp. Previously, the televisual techniques of the day involved camerawork that flashed around trying to find the ball while the commentator's voice tried to get into its dinner jacket, and so the era of Burgess, Ditchburn and Duquemin was lost. Afterwards, football was swathed in Brian Moore familiarity. The early 1960s struck exactly the right balance between mystery and accessibility. Even if you weren't brought up in a particular part of north London, and even if you didn't live in a Spurs household, you're not going to tell me that names like Moore, Peters and Hurst held more romance than White, Jones and Blanchflower.

Of course, there weren't any *Match of the Day* greatest hits videos – *Now That's What I Call Football!* – or UK Gold-type reruns playing over and over again. There was a bit of musty old footage, but that provided just a glimpse, a chance almost to see what it was like – Bill Brown running across the face of his goal, flat cap on tight, bouncing the ball like he's Meadowlark Lemon or something; Bobby Smith charging into goalkeepers like they were doors he was trying to open; Cliff Jones flying down the wing, taking on players, beating them, bloodying his head, scoring. Such tantalising glimpses proved that all you'd heard was true, but didn't really tell you much more; they merely confirmed what you already knew.

The other thing about Spurs is that, invariably, they're the first. They might not be the best, or the most successful or the most durable, but invariably they're the first. They were the first to win the double – and don't give me Wessex Athletic or Preston or any other such pedantic historical nonsense. Spurs were the first team to win the double and that's that. They were the first to win a European trophy. They were the first to embrace foreign stars. They were the first to embrace Thatcherite greed. They were the first to go public. They were the first to usher in the current wave of European superstars. They were always the first and, as happens with the first, they sometimes got burned. But they had the vision and they were brave enough to do it. That's style.

To a young boy growing up, the allure of Tottenham Hotspur – the dashing romance, the elegant sufferings, the triumph of style over the mundanity of result – was simply too much to resist. What greater life model could you want? What better values could you aspire to? I could not comprehend how anyone could choose to throw their emotional weight behind any other team.

It's 1966–67; the era of Greaves and Jennings, Dave Mackay and Alan Gilzean, who curiously looked older than my father though logic says he was probably only in his mid-20s. Pure white shirts, dark blue shorts and socks; nothing on the kit save the club cockerel and a number. I remember as yesterday a home game against Burnley. We beat them 7–0; Cliff Jones scored the last goal running from outside the box and flinging himself forward to meet a low cross with a diving header. As the ball flew into the corner of the net, Jones's momentum carried him through and he crashed into the post, concussing himself. It was a typical moment – one-part brave, one-part heroic and three-parts mad. Typical of Jones. Typical of Spurs.

Wildly and romantically exaggerated memories they may be but they are nevertheless my memories and they can't be polluted by cold facts. When I went to see Jones to talk to him about his greatest game, I couldn't help but ask about that Burnley game. He remembered the game instantly and started rabbiting on about it, his Welsh lilt combining with a boyish enthusiasm to bring it back to life in technicolor. Then he got to his goal.

'I think it was 5–2 or something like that. I knew it was going to happen, but I thought, "Ah, let's have some of it, see what happens."'

Now, unless Jones scored two identical goals against Burnley in two identical matches and sustained two identical injuries, one of us has got the small matter of the score completely wrong. Driving back from his house, I went from being curious to know the truth to resolving not to look in any of the 3,678 Tottenham Hotspur fact books that litter my home. The thing is, who cares what the real score was? (Most people, probably, but I'll let them look it up.) In a very real sense, individual memories become 'fact' because that's what's locked in the mind – the actuality exists only in the pages of those 3,678 Tottenham Hotspur fact books.

A reservoir of memories waiting to happen, that's what football is to me. Okay, in truth it may be that football in the 1990s is a commercial enterprise peopled by professionals making a living and fuelling a number of different parasitic worlds (including mine) that wouldn't and couldn't exist without it. But for all the talk of mega-million salaries and multi-zillion transfer fees, for all the bitchy comments about teams and their ever expanding kit collections, and for all the sleazy stories from its underbelly, football is about romance. Without it, nothing else would exist.

I am a product of that archetypal father/son relationship, the men going to the football together. Partly as a bonding tool and, more likely, as a legitimate way of ensuring that he got to see the match, every Saturday, my father took me to the football. Maybe it was because we lived just up the road in Stamford Hill, maybe because we are Jewish (stereotypes and clichés are rooted in truth). More probably it was because my father was a Spurs fan and I gave him a good excuse to go there rather than whatever the mid-1960s equivalent of B&Q was. Whatever the reason, we ended up going to the Spurs. It's a well-worn truth, but this is one of life's eternal relationships: a boy, his father and their football team. It's something that you can never escape and it's possibly the one thing that can explain someone's lifelong devotion to a Grimsby or an Arsenal. Who was it who said that you can change your wife but not your football team?

As I got older I became more and more convinced of the wisdom of my father's choice in taking me to the Spurs. Blind support, that was without question; but Spurs, as we've seen, seemed to embody all that I thought right and good. We both, I rationalised, lived in a world where you did things with a certain style, with a smile, an enjoyment of the moment.

If you were brought up where and when I was, you couldn't help but be a Spurs fan. The Orient – Leyton Orient then – was up the road, just across Walthamstow marshes, and they were a fine team, possessing in their number the legendary Mark Lazarus, an 'out' Jewish player who moaned about playing on the Sabbath, took Jewish holidays off work and had a body language laced with more Yiddish inflections than a dozen Aunt Sadies. Orient were great, but they were like a best friend, not a lover. You'd laugh at the Orient, never cry. There was also another team in my part of north London, but they inspired less romance than a night in with the phone book; just as predictable, though. Being a Jewish Buddhist, I always figured that your football club was pre-ordained, a karma deal. Maybe if you were a goat last time around, a good goat, and the gods wanted to reward you with human status but weren't sure, they fixed up a kind of probation, a provisional human licence. Arsenal fans.

Manchester United was the only option, the only other team with anything like the charisma needed to encourage a young boy to give up valuable bird-watching time. So there was Best, Law and Charlton and there was the tragedy of Munich, but even then it didn't compare with the Spurs. Distance aside – supporting a football club based over 200 miles away always did seem nonsense, bestowing instant fair-weather status – United really didn't compare. The sage that was Blanchflower, the legend that was John White, the flying bandage that was Cliff Jones, the no-bullshit John Wayne-ism of Dave Mackay – these were heroes for whom it was worth foregoing the intense pleasure of looking for herons on Hackney marshes.

Inevitably, the players chosen for this book reflect my relationship with both Spurs and football. The boom time was in the late 1960s to late 1970s when I started going with my father and then with my friends, carefully missing out a couple of joyously adolescent years at the turn of the decade when I wouldn't be seen dead out with a parent. Piqued (by this and a million other things: 'Spending a fortune on platform boots and then wearing a pair of trousers where the sole requisite was that the flare be big enough to cover the shoe! What's the matter with you? Are you mad?'), the parents retaliated by saying that I was too young to go by myself. Going to college in Manchester in 1979 put paid to all thoughts of football. There are more interesting things to do when you're a student than stand on rain-sodden terraces. There's an education to be had. A post-college early 1980s interest was soon sacrificed as I left the country, hounded out by a succession of failed relationships and the, to me, abhorrent culture of the time.

On becoming a father, I started to take an interest in football again. It was good enough for me and my father, it's going to be good enough for me and Elly. Okay, so she's only nine months old, but there's new evidence to suggest that children are developing a pre-foetal consciousness earlier these days. And what type of father would I be if I ignored all the possibilities? Suppose she heard, on the radio or something, the words 'the' and 'Arsenal' in conjunction. What then? A lifetime of conflict and analysts bills. Anyway, she goes to sleep thinking 'Spurs', or at least she would if she could read the words on her baby-gro.

This is possibly the truth, but in fairness it's also possibly a lie to cover up for the fact that certain Spurs 'greats' wouldn't talk. Jimmy Greaves, Joe Kinnear, Alan Mullery and Chris Waddle sadly never got any of my many calls, faxes or letters (for surely if they had, they would have had the courtesy to reply). One player made a wage demand so excessive it was ten years ahead of its time, and one midfielder was kept at arm's length by his not-so-daft agent.

There's always a danger in meeting your heroes: odds-on, they're going to disappoint. At the very least, they'll be distressingly ordinary. The potential prat-fall here was obvious. You're dealing with a group of people whose greatest achievements are in the past, whose fame came when they were still in short trousers. Generally though, the players I spoke to were absolutely lovely, real gems.

Only one player managed both to upset and disappoint, and this was without us even meeting.

'I'm putting together a book on Spurs . . . '

'I'm not interested.'

'Give me a minute, please. Let me sell the idea to you. '

'Go on then.'

'I want to get players from the dou . . . '

'I thought you said you were going to sell me the idea. Look, I'm a working man.'

'Are you asking for mon . . .' (Sound of phone being put down.)

Anyway, who needs to speak to an early 1970s skulking manatee of a centre-forward who always looked miserable as sin? Great player, crap dinner party guest.

Of the players featured, none need a special reason for being here. But . . .

Cliff Jones was my very own boyhood hero. A great player, he was mad, passionate and joyous to watch – everything a sportsman should be. It was he who inspired me to be a Spurs boy and, in keeping with this, he was the first person I approached. A Spurs team with no Cliff Jones would be like a Tory government that worked. Ron Henry was at Spurs 20 years as a player and, so far, has been there for 20 years as a coach. He joined when Bill Nicholson was in the team, he played in the great double team and he nursed Glenn Hoddle when he was a boy; a diamond. Ralph Coates was a legend in his own time, always top value for money, guaranteed entertainment. But if hair gel had been invented ten years earlier, he might never have made it here. John Duncan was the one bright light in an otherwise very sad, dull period. Bill Nick went, Terry Neill came; Pat Jennings went, Barry Daines came; Division One went, Division Two came. Sad days, those years. It really doesn't matter whether or not John Duncan would have got into Spurs teams of other eras. That's picky. His goals got us back.

Glenn Hoddle was simply the best footballer, Spurs or otherwise, I've ever seen, and living proof that God felt guilty after so selfishly selecting John White for his team. Garth Crooks flourished in potentially the best post-double team Spurs had. The team went to

Wembley seven times in 18 months, and anyway, if Steve Perryman says that that's the best Spurs side, then that's the best Spurs side. Also, this was the era of Archibald, Burkinshaw and Scholar. Fun times. Gary Lineker is a great striker and played in the 1990 team that I started watching again when I came back to England. Jürgen Klinsmann made the sort of impact in one season that most players couldn't manage in three careers.

Finally, if you need an explanation of why Dave Mackay, Pat Jennings, Steve Perryman and Gary Mabbutt are included here, stop reading now.

Great players all, but consider it as a team: Jennings in goal; Henry, Mabbutt and Perryman at the back; Mackay just in front of them supporting Hoddle and Coates in midfield; Crooks, Jones, Klinsmann and Lineker up front and Duncan on the bench. The way teams win doubles these days (do they come free with six packets of Rice Krispies or what?), that team would win a quadruple. They'd be lining up to score. At the end of each season, they'd walk away with Safeway's bags full of silverware.

There was only one player I wanted in the team (and I mean *really* wanted) who I couldn't get – the Scottish soldier, Alan Gilzean. 'Campbeltown Loch, I wish you were whisky, then I'd drink you dry' – that was his favourite song. Bacardi and Coke Gilly we called him. What a player, what a character; lovely man. When I pointed out to Cliff Jones that no one knew where Gilly was now, he laughed his Welsh laugh.

'And most probably Gilly doesn't know either. Someone said he'd gone back to Scotland. He had his problems. He liked the ladies and they liked him, being the type he is. Aye, he was a bit of a lad. I don't know where he is, God bless him. When you do find him, give him my best.'

Alan Gilzean was the king of White Hart Lane. Initially, I wanted to meet Gilly because he was a great player, a real boyhood hero. But he wasn't only that; he was also a great comic hero. Mention Gilzean to any Spurs fan and they'll have the same mental picture: a bald, greying man, who looked nothing like a top-class professional athlete, delicately and expertly flicking the ball on at the near post. The notion of finding Gilzean became a bit of an obsession.

Bill Nicholson said: 'Ahh, Gilly. The mystery man. No idea. I've no idea where he is.' Then, for a minute, Nicholson went off, back in time. 'Great with those flicked headers. The way he could just . . . flick . . . the ball . . .'

Ralph Coates said: 'Ahh, Gilly. If I had a pound for every time someone asked me where Gilly was. But no. No idea.'

I chased a few journalist contacts. Nothing. My publishers, who are based in Scotland and who pride themselves on knowing everything and everyone in Scotland, suggested a town where he might or might not be. Might not.

There's a story in Hunter Davies's classic book *The Glory Game* about Joe Kinnear, then a 24-year-old lad about town, and Gilly: 'Joe said he'd once gone with Gilly on a Saturday evening on the town but had to give up half-way. He couldn't stand the pace.'

This is the footballer who looks like my Uncle Alf. The game's over and he goes partying. Increasingly intrigued, I started watching old tapes of pre-Alf era Gilzean, round about 1965. It was delightful. The way he moved was like no one else. Where Greaves lacerated, Gilzean danced. He was like a ballet dancer, consummately skilful, running on tip-toes as if the ground were made of ice. For a big man, he had beautiful balance, beating players by look. And even then, he could flick the ball.

The more I found out about Gilzean, the better it got. The first time Spurs ever clapped eyes on him was on 11 November 1964 in the John White memorial match; destiny angel. Every player I interviewed for this book I asked, 'Oh, one last thing. Have you any idea where Gilly is?' The older players, like Ron Henry or Dave Mackay, all laughed. Who was that masked man? The younger players knew less than I did, but said so in a tone laced with awe and respect.

Mackay was Gilly's room-mate in the old days.

'He's okay, is Gilly. He was my mate. He's back at Arbroath now, isn't he? I've been back every couple of years and I've asked after him, but no one's heard about him. He's a bit of a recluse.'

He was a bit of a lad then?

'Och aye. You're only young once. Enjoy yourself while you're in the pink.'

John Duncan said that Gilly knew his wife when she was growing up in Dundee. And now?

'I heard he's in London. Isn't he?'

I found out a few things. Of all the Spurs players, past and present, Gilly's the only one who has never returned to White Hart Lane, the only one who's never taken advantage of the courtesy luxury boxes that ex-players can have. He never gives interviews. He considers that his Spurs career was a great part of his life, but a part that's over. It's a wonderful, admirable attitude. I checked the newspaper cuttings libraries. Nothing.

By now I was feeling the same way about Gilly as I felt about the Loch Ness Monster or the Yeti. I do believe he exists – there's conclusive film evidence and loads of personal testimonies – but live and let live and respect his wish to be left alone. I knew he had a son, Ian, so I tracked him down and asked him. Ian said he'd love to help, but he had no idea. Let me take your number and I'll call you if I hear anything.

My wife got in touch with a friend of a friend, a man familiar with the workings of the bottle who now lives out near Inverness but still knows the wallpaper patterns in every bar in Scotland. If Gilzean was there, he'd find him. A couple of days later he phoned back and told me that Gilly drank at a particular bar in Edinburgh. (It'd be unfair to name the bar. The last thing they need is millions of tourists and sightseers.) I'd heard of it. It was a bohemian hang-out, a French House, a La Coupole, a place with a reputation for sheltering philosophising bar-flies, lush artists and nocturnal dreamers. The bar manager had never heard of Gilzean. Naturally.

But for any book about Spurs, there's only one person to talk to, one place to start.

1

THOUGHTS OF A MANAGER

Bill Nicholson

Bill Nicholson: 'Perhaps the greatest game was winning the Cup-Winners' Cup beating Atletico Madrid in Rotterdam. It was a wonderful atmosphere there, the stadium is very nice at Rotterdam and we were allowed to take our wives along, which was unusual at the time. When you went to Wembley, you took your wife. Well, they didn't come with us, but they were there. But my wife had a bit of a jinx about her – when she came we invariably lost, and she didn't come very often because of that. We all tried to keep her away. The players used to say, "Your wife's not coming, is she Bill?" and I'd say, "Oh, no." And they'd say, "Oh, that's all right then." But in the European Cup ties, she used to come after the match for the reception which were very nice occasions.

'I'm pretty sure that she was in Rotterdam but that was one of the occasions when we won. It was at the time when we did the double and the following year we played in Europe and we got beaten in the semi-final rather badly. We should have won that one. That was Benfica. I said to the lads, "If we can beat Benfica, we can win the Cup," because I didn't fancy Real Madrid. We'd had a bit of bad luck around the penalty area. You can always say these things about the referees and what have you, and we complained about them, but you've got to take the rough with the smooth. When we played them here, we did enough to win the game handsomely. We hit the crossbar, the woodwork and did everything but score. But at the same time we lost the European Cup, we won the FA Cup so the following year, because we hadn't won the League, we were in the Cup-Winners' Cup. I used to say we're nothing if we're not in Europe.

'The attitude at the time was good and everybody enjoyed it. Terry

Dyson scored two goals for us and he did very well. It was probably the best game he ever played for Tottenham. He was a grand lad and played just in front of Dave Mackay. They were very good friends and Dyson, who hadn't been playing all that regularly, played well. Now Dyson is only the size of two pence a cuppa, he was even smaller than Jonesy, but he had a good left on him. He played more like a winger, but at the same time, cutting in when possible. I think that if you're rigid in your play, you become rigid for the opposition; Whereas if you're elusive, you're elusive for the opposition, they're worried about where to find you, whether you're going to do this or that. If you're set in your ways, that makes it easier for them.

'Jonesy, yes, he was one of my favourite players. But strangely enough, he wasn't a regular player. I think he was injured a lot. He broke his leg or something. But Jonesy was a good player. Most of the full-backs were afraid of playing against Jonesy. He was very fast for his size, good in the air. He was a really good bloke – no doubt about that.

'Now Jonesy could take a ball past a player easily. He was playing on the left as a right-footed player. When he ran at someone, he'd run past them on the inside, so he was going into danger, but he was also going into the opposition because that's where they are. And when the next bloke comes along, he runs past him too, so now we're back in the middle of the field right out in front; he can either have a whack himself or he can push the ball to someone over there because he sometimes meets two men on the way. As I used to say, "If you beat one man, you've automatically beaten two men," because the next one's there to be beaten. So now he's beaten three because he's going to beat the third with his pass.

'I think the players in those days used to cross the ball more accurately. Anyone should be able to cross a ball. If you're playing in the Premier League, you ought to be able to miss a bloke coming at you. You don't want to hit him with the ball – if you do, you've given the ball away and you don't want to do that. You want to get past him, so you look for a white shirt. So many times you see on the television somebody who tries to cross the ball, and you wonder what they're doing. I feel like saying, "What's your objective? If you can't bloody do it, then don't bloody go for it. Go for something that you can do."

'When someone kicks the ball forward, they've already got more men than we've got and they nip in and intercept it. Very often, if the ball goes long, they've got more players and it's the same thing.

And someone somewhere along the line must feel responsible for saying well that's how you play. You don't give the ball away. And I say you've got to give the ball away in the end – you've got to go forward into a defence which outnumbers your attack. Think about it. If you lose the ball you become a defender, but when you win the ball, you become an attacker. That applies to everybody in the team – it doesn't matter whether you're a centre-forward or a centre-back, a centre-half as it used to be. When you attack, you try to lose the opponent. This used to be, in my opinion, one of our good habits. We had a lot of slogans in those days and we would say "engage or disengage", a simple thing, anyone could think about that. So you kick the ball and your team-mates are thinking about disengaging. When you're in charge because you've got the ball and your team's in possession, if one of your team-mates disengages, you can pass him the ball. But as soon as we lose possession of the ball, we think about engaging. Look for your man – where is he?

'I used another slogan: "The man without the ball – he makes the play." When the other team gets possession, there's only one man who's got the ball. Who's he going to pass it to? It depends on who makes themselves available, doesn't it? That was, I think, a very practical way of employing simplicity. Players think about that while they're playing, because they don't think about many things.

'When we first started, it was three at the back, two wing-halves, two inside-forwards and three up front. When you talk about the game now, you hear about this system. What is it now, the Christmas tree? But when you get playing, players have got to move. Movement creates movement. Don't bloody stand there – move. The fact that you move from here to there means that you leave a space, someone fills it in and creates another space.

'A lot of people say that the game has changed, and I say, "I don't agree. Tell me how." Some of the players think that the game is harder now and again I say, "How? You play for 90 minutes. The pitch is the same size as it always was. The goal's the same size. The game's still the same, you've still got to score goals." But, you know, we used to play in leather boots and we had leather balls. I suppose the boots they wear now are very comfortable. We used to sprint . . . you'd spend no end of time breaking your boots in in those days. You got a new pair of boots. You put them on, without any socks or anything, because you had a job to put them on. Then you put your feet in water, with your boots on, do some running with the boots on, a bit of kicking, but it was several weeks before you could play in them boots. We used to say, "We've got to break the boots in, so let's make them last as long as we can." I don't know whether or not the club asked you to do that to save money . . . No, definitely not. It was a bloody awful job. You don't have to do that now because the boots you get now are so good.

'I think that the best colour we ever played in was all-white when we played in Europe with white stockings. A white shirt looks beautiful. A couple of weeks ago, my wife came downstairs wearing a football shirt with Spurs' cockerel on it. It was one of the old type, no buttons, just a round neck, and I said, "Good God, where d'you get that?"

'"I bought it," she said.

'"Where did you buy it?"

'"Down the Spurs."

'"That's bloody better than what we're playing in now."

'They're lovely shirts – it looked good. We did wear blue shorts in the League matches. In European matches we wore white. A lot of teams play in white, don't they? It must be a favourite colour. I don't know if the people who make the modern shirts try to persuade you to use a colour that they would like as a substitute. If I were the manager I would say they'd have to suit me; I want what's right for the players.'

These days the sign on the door of Bill Nicholson's office at White Hart Lane says 'Consultant'. In there he sits, reminiscing, talking, consulting. In a society that so readily consigns its elders, the holders of wisdom, to the dump, and years after Spurs treated Nicholson with unbelievable disrespect, it's good to see; an example of how things should be.

On the wall behind his desk hangs a picture of the 1971 team. It's the only team photo in the room. Why? Is it not an odd choice?

'Because it was on the wall when I moved into this office.'

2

A RARE AND CLASSIC THING

Ron Henry

> I remember when we won the Cup-Winners' Cup, Bill Nick said, 'Well, what do you want for winning it?' We'd already got a watch. And they bought us a set of suitcases. A man's suitcase, a lady's one, a white one, a small one and a briefcase with your initials on. And I said, 'Bill, what's the good of these cases? We can't even afford to go away on holiday.'
>
> Ron Henry

Ron Henry. Those two words had been firmly implanted in my boy's brain since before I can remember; part of a mantra that had been drummed in and which had taken seed in a way that, say, the seven times table never could have done. After the regular evening ritual – 'Off you go. Bedtime.' 'But I'm not tired. And anyway, you're not going to bed' – had been played out, I'd lie under the covers with my copy of the *Observer's Guide to British Birds* checking out the underwing configuration of all manner of exotic creatures, and with my Spurs books and football annuals looking back through the glorious 1960s, absorbing the deeds and the names that were part of my heritage: Bill Brown, Ron Henry, Peter Baker, Dave Mackay, Danny Blanchflower, Maurice Norman, Terry Dyson, Les Allen, John White, Bobby Smith, Cliff Jones. I also knew Terry Medwin and Tony Marchi, even though there were no such things as substitutes back then.

Consider the relative usefulness of my mantra as opposed to the seven times table. Look at it another way. Even after living in Tokyo for the best part of two years, I still haven't come across a calculator that will tell you who the full-backs in the double team were. Seven multiplied by eight? They'll all do that; even the simplest calculator will tell you that. But who played right-back in 1961? No gadget will tell you that. You have to learn it. You have to study. No pain, no gain.

Of all the star names, all the glittering legends from that great line-up, Ron Henry's was one of the smaller ones; the lesser-spotted full-backs, as he and Peter Baker – the only two locals in the side – were no doubt known in the old bedtime days. That he stands out from Baker is due to two things. Firstly, Baker's blond anodyne looks, hair slicked back – it wasn't even a quiff like the other blonds, Jones and Dyson. It was slicked back like someone who might admire the works of Richard Wagner. Henry, on the other hand, had hair to kill for. Dark, thick and uniformly wavy, he had the looks and the presence of Victor Mature's younger brother. Secondly, there was the name. Ron and Henry were both classic 1960s names. Ron was one of the Krays, Henry was Cooper. It was a classic combination. Peter Baker, on the other hand, was the perfect name for a composite iffy Tory minister – 'The Conservative minister for Twatford East, the Rt Hon Peter Baker, resigned today after a series of compromising pictures involving his pet goat were passed on to the *News of the World . . .*'

Ron Henry is that rare and classic thing in football: the young lad from the terraces who goes every week to watch his heroes, and ends up playing for the team, becoming one of the heroes.

'I can remember when I first started to support Tottenham – I think I was about nine years old and my uncle came down here for Christmas. He lived in Stamford Hill. On the Boxing Day morning he said to me, "Ron, would you like to go and see Tottenham play?" The first thing that came into my mind was, "Well, how can they have a football pitch in London?" I thought it was all roads and concrete. So I said, "A football team in London?" and he said, "Yeah, come on, we'll go out." They were playing Chesterfield, and as I walked in at the Park Lane end, I thought, "How marvellous." Little did I dream that I would ever play on it, but it was absolutely marvellous.

'It was the Christmas atmosphere, and it was a better atmosphere than you get today – I'm talking about old people, they've all got their flat caps on. I stood up behind the goal and I said to my uncle Sid, "Can I go next week?" and he said, "Well, there's not one next week, there's one the week after," and I hardly missed a game all the way through from then until I went into the army.

'I can remember the first time I went there as a player and Cecil Poynton, the old trainer, said, "Well, there you go son, strip off, there's your kit there," and there was number one peg, number two peg and number three peg, you know. I stripped at number two peg, and when we came in from training, I found that I was stripping next to Ted Ditchburn, the goalkeeper; the other side was Alf Ramsey. To me these people were legends. Ted Ditchburn was one of the perfect professionals and he looked after us young kids. But I mean, Nicholson, Ramsey, Eddie Bailey – Eddie I'm still great mates with – they were my idols and I really looked up to them. When I got into the first team, it was just something a schoolboy would dream of. They were all so helpful. Bill Nick was a player then and he played in the A team with me – and I learnt a lot off Bill.'

Henry was lucky. Though he'd been at Spurs since 1952, his role had been mainly as Mel Hopkins's understudy. It was only after Hopkins injured himself on international duty with Wales in 1959 that Henry got his chance. Thus while he missed out on the 1950s teams with people like Tommy Harmer, Harry Clarke and John Ryden, when his time came, he was well and truly ready.

'I felt sorry for him really because he was a good player, but then in this game you look after yourself. Mel always came up to me and said, "Have a good game, Ron." There was no bitterness about it between us. And of course he missed the double; I played well enough during that period to keep Mel out of it. I never missed a game; I think I played for something like four years running with 42 League games under my belt each year. Bill had a lot to do with forming that team, I know, but I think someone up there had a lot to do with it as well because it was such a great team – not because I played in it, but it was such a great team to play in. Everyone knew what everyone else was doing. Everyone knew where everyone was. We never used to think about winning, we just used to think about how many goals we were going to score. It was just a formality to go on there and play.

'We'd already got John White. I don't think we saw the best of John White at all, not at all. Bill Brown was there and Bill Nicholson bought Dave Mackay. I used to get on very well with Dave, he used to play just in front of me. I did a lot of work for Dave and he did a lot of work for me. Sometimes his inside-forward would be bringing the ball and you'd think, "Well, where's bloody Dave?" And he's out there, upfield somewhere, so I'd have to jockey with the two of 'em – my winger and his inside-forward. But he always got back, he was always there in support at the death – a great player.'

Cliff Jones said – and he wasn't the first or the last to say it – that Dave Mackay was the important one, the final piece of the jigsaw.

People came and people went, but Dave Mackay was the crucial signing. If Danny Blanchflower was the brain, the bridge between the management and the workers, then Mackay was the heart. Spurs were a good side, but the signing of Dave Mackay made them a great one.

'I would agree with Cliff about Dave. I would say he was the perfect player. You could always look to him to pull you out of the soup if need be. He was tremendous – he would bring you back to life. If you went a goal down, he'd bring you back. I would say he was one of the best players, not the most skilful player, but one of the best players I've known at Tottenham. You see, a lot of people in that side were unnoticed. There was Les Allen for instance: I mean, the year after the double they went and bought Greavesie.'

Despite being an integral part of that team, there's something of the Pete Best about Les Allen – almost but not quite. That may be a ridiculous thing to think about a member of the double team, but imagine it. You're an ever-present, you score 21 goals and the manager buys someone to replace you. You want to complain, you want to moan about the injustice of it all. How can he? And then you realise that the player they've replaced you with is Jimmy Greaves. What can you do? You're second best.

'Les Allen was a tremendous player. I know they bought Greavesie, but Les Allen was a good worker. I mean Jimmy was a goalscorer but Les was a goalscorer and a worker. Les would do his share of the navvying and whenever I'd got the ball, I could always find him. They talk about John White always getting into spaces – so did Les Allen. I felt for Les when they bought Jimmy Greaves because Les scored a hell of a lot of goals, and he was a good foil for Bobby Smith. I think Jimmy was a good player with anybody, but Les didn't get the recommendations that Greavesie got. Les was a good player.

'I remember one incident that happened with Greavesie, though. When we played the Burnley final [the 1962 FA Cup final], We walked on to the pitch on the Friday morning, Cecil Poynton and Jim and me, and I said to Jim, "I'd love to win this one tomorrow – that'd give me two Cup final medals," and Greavesie said, "Well, I've got to win tomorrow because I haven't got any." I said "No you ain't Jim, have you?"

'"No, but I'll have one tomorrow because I shall score in a couple of minutes."

'And he did. Now that was fantastic, wasn't it? Exactly after two minutes, he scored a goal. He told me that on the Friday morning. Of course, Burnley drew level, one each, and then we went and scored two more goals.'

Playing in a side like that, wasn't it a danger that you'd get a large dose of arrogantitis, that you'd get big-headed, start to think that you were unbeatable, fireproof?

'No, we never used to get carried away because we just used to enjoy playing. When you're playing so well, it's just a pleasure. It's not hard work. We used to love playing in front of a big crowd. I can remember an instance when we were playing Dukla Prague at White Hart Lane in the snow. Their outside-right, Dave Mackay and me all went down in a bundle. We didn't know where the ball was so we started making footballs from the snow and throwing them at each other; the crowd loved it. Things like that happened. It was a good team spirit, everybody worked for everyone else. No one was big-headed in that side, because no one thought they were better than anybody else.

'I think that the crowd at Tottenham were the same – they were fantastic. I remember getting voted Player of the Year by the Supporters Club two years running – 1961–62, 1962–63 – even though Greavesie, Mackay and all them were there. You know, the supporters were fair – they picked a lesser-known player. The full-back isn't as recognised as much as the forwards. But it never bothered us. We used to think we were just as important as them up front, because if we let goals in, they're not going to get the limelight for scoring them, are they? That's how we thought.

'Actually, to tell you the truth, I never used to play a lot. I used to stand at the back and watch them play. I can remember playing at Wolverhampton because we still hold the record for winning the opening 11 games of the season. We beat Wolves 4–0 for the record, and Billy Wright came into our dressing-room and in his Midlands accent he said, "If there's a team that's going to beat you, I'd like to see it."

'That was coming from Billy Wright. I try to explain to people about it today, it was so simple the way we played. We never used to get injured because we never got caught in possession of the ball. If you don't get caught in possession, you don't get kicked about.

'We never tried to beat people. It was just look up, pass and move, pass and move. And you can't stop it. This stuff on television now, I can't watch it. You know I haven't watched a Tottenham first-team game for nearly ten years. Admittedly I go away with the youth team on Saturday mornings, but after that I'm out of the car-park at ten to three in the afternoon to come home. I can't sit and watch it. I don't know why it is. I'm not running the side down, don't get me wrong, but it's not like I've been used to. The football has changed. Every side has changed.'

Asking the question, 'What was your greatest or most memorable game for Spurs?' of any of the class of 1960–61 is like saying to Hitler, 'What was your favourite war?' You know what he's going to answer. It's not as if there's a choice involved. History has chosen.

Tottenham Hotspur 2 (Smith, Dyson)
Leicester City 0

FA Cup final
6 May 1961

Tottenham Hotspur: Brown, Baker, Henry, Blanchflower, Norman, Mackay, Jones, White, Smith, Allen, Dyson.
Leicester City: Banks, Chalmers, R. Norman, McLintock, King, Appleton, Riley, Walsh, McIlmoyle, Keyworth, Cheesebrough.
Attendance: 100,000

That day Spurs won the Cup, won the double, re-wrote the history books . . . did a million things. For Ron Henry, there was another cause for celebration. It was the day when the football world finally realised his worth. It's a match laced with lovely ironies. Spurs win the double by playing it safe. Tiny 5 foot 3 inch winger Terry Dyson heads the winning goal from a cross by burly centre-forward Bobby Smith. The manner of it was from the same Irony Superstore. To quote *The Times* newspaper of the day:

> One wondered if the occasion were going to prove too much even for Tottenham. Certainly the expected domination at wing-half was not forthcoming. Mackay, normally a player of gale force, was like a zephyr until the closing stages, while Blanchflower, brow furrowed, looked careworn and played in the same way. It was the less publicised of Tottenham's men who took the honours. Most of the glory this season has been attributed to the expensive forward line and the wing-halves, while the

> contributions of Norman, Baker and Henry usually have gone unsung. Now these three – calm and unruffled – took the strain, building up confidence from behind. Henry was outstanding and never put a foot wrong.

Ron Henry: 'My first Cup final, the game against Leicester, was something that everybody dreams of. I can remember being in the hotel, on the ground floor, Peter Baker and me shared a room. It was a lovely morning, May the sixth; and the window was up and as Peter Baker woke up two young lads leant in and said, "Ron, Pete. Can we have your autographs?" I thought that was tremendous.

'We went to Wembley by coach and it was marvellous. I said to myself, "Leicester are not going to score." I studied Howard Riley who was playing outside-right; I'd already played against him twice that year in the League. I thought about him and it came to me: let him have the ball and he'll make his own mistakes, and he did. I just closed him down when he got the ball, but he would make mistakes. He could knock it a little too far in front of him, he'd knock it over the by-line, things like this. He would go by and come back and get beaten again and I loved it. I got man of the match for that game which I thought was tremendous.'

Curiously for a manager who'd just typed his name in the history books, Bill Nick's thoughts were of a double disappointment. Firstly, there was the League. He was disappointed that Spurs only tied with the Arsenal record of 66 points. He wanted, quite rightly, to break their record. Secondly, there was the FA Cup.

'Bill was disappointed with the FA Cup final because we didn't put on a good show,' said Dave Mackay. 'I think in his heart he was delighted that we'd actually done the double, because we'd deserved to, but really he wanted us to play them off the park. It was a scrappy game – once they went down to ten men, they were battling away.'

Leicester full-back Len Chalmers was injured in a tackle with Les Allen after 19 minutes and had to go off. That, effectively, ended the final there and then.

'When they went down to ten players, I remember thinking to myself, "Hey, hold on a minute . . ." I mean I was always one for pushing forward and doing this and doing that but I remember saying to myself, "I'm just going to sit here and wait and be patient until we score the first goal and when we get the one goal, we've won it." And actually it worked out like that. I wasn't scampering all over Wembley like I would normally do playing for Tottenham. I was just sitting there, making sure that it was nice and safe and that we gave nothing away. It turned out that Bobby Smith scored the first one and Dyson got the second and we were quite sure, quite safe.

'When you get to Wembley, the one thing you don't want to do is lose. You can see them when they go up for the medals – the winners and the losers. There's a great difference.'

Was it done as an example to the others not to get carried away? Was it Danny's orders?

'No, that's why I took it on myself. I thought, "Hey, take it easy, and concentrate on defending and making sure that they get nothing." The manager never told me that, I just felt it myself. And Danny never told me, "Sit there and don't do this and don't do that." For the first time in my life, I just thought, "Hey, this is a great chance." I'm thinking about the double – we wanted to be the first ones to win the double. I don't think that Blanchflower would've noticed what I was doing, I don't think anyone would have noticed it.'

Towards the end of the match, Mackay slowed down again, but this time there was a different reason. Ron Henry: 'I can remember Dave coming up to me when we'd scored the second goal and saying, "There's something wrong with my eyes, mate. I can't see a lot." It was about ten minutes from the end. No one knew this, and he said, "My eyes have gone all a blur." He must have got a knock or something. I said, "All right, Dave. I'll shadow you," and that's what I did for the last ten minutes. But no one knew and Dave never told anyone when we got back to the dressing-room. He was all right afterwards; it settled down. But I can remember that game. We never played well that day. Our better-known players didn't play well, the Blanchflowers, people like that. Perhaps they deserved a day off, I don't know. We had to play bloody well at the back, but we did. It was a great game I feel – in my book.

'After the final whistle I went and shook Bill Nicholson's hand and I said, "Well done, Bill," and the words he said to me were, "Yeah, but I'll tell you something, Ron. No one will know what we've done until 20 years' time." And he was right. I didn't know. I sit here and think about it now, and when I saw that United won it, I thought, "Well, I did that." You don't realise it until after . . . a long time after. And it will never be the same. We were the first ones to do it.'

After the game it was . . . what? Straight down to Stringfellows (or the Stork Club or some such 1960s equivalent)? Lie back in the dentist's chair and wait to be showered with tequila? A quick jump on to the nearest Cathay Pacific plane for a good old-fashioned singsong? Probably not. In the days of old when knights were bold, our heroes didn't do such things. So how do you celebrate after you've done the undoable? Where do you go? Do you party?

'Yes, at the hotel. I don't know what it was – the Hilton, or somewhere like that up in London. I had a wonderful night, a great night, got home in the early hours of the morning. It was a proper club celebration. They're not now are they? They invite anybody. If you want to pay 50 pounds you get a ticket and also go to the reception, but it was just the club and it was wonderful – beautiful. I'd like to go through it again. You know like some people go through their marriage vows again, I'd like to go through my Cup finals again.'

Epilogue

'We played because we enjoyed it,' says Henry. 'I got two things out of football, two very important things. I got a lot of pleasure and a lot of friends, genuine friends. We didn't get any money out of it. I took a job at Tottenham for five pounds a week, but before I went in the army I was at a rubber company in Dunstable earning eight pounds a week. My wages when I came off the Wembley pitch after winning the double were 16 pounds, eight shillings after stoppages. I've still got the pay packet upstairs if you want to see it. That was standard.

'My wages were 18 pounds per week and with your income tax and stamps, it took me down to 16 pounds, eight shillings. I used to say to Edna, "You can invite mum and dad round for tea this week, and get some salad in because we're only playing Nottingham Forest. We'll easily beat them and we'll have a four-pound bonus." A four-pound bonus was a lot of money – that made it 22 pounds a week. If you missed that bonus, you were like a bear with a sore head until you won the next game. We didn't miss it very often but because we wanted to play – we didn't play for money.'

Now, legend has it that, as a reward for winning the double, the Spurs team members were each given an inscribed gold watch. It's a recurrent theme, I know, but again, from this vantage point, it sounds so lovely, so real. I know money's important and, yes, it's great to have it, but a gold watch. Imagine it. Manchester United have won the Premiership and they're about to play in the FA Cup final. The morning of the match you read in the tabloids that the United players are on a win bonus of an inscribed gold watch. Fills your heart with human happiness somehow, no?

'The club paid a lot of money for them; they were the Rolls Royce of watches, Longines. The club paid 130 pounds for each one of them. There you are. And I've got an Atletico Madrid one for winning the European Cup-Winners' Cup. It's never been worn, never been on my wrist.

'I remember when we won the Cup-Winners' Cup, Bill Nick said, "Well, what do you want for winning it?" We'd already got a watch, so they bought us a set of suitcases. A man's suitcase, a lady's one, a white one, a small one and a briefcase with your initials on. And I said, "Bill what's the good of these cases? We can't even afford to go away on holiday."

Hold on a minute. The Cup-Winners' Cup was in 1963. This is after George Eastham, Jimmy Hill and the abolition of the maximum wage. Surely in 1963 you were on a proper wedge?

'I had about 18 months of the no-limit wage and the most I ever took was 40 pounds a week. It was 20 pounds one week and we went to Holland on tour. Bill Nick took us aside one by one, gave us our new contracts and told us what we would be getting. I was on 40 pounds a week. That was the top wage that I ever got. It was nice because I'd never had 40 pounds a week before. We didn't go out and buy big cars and that, not that I'd have wanted to. As I say, we didn't get money out of football. The thing was, you were doing something that I personally would have paid to do. Instead of me taking five pounds a week from Tottenham, I would have given them five pounds a week to play for them. That's the difference, to put that Tottenham shirt on and go out at White Hart Lane, I would have given them five pounds a week. I don't know where I would have got it from, but I would have done it. That was my attitude on football.

'But if I had to pack up at Tottenham, I wouldn't go to another club. I never thought of going anywhere else. I'd never want to go to another place, even today. I've been there for 42 years now. I've been doing the youth team for 20 years, and I had 20 years there as a player. Tottenham have never given me anything, but they've never cheated me out of anything and I think that's how life should be. I've done a good day's work for a good day's pay and that's it. I've never wanted any more from Tottenham than what I've had and I've always given my best. I can't understand how these players go from club to club every other year, you know. That wouldn't do for me. Well, it's my life. Tottenham is my life, although I run this business here [a garden nursery specialising in potted plants]. I've got the best of two worlds. When I get fed up with Tottenham I come home and when I get fed up with the nursery I go to Tottenham.

'We keep in touch, I still see some of the lads – Jonesy, I see, Terry Medwin, Terry Dyson, Maurice Norman, people like that. We always send each other Christmas cards. They're all nice boys. Most of them come here to get their plants.

'Bill Nick's coming down here next week. He comes down two or three times a year and we go out for a meal. Keith Burkinshaw comes here, I see him quite a lot. Eddie Bailey . . . They come down to pick their plants up. I see quite a lot of them down here.

'It's a shame age catches up with you, but I've got my little job and I'm contented. I've got no regrets. I've enjoyed my life.'

3

THE ULTIMATE WARRIOR

Dave Mackay

> I suppose most people would assume my choice for my greatest ever signing would be Jimmy Greaves because he was the best striker of his era and the game is all about scoring goals. But I think I must select Dave Mackay. I knew we needed to make a new signing as we entered the 1960s, and Mackay probably did more than anyone to forge a team capable of winning the double. Not only did Mackay make an enormous contribution on the field but his dynamic character was also a major influence in training. The effect he had on the other players was truly remarkable . . . He was truly a great player with far more skill than he was ever given credit for. He had a delicate touch, two good feet and was such an intelligent reader of the game that it came as no surprise to me that Brian Clough converted him to a sweeper at Derby.
>
> Bill Nicholson

Dave Mackay. As a footballer, he was a legend; as a concept, he was perfect. For the quintessential Dave Mackay moment, forget cups, forget leagues, forget even doubles. This moment, this classic moment came in the middle of a match at White Hart Lane on 22 August 1966, and it's one of those moments that has been frozen in time in a photograph that, in itself, justifies the invention of the camera. It's a sunny day and there's a huge crowd. On the left of the photo, Terry Venables is walking towards the centre, but you can tell he's not walking that quickly. Like a gawper at the scene of a car crash, he wants to see what's going on, but he's scared of getting involved. On the right of the picture, the referee is also moving to the centre, but he's moving with more urgency. His whistle is in his mouth, like a boxing referee saying, 'Break it up, break it up.' At the centre of the photo are Dave Mackay and Billy Bremner. Bremner, one of the hard men in a hard Leeds team, is standing still, looking very small, very young. His eyes are pleading, saying, 'It wasn't, it was him . . . no, no, okay, it was me, it was me. I'm sorry, really.' Facing him is Dave Mackay, chest out, chin out, cow pies coming out of his ears, looking very tall, very big. He's marching towards Bremner, which is a bit of a concern because he's about a foot away from him. In his right hand is a lump of Bremner's shirt. His face is saying, in classic brogue, 'You and me, pal, we're gonna talk.' It's a wonderful moment. The Sultan of Brunei could be standing next to you, saying, 'Have it all. You can have it all, but only if you swap places with Bremner,' and you'd laugh in his face.

Bill Nicholson: 'From what is known of Bremner, it could be safely said that he probably asked for it. Dave Mackay had a strict code of conduct. He tackled robustly, but always fairly and expected similar treatment himself. But if anyone went outside the rules, he became very angry indeed and the Bremner incident was one of those occasions.'

Curiously, Bill Nicholson was just that far from not signing Mackay at all. He was a player Nick had seen while assistant to Jimmy Anderson and, as soon as he became manager, he was on the phone to Hearts manager Tommy Walker. No go. Walker said no. Well, he would, wouldn't he? So Bill Nick went off to Swansea. He'd heard that Mel Charles, brother of Big John, was available. Although Nicholson was admittedly 'not excited' by Charles, he was a good player and would have been a useful addition to the ever-strengthening Spurs squad. Nick and Charles spoke and Charles said that he'd give his answer on Saturday night.

'Sorry Mr Nicholson, but I've decided to join the Arsenal.'

'Okay, son. Thanks for ringing and I wish you all the best with the Arsenal.'

With that, Nicholson was back on to Walker. It was Saturday night and the transfer deadline was midnight on Monday. It's odd, but there seems to be an unwritten law that such matters must be carried out as the clock is ticking towards the transfer deadline. Nicholson pushed, and Walker, possibly knowing that he was being a touch King Canute in the face of destiny, relented; £32,000 later and Big Dave was a Spur.

Before even talking to Mackay, you know that the feet are going to be on the ground, studs first, solid and secure, just as it should be.

What was it like, playing in that team, waiting for the angels to give the nod to the orchestra, knowing that Zeus had ordered it?

Dave Mackay: 'Actually, when I went there it was to save them from relegation. They were second bottom of the League. There were eight games left – I only played four because I had a little injury, but I never lost a game. I don't know if we won them, but we didn't lose them. Tottenham never lost a game until the end of the season – they either won or drew every game. Then we picked up straight away, and almost won the League the following year. By that time, Bill Brown and John White had come as well as Cliff Jones and myself, and it just seemed to take off from there.

'John White was very important. He was good as soon as he came down from Scotland – you had to fit in right away. They used to call him the ghost because he was good at flitting in behind people. He was a wonderful player and had great stamina. Cliff Jones and him, when you saw them among the autograph hunters, you didn't know who was who. Marvellous player though, John White. Could kick with both feet. Much stronger than he looked.

'The thing was, in those days, you didn't really get near the double and so people weren't talking about it that much. It was not like now when it's so common. Nowadays, as soon as you look like you're going to win the League, people – the media – lose interest in the League; they're only interested in the double. Then, the double had never been won by anybody so it was a little bit different. Now they're doing double doubles and in the future they'll be doing treble doubles and even more. But being the first in anything, that's always special; and to do the first double this century, that was going to be an achievement.

'In those days it was like an eight-week wait before the Cup final after the semi-final – you still had a good few matches to play in the League before the final came up so we concentrated. We weren't thinking too much about the Cup, but mainly to get the League finished first.'

Despite what Mackay might say or think, the double was on the agenda, possibly far more than it was a decade or so later when the Arsenal won it. Both Manchester United and Wolves had gone close in the late 1950s, both failing by a single match. As Phil Soar records in *Tottenham Hotspur 1882–1995*, Danny Blanchflower was thinking of little else: 'Joe Mercer recalled coming back from Sweden after the World Cup in 1958. On the plane, he said, Danny could talk of little else. He told us over and over again that it was going to be done. "And we'll be the ones to do it," he said.'

Bill Nicholson was more Bill Nicholson. 'I felt that we would have a good shout in the League, but in the Cup? Well, who knows about the Cup? One afternoon on a strange pitch, an awkward ground, one or two things going the opposite way and . . . bingo! You're gone. It's different again, the Cup.'

You can take the man out of Yorkshire . . . Then again, it's part of the manager's role to keep his players' feet on the ground – Feet schmeet, as my father might have said.

One of the most remarkable things about the whole remarkable double season was the way in which Spurs started off. Having missed out on the championship the year before by a gnat's whisker – that heart-stopping missed penalty against Manchester City – it was as if this time they wanted to get it settled now, as quickly as possible. As the sun was still shining and the days were still long, Spurs cast a shadow over the entire League and danced through their first 11 league games without dropping a point. A record 11 wins on the trot and our heroes were in danger of slipping out of view, of lapping their retreating shadow. Then it happened – they drew 1–1 at home to Manchester City. The same Manchester City who they'd screwed up against the previous year. Curiously, Bill Nicholson didn't go out and spend a mega amount on a hugely skilled but team-disrupting South American. He kept faith with his boys and they kept faith with him. They won another four on the bounce. Burning rubber on the opposition, they amassed 31 points out of 32; unbeaten.

But all things must end, and on 12 November, Spurs went up to Hillsborough to take on their closest challengers, Sheffield Wednesday. Stylistically, Wednesday were the Colonel Mustard of our story – ready to have a go with the lead piping but always short of a few cards. Spurs, meanwhile, were an amalgam of Captain Scarlet and Captain Black: the near paranormal indestructibility of the former aligned to the stylistic nous of the latter.

Serious, hard and seriously hard, Wednesday were solid. Sadly though, the team is best remembered for being at the centre of the biggest bribery scandal of the era. But they were good. In another era, round about 1970 to 1971, they'd have walked the League and probably won the Cup as well; not much going on in those years, apparently. They had some good players, too, names that few outside of Sheffield will know now – big John Fantham, who appeared on more than one cigarette card in his day, and Don Megson. Two of their teammates, Peter Swan and Tony Kaye, were involved in that bribery nonsense. One hundred pounds. Really! Such a quaint lack of ambition. Hadn't they heard of Far Eastern betting syndicates? Swan and Kaye were instrumental in Wednesday's 2–1 victory over the Spurs. In truth, it was probably a blessing for the glory boys. Every week it was, 'Is this going to be the week that Spurs get beaten?' Well, now they had been beaten and the pressure was off.

On 18 March, Burnley did the bridesmaid's shuffle at Villa Park as Spurs secured their FA Cup final place. The final was nearly two months away on 6 May; in between was Sheffield Wednesday.

Tottenham Hotspur 2 (Smith, Allen)
Sheffield Wednesday 1 (Megson)

17 April 1961

Tottenham Hotspur: Brown, Baker, Henry, Blanchflower, Norman, Mackay, Jones, White, Smith, Allen, Dyson.
Sheffield Wednesday: Springett, Johnson, Megson, Hill, Swan, Kay, Finney, Craig, Ellis, Fantham, Wilkinson.
Attendance: 61,200

Sheffield Wednesday in one of those turns of fate that makes football such a funny old game, it had to be Sheffield Wednesday. (John White made his debut against Wednesday on 17 October 1959 – irrelevant to this story, but useful for fact junkies.)

'Wednesday,' says Mackay, 'were our biggest challengers. There were five games to go, I think, and we won 2–0.' (Four games and we won 2–1 actually, but that's detail.) 'Had they beaten us we would still have won the League, but by winning that game we went way ahead of everybody and we stayed in that particular position all the time, you know. It was just this one game where they were lying second – they finished second I think – but had they beaten us we would have had to wait another couple of weeks or something like that. So it was a very important game for us.'

Like that first match at Hillsborough, the evening game at White Hart Lane wasn't a game for the purist. Full-blooded is a fair description. As a point of discussion, consider this. Why is it that the really exciting games are always in the evening? The great Cup nights, they're always in the evening. How many times have you seen dull, lifeless FA Cup finals played out on the Saturday afternoon, only for the evening floodlights to bring the replay to life a few days later? It must be something to do with the lights concentrating the energies on the arena, creating a Colosseum effect.

In the first half, both Mackay and Wednesday's Peter Johnson were booked as the men sorted themselves out. The story was quite straightforward. If Spurs won, the championship was theirs, and that's what the crowd had gone to see. If it was football that they were after, they would have saved their money until the next week. This was scheduled to be a Glory Night.

What was the crowd like? Did they respond in that same evening way, like it was a Cup tie?

'They were fantastic. I came from Hearts where we would probably get half the people they'd get down here. At that time at Spurs, they didn't have the other big stand; they had the small stand and you just couldn't get in the ground. They were fantastic – really – very enthusiastic and appreciative. I mean that. You talk to one or two of them now and they say, "We just used to love watching the boys warming up." We did little tricks on the ball just to please the crowd. For the Cup final I should think we did exactly the same – not that it mattered, I mean half of them wouldn't understand but we always used to do it anyway. Not all of us – Blanchflower, John White, Cliff Jones and me.

'Most of the time in the League at Tottenham, it was quite an electric atmosphere and I'm sure that the fans got their money's worth every week. We did play good football, very entertaining stuff, and the crowd were always exceptionally enthusiastic. But this game was special. It was more like a Cup tie.'

Though Don Megson's pipe-opener shut a few mouths, it was never going to be more than a dying man's last request. Almost immediately after Megson's free kick, Bobby Smith – big, bad and blessed with the touch of a district nurse – flicked the ball over England international Peter Swan and swiped the bouncing ball home on the half-volley. A touch Gazza. The crowd were still flapping their caps in the air (as they did) when Danny Blanchflower's free kick was flicked on by Maurice Norman and Les Allen leapt up to crack in a shoulder-high volley; 2–1 and time to wrap up the birthday present.

In the second half, it got hotter. Big, bad Bob shoulder-charged Wednesday's England goalkeeper, Ron Springett, into a goalpost and, not unreasonably, both Springett and the post were carried off. But this being a time when men were men and substitutes were still the stuff of science fiction, Springett crawled back on minutes later. Soon enough, the crowd were on the pitch thinking it was all over. Referee Tommy Dawes, who'd blown for time a few minutes earlier, said that it was now and that was that.

It was one of those games when Spurs weren't great, but they were as great as they needed to be. *The Times* noted that:

> Certainly the Tottenham forwards have played better than this and Blanchflower too seemed below par. But such is the make-up of this remarkable side that if one or even two departments have a day off, another is more than ready to accept the responsibility. Baker and Henry were both magnificent and that was enough.

As already quoted, almost exactly the same words were written after the Leicester FA Cup final eight weeks later.

Spurs finished eight points clear of second-placed Wednesday and nine points clear of third-placed Wolves. Blanchflower was, for the second time in four years, voted Footballer of the Year.

Bill Nicholson: 'Mackay was a carefree type of person, the opposite of Blanchflower. But they had great respect for each other.'

Blanchflower's place in the team was an odd one. It's curious now reading about Blanchflower. He seems to have been not so much a footballer as a foreman. At 34, he was considerably older than everyone else, and he was not so much one of the players, but more of a bridge between the players and the management – the deputy manager in all but name. It's a testament to Nicholson's management that he let him operate in this way. Can you imagine a modern manager allowing one of his players the amount of rope that Nicholson allowed Blanchflower? It may also be relevant that Nicholson didn't sign Blanchflower, Arthur Rowe did, and until the great year it seemed that no one was quite sure what to do with him. He was in the team and then he wasn't. He was made captain and then he wasn't. Blanchflower was the quintessential maverick and we all know what a maverick is: a hero in his/her own mind and a lippy, stroppy bastard in everyone else's. As Nicholson said, 'In a poor side Danny was a luxury; but in a good side, his creativity, his unorthodox approach was priceless – a wonderful asset.'

Even forgetting about talk of doubles, the atmosphere at White Hart Lane must have been like a carnival? Well, yes and no. Celebrations are for fans. For the players, there's still work to be done. And League or no League, for managers there's always room for improvement.

'After that Wednesday game, we lost a couple of games which I'm sure we wouldn't have lost if we had had to win them. We lost 4–2 at Burnley and 2–1 to West Bromwich Albion at home the week before the Cup final. So after more or less guaranteeing that we'd won the League, I think everyone lost interest a bit. I remember Bill Nick was upset because he wanted to beat the Arsenal's record of 66 points. We had 64 and out of the last three games I think we won one and lost two.

'It's not what you should do, but I'm quite sure that everyone wanted to play at Wembley and so made sure that they weren't injured before that particular game. It was never a question of who was going to play, nearly everyone picked themselves, though we did have one or two excellent reserves. Our reserve team could have near enough played as a first team for someone else. The boys who were in that first team – we'd had such a successful season that year that nobody would get replaced right away.'

It's a stupid question, but it's one that's just so tempting to ask any member of that team. Is it just that history has filtered the truth through its very own rose-tinted specs? Has the legend exceeded the truth or was it really . . . 'Every team always has its weak parts' . . . invincible?

'I think back now and if we had concentrated . . . we probably wouldn't have enjoyed it as much, but if we had concentrated on winning games rather than entertaining, we could have done a lot better in terms of trophies. But the way we played, if we went to play at Manchester City or Blackburn or wherever it was, we just went out to play, you know? Regardless of the score, we just kept playing. We didn't think, "Oh, we're getting beat 2–0, we'll try and keep it down." I remember going to Manchester City – we were losing 6–0 and we ended up losing 6–2. And we lost 7–2 to Blackburn Rovers, so no, we weren't invincible, we did get beaten and sometimes we got hammered, but it was very rare, so we didn't think, "Oh no, we're two down, we'd better play it tight at the back or something." We never played like that. We just played good open football all the time, attacking and trying to entertain.'

It's one of the great ironies that Spurs did just that – attack and entertain – except on one occasion: the FA Cup final. The one time everyone would be watching, the showcase, the chance they had to show everyone what they could do.

Dave Mackay: 'I think that it was a disappointing final because Leicester went down to ten players and there were no substitutes in those days. We just said to ourselves, "Hey, we're going to win here" rather than going flat-out entertainment-wise and risking getting beaten.'

The team as a unit must have been very level-headed and sensible to have broken a mould and achieved such a thing.

'It was a team that had a good harmony – not on the mornings when we played in the gym, but when we played on a Saturday. Everyone played for each other and helped each other. We used to fight in the gym, but that really was just the six-a-sides. Seeing it, you'd think that nobody had got any friends at all. But once you'd had your shower everything was forgotten and you just waited for the next day. I don't know if that team had a higher percentage of good pals than other teams. We used to have fights in our training, the same as everybody else, but when we'd finished we'd just do our jobs.

'Level-headed? I think if you'd seen me that night you'd have thought differently. But no, in football these things come and go and you've always got to remember that. It's like . . . my biggest disappointment in the game was beating Benfica 2–1 at Tottenham in the semi-final of the European Cup and they went through because they beat us 3–1 in Lisbon. We finished up losing out to them when we should certainly have beaten them, no question. But that's football you know? We would have loved to have won the European Cup, but we didn't.

'But they were level-headed guys anyway. I think when we had that team that won the League, we thought we could win any game against anybody any time. It didn't always happen, obviously, but we were so confident – not just of our own ability, but of the team's ability.'

Epilogue

Bill Nicholson: 'Mackay is a great man. There aren't enough words in football to describe that man. You take him to that ball court and we'll work him in the ball court. We're volleying the ball against the wall, and you volley it with your right foot, then your left foot, then your right foot and your left foot, and the ball doesn't come down – it stays up all the time. That's the exercise. If a player does between 12 and 15, he'd be doing well. Mackay will get 20 to 25. He's that much better. When he's out on the field, the way he walks around, he sticks his bloody chest out. You've got that photo with Bremner, you must have seen that one. It describes Mackay. He's not a dirty player on the field – he's a very strong player without being dirty. A great left foot – total control of the ball. Excellent.

'He was a very, very good player for Tottenham; very skilful. He used to read the game well and he could score goals. From a playing point of view, if you're picking the team, there were several players who would come automatically, and he would be one of those. He was a great leader, oh yes, with the way he would storm into things with his bloody chest out and that Scottish brawn. Ha ha ha. Yes, a great guy, Mackay.'

Cliff Jones: 'You daren't play against Dave Mackay in a five-a-side match. He was the ultimate competitor, the ultimate warrior. That was Dave Mackay. They talk about hard players today, and I've seen some – take Vinnie Jones, bless him, but he can't play. Dave Mackay, he could play. He was a very skilful player and then a real tough competitor. Well, he's such a 100 per cent guy – 100 per cent honest and he was like that off the pitch. Top performer – the best player in that team. More important than Danny Blanchflower, more important than John White, more important than myself. We sparked off Dave Mackay – he made us tick. Bill was the most important person. Danny took the power – and he was a good captain off the pitch for us, too, he bridged the gap between boardroom and dressing-room which most footballers can't do, but Danny did that. But it was Dave Mackay who made you play. Didn't matter how the game was going, you'd look round and his sleeves were rolled up and you had respect for him.'

Bill Nicholson again: 'I will always remember the first day he arrived at our training ground after I bought him. The other players were shaken by his drive and commitment. They looked at each other as if to say, "What's happening here?" At the time, we had a bunch of seasoned professionals, most of them internationals, and Mackay was able to stir them all up. He brought a new surge into every aspect of club life, particularly in training. Suddenly, training became just as important as the matches. Mackay was a bit of a show-off when it came to the skills of the game and was also a brilliant tactician. In practice games, he had to be a winner. His barrel chest would be thrust out and he would emerge on the winning side, no matter what the odds.'

Terry Venables: 'Dave Mackay is, for me, one of the most charismatic footballers of all time. One of the best characters I've ever known in the game. There are some great stories about Dave. He would throw the opposition the ball when he ran out on the field. "Here it is," he'd say. "Have a kick now because you won't get one when the game starts."

'We used to play in the gym. Eddie Bailey would give us a ball each and there would be coloured lines on the wall, red, yellow and blue. Eddie Bailey would say – and I'm sure he just made it up as he went along – chip the ball against the blue line, catch it on your thigh, bounce it onto the red line, volley it against the yellow line, bounce it down on your chest, then your head, volley it against the white line and as it comes down, kill it dead. We would all look at each other and think, "Great, Eddie." Who could possibly understand it, let alone do it? Dave would say, "Hold on a minute," and chip, thigh, volley, back on his chest, head, volley back against the white line and kill it stone dead. "Do you mean like that, Eddie?"'

4

THE FINAL FLING

Cliff Jones

Cliff Jones: 'We were out there for three weeks and that was a long time in Russia – particularly in 1959, my God. But it certainly was an experience, no doubt about that. Looking back, you think, "Cor, what an opportunity, I should have seen a bit more of it." I think that the classic one was when West Bromwich went to China and they were taken round the Great Wall. One of the players said, "When you've seen one wall, you've seen 'em all." Typical footballer's comment. We were a bit like that. No, we didn't really appreciate what was there. We didn't do any sightseeing really, although we did see the Kremlin. We went to see Lenin and Stalin lying in state. As far as I was concerned, I can't say I like communism. We're not political people, footballers, but it seemed to work there – I mean, they all seemed perfectly happy and affluent. The shops were good. It seemed to work.

'What we did see – and we thought it was absolutely fantastic – was the Bolshoi Ballet in Moscow. We said, "Oh Bill, we're not going to see the Bolshoi Ballet. Oh God." But I tell you what, it did impress us. We were right down the front and what impressed us and Bill Nick as well, was the fitness; absolute fitness, tremendous fitness. The power . . . we were right up close to them, and we could see the effort they put in. The breathing – they were really extending themselves. You've got to admire them. Tremendous. Bill said, "I want you lot like that." I tell you, if anyone had said to me that I was going to see the Bolshoi Ballet and enjoy it, I would have said, "You must be bloody joking," but we all came out very impressed. Very impressed. It's quite unbelievable really.'

It's written in the ancient scriptures that you should never meet your heroes. Keep them at a distance. Keep them heroes. You know, the scriptures didn't get to be ancient by accident. They didn't wake up one morning ancient. They grew to be that way; and they grew to be that way because they're true. But sometimes . . .

Watching Spurs in the mid to late 1960s, Cliff Jones was the link between the now and the then, between the myth and legend of only a few years earlier and the only too real humanity of the present. Dave Mackay was still in the team, a battling war-horse exhorting the younger legs around him to do it, and he was great, but it was Jones who held the romantic eyes of a young boy. Maybe not flying quite so much, but he was there, taking people on, diving for headers, bravely, stupidly. More than anyone, it was Cliff Jones who first laid the seeds for this book. Best, Law and Charlton? Yes, but did they play for Spurs? Were they in the double team?

Cliff Jones is 61 now and fit as a fiddle (tight T-shirt, no lumps or bulges), sporting a smile as wide as the cut that invariably appeared on his head: 'I loved dribbling, and I loved taking players on, but I realised that at some point in the season, I was going to get an injury. That's the end of the story.' Resplendent in a pair of Spurs tracksuit bottoms, Jones dances along that fine line between enjoying the past and living in the past like it was a touch-line. It's a trick not many manage to do and it's a treat to see.

'It was a lovely period of my life – fond memories and affection, no regrets. As a young person, I was fortunate. I played a season of Welsh League football. That was tough. I was 16 or 17 then. Then I had a season of combination football and two seasons of Second Division football before I was established, before anyone started to say things about me. I'd learnt my trade, you see. When I first came into the game, it was like a process. Happy days, happy days.

'I came up from Swansea in 1958; £35,000 I cost. Didn't get a great deal of it. I got the 20 pounds signing-on fee from Tottenham. I got an accrued share of my benefit from Swansea which was about 100 pounds after tax. In those days, regardless of the size of the transfer fee, the ruling was that it was 250 pounds if you were transferred from one club to another; but if you asked for a transfer, you would forfeit that 250 pounds. I asked for a transfer from Swansea because I wanted to play First Division football. I could see that I wouldn't do that with Swansea even though we had a good side and a lot of talent. I could see we weren't going to do it, so I asked for a transfer and forfeited that 250 pounds which was quite a few quid in them days. So all I was entitled to was the accrued share of the benefit – plus a few bags of anthracite thrown in. That's what the old saying was – have your bag of coal and up you go. We have a laugh about that, coming from the Valleys. A bag of coal always comes in handy.'

As we talked through the familiar idea that people do things too quickly these days – too much rush, not enough time to grow – I asked Cliff if he thought that there was too much pressure. It's easy to think that it's all so different now, more professional, with so much money involved, creating such stress, but that's an arrogance of our age. When Jones went to Spurs, he became the most expensive player in the land. Imagine a young lad coming up from Swansea to the big city, the record money signing and it doesn't matter whether it's Alan Shearer for £15 million or Cliff Jones for £35,000. So was there pressure then, being the most expensive player in Britain?

'Yes, I suppose you can say that, but soon I wasn't aware of anything about being the most expensive player. When I went to Tottenham, I seemed to strike a bad piece of football – I didn't start off very well. I had a fair game against the Arsenal I think, then I got injured and when I came back, Spurs were struggling, and I never really performed. Wales went to the World Cup in 1958, and we didn't do too badly. I did quite well, but at the start of the following season I broke my leg. I'd just come out of the army. I'd played football and sport virtually non-stop for two years, and breaking my leg was good for me, although you never really think that at the time. I thought "Oh no, disaster", but in the end it worked in my favour. It meant I could stop and have a look at what I was doing and how it was going. When I did come back, that's when I started to do okay.

'That was coming up to the 1958–59 season, which wasn't a bad season for me. At the end of the season, Bill Nicholson signed Dave Mackay, and we went on a tour to Russia. We really got together and performed well, and you could see that he'd knitted it all together – particularly with the signing of Mackay. The following season, 1959–60, we should have won the League; we came third I think. And then the following season was the double year.'

Time to hit the pause button. At the end of the season, we went on a tour to Russia. You play a long hard season, slogging around through the winter mud with boots like divers and a ball like a medicine ball and then, as a reward, you go off to some strange land to play more football. Somewhere in the equation, these players have wives, girlfriends, children, lives . . . It's difficult to see where though. So this is a normal thing? To go to Russia?

'It does seem strange after a hard season, but that's Bill Nicholson. He obviously had something in mind. You've got to perform. You've got a bit of pride and, of course, they're going to perform. They're very patriotic people, and it was tough – not the type of tour you look forward to, but as I say, football-wise, it really got us together, and it was signs of things to come. That was the double team all knitted in. We performed out there. We were there for three weeks and that was a long time in Russia – particularly in 1959, my God. But it certainly was an experience, no doubt about that.

'Football-wise, that's when we clicked, and that carried on all through the following season. We should have won the League, but we had a very bad Easter. We played Chelsea away, Manchester City at home and Chelsea at home. We won the first game at Chelsea, then City beat us 1–0 and Chelsea beat us 1–0. It looked like we would be taking six points and we only took two. Burnley won the League that year and we came third. Just before half-time in that Manchester City game I took a penalty. Bert Trautmann made a brilliant save, and I followed up and put it in the back of the net. Thought I'd got away with it but, of course, it was half-time and it didn't stand. I said to Bill, "I'm not taking any more penalties," and Danny took 'em after that. I knew that it was a big penalty and, looking back on it all, you can see that the defeat revolved around it. Of course, it wasn't my fault, but you tend to think, "If I'd only scored that penalty, it could have been different."

'At the time nobody really knew what was going on. When the referee pointed to the centre circle, people thought it was a goal, but it was just for half-time. You could hear everything going round and round: "Is it a goal?" Of course, he came out with, "No goal." There were just seconds in it but you've got to accept it, haven't you? And that's the one thing about Bill Nick, he made sure that we would accept it. He wouldn't have us whingeing and moaning about it. He'd say, "I'll tell you something. You don't know the rules of the game." And he's quite right. He said, "Referees are only human – they're going to make mistakes, but they're not going to make as many as you lot, I'll guarantee that." He put us in our place. It's leadership. It's the one thing that I dislike – chasing referees. Like Manchester United, all that chasing referees – I can't stand it, and Bill wouldn't tolerate it. That comes from Ferguson. Leadership again, and you don't see enough of it. It's just values – good values.'

Of all the remarkable statistics about the double year, one of the most striking is that Spurs only used 14 players the whole season.

Eight first-team regulars – Brown, Baker, Henry, Blanchflower, Norman, White, Allen and Dyson – were ever-present. Think of the spirit that that must engender – the camaraderie. It's not hard to work out who the player was that kept getting replaced because he was injured.

'I realised that at some point in the season, I was going to get an injury. That's the end of the story.' (For the record, Cliff Jones played 29 League games in the double year, being replaced by Terry Medwin when injured.) 'They only used 14 players, and I was the one who was getting injured all the time. The year we did the double and created that First Division record of winning 11 games straight on the trot – well, I only played in three of them. The first game of the season I got injured badly against Everton. I always remember it. Alex Parker was the right-back. When I was at Swansea we had this old professional, Billy Lucas, and he said to me, "When you go on to the football field, don't trust any bastard. Don't trust them." I was in the army with Alex and I thought he was a good pal of mine – and he is but he really did me. Oh, did he do me. He came in late. I'd played the ball off, and he came in – boom – seconds late. I thought I'd broken my ankle; and I had to go off. "Oh, Alex," I said, "you came in a bit late there – I thought we were mates, me and you." "We are," he said, "but not today."

'I thought, "Billy Lucas, you were right." Alex, he was a good pal of mine, but that's professional sport – ruthless even then in those glory, glory days.'

Asking Cliff Jones what his greatest game was, I'd have put my house on him naming the FA Cup final against Leicester, the game that won Spurs the double. How many games write themselves into the history books so conclusively? And if not that game, then another watershed – the 5–1 victory over Atletico Madrid in the final of the European Cup-Winners' Cup on 15 May 1963. It meant Spurs were the first British team to win a major European trophy, it was final and total vindication of everything that had been missed and everything that had been achieved; and this without the injured Dave Mackay, and with Danny Blanchflower, aged 37, playing on one leg, against a Spanish team that spookily had a flying winger called Jones . . .

But Cliff Jones had other ideas: 'Gornik, when we beat them at home. That's the one which, to me, was the great game. There are other games you've got to talk about. The Cup final itself against Leicester when we clinched the double; I've met people who were at the Benfica game, and they say that that was the most outstanding game. Another game that stands out is the Charity Shield against Ipswich the year after we did the double. I always thought we could have done the double again the following year, but Ipswich won four points off us and they won the League.

'I can remember the Charity Shield after that. Bill Nick said, "Right. We're going to change it a bit today," because with Ipswich they had their regular wingers, Arthur Steven and Jimmy Leadbetter, playing deep, right back there, and they had Ray Crawford and Ted Philips at centre-forward. So what would happen is that our full-backs would go to their wingers and our wing-halves would be a bit lost, so there were big gaps and Ipswich exploited that. The full-backs were drawn out of position and the deep wingers would make all those diagonal runs which caused a lot of problems. This was Alf Ramsey's team and it was a very effective system.'

This point is worth a brief detour. Ipswich won the League the season before simply because they beat Spurs 3–1 at White Hart Lane by playing a system that was different. It perplexed Spurs – in fairness, it perplexed everybody – and without the blanket media coverage of today, no one found out until it was too late. If that happened now, Alan Hansen and Jimmy Hill would be shouting about it from the rooftops on day one. On day two, there'd be diagrams in the papers. On day three, Ipswich would be relegated; and maybe that should've happened then. And Spurs would win the League and everybody would go home happy.

Bill Nick later claimed that he sussed the system and had wanted to change his team tactically in the White Hart Lane game on Boxing Day. But the players disagreed, Bill Nick relented, Spurs were beaten and that was that.

After that Bill didn't mess around: 'There was no nonsense this time. I put my foot down and told them very firmly that we would play this one my way, which we did, and we beat them by 5–1.'

Back to Cliff: 'In the Charity Shield Bill Nick said, "Right – Peter Baker, Ron Henry, you're going to come in and mark Philips and Crawford. Maurice Norman, you go in spare. Danny, Dave, you're going to push down on to their wingers and see how that goes." And I tell you what, they never got a kick. The other clubs obviously saw how we played them and they adopted that system, shoving the wing-halves on their two wingers. It was quite revolutionary really, because it was considered a full-back's job to mark a winger. They nearly got relegated that next year, Ipswich. They finished about third from bottom.

'Bill was always forward thinking about the game, always looking for a new way to do things. For example, when we played against West Ham, Bobby Smith would go and mark Bobby Moore – all the attacks stemmed from Bobby Moore, you see. Centre-forward would go and mark centre-half – common sense, but I would never have thought of it. Danny might have. But that was Bill.'

Tottenham Hotspur 8 (Jones 3, Smith 2, Dyson, White, Blanchflower (pen))
Gornik Zabrze 1 (Pohl)

European Cup, preliminary round, second leg
20 September 1961

Tottenham Hotspur: Brown, Baker, Henry, Blanchflower, Norman, Mackay, Jones, White, Smith, Allen, Dyson.
Gornik Zabrze: Kostka, Franesz, Oslizlo, Olszowka, Pohl, Wilczek, Gawlik, Florenski, Lentner, Jankowski, Olejnik.
Attendance: 56,737

On 13 September 1961, Spurs went to play their first game in European competition in Poland against Gornik Zabrze. This might have been the European Cup, including the very best teams in Europe, each team the champions of their respective countries, but this was the Spurs double team, the invincible Spurs double team. Mackay, Blanchflower, White, Jones . . . Real Madrid were welcome to come and have a go. As if – Real had been beaten by Barcelona the previous season, another reason to start doing that glory shuffle. Time for a new dynasty?

In Phil Soar's book *And The Spurs Go Marching On*, Bill Nicholson tells of an advance trip he made to Poland to check the facilities.

> They took me to this terrible place and told me this is where we would be staying. I told them they would stay at the best hotel in England when they came to us, so I wanted Spurs to stay at the best hotel in Katowice where Gornik were based. They said that this was the best hotel in Katowice.

Danny Blanchflower, as Danny Blanchflower often did, took up the story: 'There were prisoners in the streets digging up cobblestones guarded by men with machine guns. Going through the park leading to the Slaski Stadium we could see women, on their hands and knees, cutting the grass with what seemed to be large pairs of scissors. The stadium, massive, lit and tall like a distant castle, was the only welcoming thing about the whole place.'

The air of disorientation obviously knocked Spurs out of their stride like a child knocking a spinning top in full flow. Within an hour, Spurs were 4–0 down and Nicholson didn't disguise his feelings. 'I was bloody upset. We showed no determination or discipline.' Jones and Dyson got two goals back and the game finished 4–2 to Gornik. It didn't matter. The next day McDonald's could have set up shop in Katowice High Street and it wouldn't have been more astonishing – or more shocking to the Poles – than what was about to come.

Cliff Jones: 'We had great expectations going into Europe – it was a new experience for all of us. We'd drawn Gornik and Bill had had them watched, but we went out there and we didn't perform all that well. At one period, we were 4–0 down and looked like we were in right trouble about whether or not we were going to go any further. We did pull a number of goals back. Terry Dyson got one and I got one to make it 4–2. It was different surroundings, different atmosphere, we were playing against the Gornik side which really was the Polish team, a very high standard. We'd gone out and played our game of getting forward – that was our game, to try to get goals – and, of course, it backfired a bit. Bill learnt from that. Whenever we played our first legs, and fortunately we had the advantage of always being drawn away first, we put Tony Marchi in and played an extra defender. I think Dyson would come out – Dyson or Les Allen – just to stop them from scoring. If we came back with no score or 1–0, it was okay. We always had the capability of coming back, no problem. We never got beat at White Hart Lane. It was always within our capabilities to pull back two or three goals. It was about the only time we played that way just to contain the opposition. Bill would go over first and have a watch, and in the dressing-room he had the dossier on each player to give us. It's always an advantage to know a little bit about each player.'

The Spurs double team, well prepared, armed with Revie-esque dossiers, firing on all attacking cylinders – and 4–0 down.

'Yes, and we did take a bad press as well. There were one or two incidents in the game which caused a few problems and we were accused of being over-physical which was possibly justified; when Bobby Smith's around and when Dave Mackay's around ... particularly Bob. And, of course, if you think about the goalkeeper... you could shoulder-charge the goalkeeper in this country, but there were different rules in Europe then. Bob still applied the British rules. Not only was he a good player, but he could also intimidate people. That has a part in the game. It isn't very pleasant sometimes and we did take a lot of criticism from the press.

'Bill was not happy about our display, and he made sure that we were ready for the second leg, made sure that we were really built up. The fans were quite amazing – they were really ready for it – and when we walked on to the pitch at White Hart Lane, well ... I wasn't prepared for it. I mean, it was quite incredible. It was electric; absolutely electric. The first European match in Tottenham's history. There were nearly 60,000 there – all up for it like the players themselves. When we played at Gornik – you'd find this with the European grounds – there was a running track around the pitch and the spectators were about 15 yards from the playing area. But at Tottenham it was different. The crowd was almost on the pitch in comparison to that – the noise made you feel a tingle go right up the old back there.

'Gornik were also up for it, but as they came out you could see them look around a bit apprehensive, and right from the off, we hit the bar – we attacked right from the off. We had the kick-off. I think it was Les Allen who smacked it against the cross-bar. That's what the crowd wanted. I tell you something – it was one continual roar for 90 minutes. I've never experienced anything like it. Not many Polish supporters there, I can tell you. And I have to say it, we swept them right off that pitch. We swept them aside. I honestly feel that in that particular game – we won 8–1 against a national side – I don't think that there's any team ever could have lived with us that night. I don't care who they are – if you put them at White Hart Lane that night they would have struggled. That night we were unstoppable.'

The 1970 Brazil team?

'That night? They would have struggled.'

Why?

'It was the motivation to do well – we knew we could do so much better than we had done out there. We'd just won the double, and we were determined to perform as we could do. Also, the crowd were experiencing something they'd never experienced before and that came across to us. Make no mistake about it, they do play a very big part. Bill Nick had got us to a fine pitch and we were all ready to go. We were still smarting from the criticism we'd taken. We were quite justly criticised for our performance in Poland; we wanted to do something about it, and we certainly did. In night games I don't know, we always seemed to be able to run quicker and for longer. They just seemed to have that bit of atmosphere. It was just an incredible game. It always sticks in my mind. I mean it, that night not many teams could have lived with us: 8–1.

'We went three up, so that put us 5–4 in front, and their inside-forward hit possibly the best goal of the game – a volley which flew into the net. That made it five all. It spurred us on and we just crashed them away.'

Curious to note that, in those bygone days when life was so much simpler and the milkman delivered milk to your door, their inside-forward was called Pohl, Ernest Pohl. It kept things easy. Who scored for them? The Pole, Pohl.

'My goals – a header, a right foot and a left foot – made a hat-trick because they were one after the other. There weren't any other goals in between. I think it was in the space of about 12 minutes. Everything just seemed to come off. I was just . . . well, absolutely exhilarated by it all. It was for me one of the greatest moments of my life – next to scoring the winning goal against England at Ninian Park. Being Welsh that's got to be my top, the winning goal, but that's another story.

'That night, that was the greatest; it stands out in my mind – the speed, the pace, the power. At half-time, we knew the game was won. We didn't want half-time to come. We really couldn't wait to get out there and finish the job off, which we did. We could have still been playing now, I reckon. We didn't want that final whistle to go. What an incredible night. I think that was the start of the headlines – the glory, glory game, the Hot Spurs. I mean, we were tremendous; unstoppable.

'Bill was happy and he said, "That was all right" which meant you had really done well. Bill was a bit like that. He said to me one day, "That was a bit better there, Jonesy." "You're giving me a pat on the back, are you Bill? That's unusual," I said. "Yes," he said, "but remember, a pat on the back is only three foot away from a kick up the arse. All right?"

'John White was involved in all the goals. For me, John White was the Glenn Hoddle of his time – he was that kind of player. He had all the great skills, the control, the craft; possibly he made himself a bit more available than Glenn did. Every time he picked the ball up, he'd always have one pass on. That was his game you see, he was a very fit boy, trained well. He was the army cross-country champion. Bill Nick enjoyed that. When he found out he was a cross-country champion, he said, "I'm having him," because he needed someone to be a machine. John was such a lovely character. He was my best mate. If you're going to criticise, he could possibly have got a few more goals because he had a great deal of power in both feet, and great accuracy, but there we are. He was one of the greats. I still keep in touch with his wife – she's moved down to Sussex now, remarried with a family. Great lad, cracking lad.'

Epilogue

Talking to Cliff Jones now is like seeing the leaves of a photo album come to life. But meeting him, it became clear that that was my history, not his. One of the most gifted players in the most glittering football team this country has ever seen, Jones exudes the contentedness of a man who's satisfied.

I asked him, is there anything you regret? Is there anything that you didn't do that you wished you had?

'Oh yes. I would have loved to have played abroad. It nearly happened. In 1963, I'd just had my best season and we'd won the European Cup-Winners' Cup. We played Juventus in a pre-season game. I annihilated the Juventus defence and they'd just won the Italian championship. Obviously it stuck with them; we had a terrific season and Juventus came for me. The director and the president of the club both came to my house in Palmers Green just outside London with Tony Marchi as the link-up. Marchi had been to Italy on loan at the turn of the decade.

'But Bill Nick said, "No – you ain't going" and that put an end to it. I'd just got the business set up, and I'd got the four kids in school, so in many ways it was a good thing. I didn't want to disrupt that side of my life. Looking back, if I could make any changes I would have loved to have gone and experienced Italian football; I think I could have done well, but it's something I'll never find out. Bill said no, and when Bill said no, that was it. You didn't argue. The deal would have been £125,000. I was going to get a £20,000 signing-on fee for a two-year contract – good money then. They wanted someone who was an individual, who could score goals and be entertaining and effective, someone who the Italian crowds would like. I could have linked up with John Charles. It would have been a good move. I wasn't a jack-the-lad but a family man; I was disciplined. But we'll never know.

'He did give me a rise though. It wasn't too much, but there you go. It was nice to know that Bill still wanted me that much and it was nice to know that Juventus wanted me too. Now and again, I just wonder what might have been. One thing I have learned is that there's no point in living in the past. You have to get on with today. As Danny said, "If you can get today right, it makes yesterday a pleasant memory and tomorrow a vision of hope." Isn't that nice? A number of sportsmen tend to look back and live for the past and you can't.'

Before leaving Jones, I had to ask him about my favourite Spurs game – Burnley, 7–0 at home. There's one game I must ask you about . . .

'Burnley,' he said laughing. 'People always remember that one. 1966, '67. Yes, that's another period when we were playing great football. Mackay had gone. There was Alan Mullery, Venables, Jennings, Knowles, Kinnear, England – the Cup final team. It was a header that goal, but I collided badly with the post – not always the best thing to do – and I eventually had to go off. I can remember getting the other goal, but after I'd got that whack, I couldn't do a great deal with the ball. Bill Nick always said that I was more effective when I passed the ball. "Let it go," he'd say.

' "What do you mean?" I said. "Pass the bloody thing," he'd reply.

'I think it was 5–2 or something like that. I knew it was going to happen, but I thought, "Ah, let's have some of it – see what happens." Lovely days. A lovely period of my life. I was fortunate. I look back and think of it as a privilege.'

5

ENTER PAT PENDING

Ralph Coates

> I thought back to when I played and I was lacking in confidence. In some matches I was feeling like, 'I don't want the ball – don't give me the ball' because I was frightened that I'd make a mistake. Once your confidence has gone, you don't want it – and that shouldn't be. You should want the ball all the time, and if you make a mistake, so what? You've tried.
>
> Ralph Coates

Bill Nicholson: 'Ralphy played at Burnley, and whenever we went up to Burnley it was always Coatesy who gave us problems. So I went and signed Coatesy. I met him at a hotel up the motorway – the M6 I think – in Stoke. It's where I interviewed and signed him. I got him back down here and the first thing he said to me was: "I don't take corners, Bill." I said "What?" He said, "I don't take corners," and I said, "Why?" When he told me why, I said, "Well, you'd better bloody learn how to do it then. With your bloody size, you're not high enough to nod the ball into the bloody net, but you should be good enough to kick the ball into that area for someone else to do it." I don't think that pleased him all that much.

'Some of the players . . . I had to say to them on more than one occasion when Coatesy wasn't playing, "Hey look, you've got to give him a fair crack of the whip. I know that he's been disappointing since he came here and I signed him and I should take the rap for this, but I tell you one thing. Whenever we played at Burnley, and nearly all of you lot have played at Burnley, who was the man up there who always gave us all the bloody problems? It was Coatesy, wasn't it?" And they'd all go, " Yeah, yeah." I said, "Well, if he can play like that for Burnley why can't he play like that for Tottenham?" I said give the boy a chance, give him a break; he got a good break because he played in one of our European Cup ties – where was it? In Russia somewhere – and he scored a goal. He was thrilled to bits and all the lads were pleased because it was a good goal.'

I was at work thinking of ways not to be at work when the phone rang.

'Hello. This is Ralph Coates here.'

Before overcoming the shock of being phoned by Ralph Coates, my right hand, without thinking, reached over to my left ear and swept a great swathe of hair over the top of my head and onto the other side. Okay, so my hair isn't as young as it once was, but this was not a hair gesture. This was a subconscious acknowledgement of one of the great sporting tics of the post-war era; right up there with the McEnroe wail and the Ali shuffle sits the Coates sweep. It was as if Ralph had seen Bobby Charlton, sat and thought about it and, like the artist he was, developed the idea, taking it as far as it could go. Not for Ralph a few wispy strands of flyaway hair. No, he had a kind of elongated ginger brillo pad flap that attached itself just above his left ear. The other curious thing about Ralph's appendage was that it seemed far longer than his head. To see it flying in the wind, pre-sweep, you'd think it was some bizarre Vivienne Westwood scarf, or an unfurled turban.

You did not have to be a Spurs fan to find something to appreciate in the Ralph Coates experience. You didn't even have to be a football fan. Seeing him in full flight, tearing down the wing, hair trailing behind him like a pre-war airforce pilot's white silk scarf, the ones held in place with metal coat hangers at right angles to your head, is the sort of thing you'd tell your kids about. Ralph Coates – there was always something about him that was less George Best, more Professor Pat Pending, something a little Hanna-Barbara.

As a Spurs player, Coates's appearance made a curious kind of sense. Consider it this way. Given that he was bought to replace either Alan Gilzean or Roger Morgan, his ear quiff fitted the bill perfectly. There was Gilzean, timelessly bald and grey, not a man you'd pick out of a police line-up as a highly paid professional athlete. Yet he was as elegant as a gazelle, as mobile as mercury, a ballet dancer; one of the finest forwards of his time and a footballer of such ability that he was able to be the perfect foil for such diverse and formidable talents as Jimmy Greaves and Martin Chivers.

Then there was Roger Morgan, a style victim from an era when men didn't have to try too hard; an Alan Gilzean from a parallel anti-matter universe. Remember those photographs that used to stare out of the windows of barber shops? That kind of second division Jason King cossack look? Watching him play, you had the feeling that if Roger Morgan had been a racehorse, his favourite result would have been a photo-finish. He looked good but, in football speak, he didn't produce the goods. If we all aspired to be elegantly wasted, Roger Morgan wasted elegantly. The perfect Spurs player? Okay, so he was unlucky with injuries and was kept out of the first team for over a year . . . Let's not get bogged down in detail here. Morgan flattered to deceive, so much so that he was described by an early '70s tabloid as 'one of Bill Nicholson's expensive mistakes'. *One* of? What – or who – could they have meant?

When Bill Nick went up the M6 to the Staffordshire Post House Hotel to sign Ralph Coates, his wife probably thought he was popping out for a bag of wine gums. Nicholson's deals always had a touch of the Agatha Christie about them.

'It's raining today in Sheffield, isn't it?'

'Yes. And the sheep are green. So, you want Ralph Coates, then?'

Far from implying that there was any impropriety going down – brown paper bags and the like – the reason for this was the exact opposite. Keep publicity down, keep the price low. It might have worked for Spurs, but when Coates walked out of that hotel he became, at £190,000, the most expensive player in Britain. Was that much of a burden?

'Very much so. Burnley was a smaller club – no disrespect, it was a terrific club, but it was a small, family club. The players got together two or three times a week. Being the best player and the greatest asset that they had was a responsibility. But after the transfer, there was the responsibility of having a £190,000 tag, a record at the time. Coming down and playing with such great players, you had to establish your own identity and your own quality of play which is a lot more difficult when you've got another ten players of equal or better quality than you. It was hard to adjust. The first season was difficult for me and I didn't fulfil the potential which was there, waiting to come out.'

The thing that people have got to remember with that whole 'didn't fulfil his potential' deal is that the potential is only someone else's projection. It also relates to a well-known law that's effective in offices and other business areas. Sometimes known as Peter's Law, it works like this. Person X is very good at his job and is seen to be very good at his job. So he gets promoted. Person X is very good at the new job, and gets promoted again. This happens again and again until Person X finds himself in a job he can't do so well, doesn't get promoted, stays there. And people around him moan. But is it his fault?

'You know the crowd are saying, "Okay, so where is it? Why did they pay that?" and you know you're not justifying it. You know you can do better if you only get the chance. It was a difficult year because I was playing out of position. The price tag was a burden, and in the first season I wasn't too happy with it. The second season was a lot better and I was voted Spurs Player of the Year, which was quite pleasing. The supporters were very patient with me. At the time I'd heard that if they didn't like a player, they let the player know. [Terry Venables, another player who got a famously hard time from the Spurs fans, once said that they weren't too bad. They gave you at least three games before they started getting on your back.] But I can honestly say, hand on heart, that they gave me a great time at Spurs. I think it was my kind of play that they appreciated. I could have had a poor game, but it wasn't through lack of trying and I think that the crowd appreciated that. I gave 100 per cent every game.'

Coates's efforts and comparative lack of success contrast nicely with another Spurs star of the time. If Coates would run and run and then trip over his shoelaces at the vital moment, this other star was the complete opposite.

'Very difficult, it was. A number of people have mentioned that to me. Martin Chivers had two terrific seasons where he couldn't do anything wrong. I mean, every time he shot for goal, it ended up in the back of the net. He reached a colossally high standard of play and that's very, very hard to maintain. The type of player he was, he needed the service; and whether or not he got that service, or whether he wasn't trying to get the service, only Martin knows. But whereas I was busy all the time, Martin wasn't. It could be disillusionment.'

Coates came to Spurs on the cusp of what was the start of the proper money. In 1971, £190,000 was a lot of wedge in anyone's haircut. But when he signed in that hotel in Stoke, he made a decision to exchange a luxury bungalow surrounded by lush fields for an upstairs flat in a grotty part of Palmers Green, a nondescript area in urban north London. His wife, Sandra, had a job as an occupational therapist and though his two-year-old daughter was pre-school, it was still an upheaval.

When Ralph Coates announced he was leaving Burnley, people came to his house and cried on the doorstep. More than a big fish in a little pond, he was a whale. The journey to Tottenham might only have been a few hours down the motorway, but as far as Coates was concerned, it was so far it would have taken the Starship Enterprise about three episodes to get there. The Burnley manager used to ask his advice when he picked the team. (Close your eyes and try to imagine Bill Nick doing that.) When he was injured, the club was scared of leaving his name out of the match programme for fear that no one would turn up. Towards the end of his time there, Coates was on sleeping pills, such was the pressure of expectation. Even with his record fee, at Spurs Coates was just another star, the latest cheque-book Charlie. Then he turns up with his hair and announces to all the world that, no, he doesn't take corners.

Ralph Coates: 'No, it wasn't exactly like that. Going back to my three or four years in midfield at Burnley, I used to hang around the box and I'd never take the corners. Anyway Bill says – and it was in a practice – "Right, you take the corner." I took my position as I always did by the box so that if the ball came out I could get the goal, and I said: "Bill, I haven't taken the corner for three or four years," and he said "Well you're taking one now."

'In hindsight, I wished he told me before because I could have taken a bag of balls and practised. I was a perfectionist and I would have practised my corners. As a winger I used to go back in the afternoon and practise crosses till my leg ached. It wasn't a problem but I was just taken aback. It's a skill to put that ball where you want it. I didn't mind doing it, but it's a skill. I took corners in the game and I practised them and it wasn't much of a hassle. It was just a shock and that's when I knew that there were changes going on. I was having to play positions I hadn't played for a long time and it was a very difficult time. But I'm not one for banging the manager's door down. I'd rather sit down and talk about it realistically and come to a balance and appreciate his problems too.'

How did the other players react to you? How did they relate to what you were going through?

'Generally, the other lads were very patient.'

Did they take the mickey much?

'They took the mickey all the time. They took the mickey out of me so much that I would be disappointed if they didn't. I really didn't mind that – my shoulders were strong. Some of the lads would react a bit more violently if someone took the mickey out them, but I didn't mind it at all. I used to quite like it because it showed that I was one of them. Some people would say, "How do you stand for that," but I'd rather have it that way.'

There's a very cute story in Hunter Davies's *The Glory Game* which tells of how Cyril Knowles – naturally – had wound Ralph up, telling him that the style of the club was such that players weren't allowed to wear the same shirt two days running. Another story tells of how Ralph – a young lad from Burnley – was so concerned about the dress thing that he went out and bought himself a floral shirt for his first day.

'Well, yes actually, the lads did give me a bit of stick about that. They were telling me about the fashions and how they'd changed and Carnaby Street and this type of thing.' At this stage, you want to hug Ralph. 'But the shirt? No, my wife bought it for me. She said, "You can't look out of place," but she went a bit over the top. I still wore it, but the lads gave me a bit of stick because it was way beyond what they were wearing. It was quite funny and it broke me in with the lads – plus the tie I was wearing didn't go at all. But then again it was good. It broke the ice.'

Coming to the big city, pockets bulging with notes, was there a huge temptation to become a bit of a lad?

'No. It wasn't in my nature, coming from the north east. Mind you, hearing some of the stories about Gazza . . . But I've always been a basic, feet-on-the-ground sort of person, and I've never let anything deter me from the knowledge that my grassroots are in the north east. I'm not a playboy and I'm not one for clubs. I'd rather go to my local pub for a couple of pints and a chat than go to Stringfellows disco, no disrespect to Stringfellows. I'm not the type of person for the bright lights and the highlife.' Everything you want to know about Ralph Coates is summed up in that phrase – no disrespect to Stringfellows. He can't even be rude about Stringfellows. Maxwell C. Wolf, my dog, is rude about Stringfellows.

It's somehow symptomatic of Coates's time at Spurs that, despite scoring the winning goal in the League Cup final in 1973 against Norwich, the match that sticks in his mind was played about three million miles away from White Hart Lane, out in the wilds of darkest Russia.

Dynamo Tiblisi 1 (Asatiani)
Tottenham Hotspur 1 (Coates)

UEFA Cup, third round
28 November 1973

Dynamo Tiblisi: Gogia, Dzodvuashvill, Chelidze, Khurtsilava, Kanteladze, Ebralidze, Asatiani, Macharidze, Kipiani, G.Nodia, I.Nodia.
Tottenham Hotspur: Jennings, Evans, Knowles, Pratt, England, Beal, Naylor, Perryman, Peters, Chivers, Coates.
Attendance: 45,000

They were a fantastic team. It was an afternoon kick-off, in front of a crowd of what seemed to be soldiers. We went out to look at the pitch and there was this cockerel hanging up by its neck as we walked on to the pitch. They were a very good team. I remember in the warm-up they were doing a dozen full sprints the length of the pitch. We looked at them and thought, 'Phew, they'll be tired by the time the game starts.' But they weren't tired and they ran as quickly in the game as they did in the warm-up. We were probably lucky to get that result, but we absolutely smashed them at home with the aerial ability of Gilzean and Chivers and Peters and the long throw-ins, near-post corners. We beat them on those extra bits of the game rather than passing it around from A to B to C to D. But pound for pound they were a fantastic team.

Steve Perryman

'I was in my early 20s – 23 or 24 – and though it's a big adventure going somewhere like that, you don't really get a chance to see the place or do anything. It's a case of flying in there, having your night's kip, spending the day relaxing, playing the game and then flying out the next day. So you don't get a chance to see the place you're in. You meet the other players only after the game. Once the game's over there's normally a banquet or a meal and a presentation to the referee or the clubs exchange presents. It's not like the western world – there's the shops in London, your Harrods, your Oxford Street and what have you, and then you go to Russia and you've got your basic shop-front. We did have time on the afternoon prior to the game to look around – I was going to buy my wife a present, but there wasn't a lot that she'd appreciate. It was bit of a shock to see the different cultures.

'I'd been at Spurs three years up until that point, as a winger. Not many people know this, but in my last years at Burnley I was employed again to go where I wanted. Jimmy Adamson, who was manager of Burnley, told me just to get involved with the game and make a nuisance of myself, and I thoroughly enjoyed it because I wasn't restricted. And then I moved, as everyone knows, to Tottenham and was very surprised when, prior to the pre-season games, Bill said, "I want you to play wide as a right-winger." It shocked me a bit and then I felt restricted, relying on other people to give me the ball. I couldn't get involved in the game as much as I wanted to.

'I think that in a number of cases managers do buy players for certain positions, but in my particular case I didn't give it a thought, because I assumed – wrongly – that after playing for three years at Burnley in a free role, Bill Nick or the reps or the scouts would have seen me in that role and want me to do the same at Spurs. So I didn't question what position they wanted me for. I hadn't played on the wing for three years and although I had a bit of pace, my control was good and my quickness off the mark was good, it came as a bit of a surprise. At that time, Alan Gilzean was playing that wide type of attacking role, and I think that I was bought to fill Alan's position because – no disrespect to him – he was getting on a bit, as he admitted himself. But I just couldn't quite get to grips with the position after playing in a free role for Burnley.

'I didn't question it. I gave it the season; I gave it a go. I wasn't too happy for that first season at Spurs and I didn't give what I thought were my best performances and so eventually I went to Bill and said, "Look, I've got to go into midfield, I'm not enjoying the football."

'Although the first season was quite good, my own performance didn't reach the standard that I wanted it to. He changed my position to wide midfield, which was a lot better, but it still seemed a bit restricted on that right-hand side. It wasn't until the UEFA games came along when Bill thought "give him a go" that it suddenly clicked.

'I thoroughly enjoyed the game. The goal itself was very pleasing inasmuch as it was laid back to me and I'm not renowned for my shooting expertise. It came on to my left foot, which wasn't my favourite foot; I kept it down, swung the old leg and it went right in the top corner. It actually had so much power in it that it bounced out, right back to where I was standing. Whether the netting was too tight or what we don't know. Martin Chivers, who laid the ball back for me to shoot, said, "Where did you get that one from?" And I couldn't answer. I just laughed and said, "I don't know."

'It was an instinctive shot – it happened so quickly – the ball was laid to Martin, I supported him, he laid me off and I hit it. My main objective was to keep it down and not sky it over the bar. The ball was rising as it hit the top corner of the net, and the keeper, although he made a terrific effort for it, just didn't have a chance to save it. I think I was more surprised than him. In his broken English, the keeper did congratulate me on the goal which was very pleasing, but the team's overall performance and my involvement in the game itself was terrific. I just went wherever the ball was. I made some important tackles in my own box and came out with the ball; it gave me an incentive. We used this ploy for the rest of the UEFA Cup, for me to go where I wanted, and I got more involved in the game because of it.

'In the competition we had a good run. We beat AC Milan in Milan. We got to the final where we lost to Feyenoord – drew 2–2 at home and lost 2–0 at Feyenoord which was very disappointing, but it was an honour to get to the final. I thoroughly enjoyed my European games. It was one of the reasons I went to Tottenham, because they were in Europe. That's what I wanted to do.'

Epilogue

'I'm doing a psychology course at the moment,' says Ralph Coates. 'I think that psychology could come into football more and more, to get players in the right frame of mind to go on that field and perform to their best. You've got the managers and the coaches who do it physically and tactically, but there isn't anyone there to prepare them mentally; it's a very important aspect that we're not utilising. I'm 110 per cent certain that the psychology side of things could tip the balance between being a successful team and an unsuccessful team. Players think that they're there, but often they're not. That little bit extra could make all the difference – I'm totally convinced of this. A player can be sitting in the changing-room and look as though he's really ready, but in actual fact he's thinking about that row he had with his wife earlier in the morning.'

'The nearest we got at Spurs was the manager and he was like a sergeant major. "Come on. We've got to win, come on we need the points" – but I really think in an ideal room with the right temperature, you can relax a player. I'm always one for getting them in a huddle just in the kickabout, and saying, right, we're in the right frame of mind, we've done our preparation, and now you've got to do this, etc. I'm sure that it's a better preparation. Only time can tell. I'd just like to be given the opportunity to prove it.

'It is an attitude. I mean, you can go to extremes, like with the colours of the dressing-rooms. Some players might be affected by colours. If you can, get the players together and ask why the dressing-room is white; would they prefer green or pink. See what the majority of the players want to make them happy. If it's just a tenth of the preparation, then why not do it so that we can honestly say we've done everything to prepare ourselves. I can imagine Bill Nick and Bill Shankly saying, "What are you talking about?" but times have changed and you have to grab every chance you can. Now I'm a positive thinker. I'm more deep-thinking than before. I'm sure that if I'd had this attitude earlier I'd have been a better player – a more positive and confident player. I really do.'

From Pat Pending to positive thinker and feng shui advocate. Though by all accounts never a confident lad at the best of times – taking sleeping pills because of the pressure at Burnley? – his Spurs experience must have stripped a threadbare supply almost totally. It's good to see him reclaiming it from football, albeit a good few years later.

Are you still in touch with any of the other players?

'Oh yes, it's only recently that I've stopped playing with the lads for the charity games. My knee's a bit slow now, whereas in the old days, you'd give it a bit of a knock and it would be fine the next day. I've decided to give it a rest. I'll see if it's improved next season. It's good to play with the lads – we get on the coach and the first words are "Can you remember . . .?"'

6

THE SPIRIT LEVEL

Steve Perryman

Steve Perryman: 'The interesting thing was, with Bill Nick being very clever, we go back to Italy, shielding this one-goal lead. People talk about Shankly going to visit every hotel room to check that there's no traffic, no noise or this or that, no way that people could interrupt you. We got granted permission to use Inter Milan's training ground. I don't know how he got it. I think it was more out of respect for Bill Nick. I think he asked the question and got the right reply. It might have been an anti-AC feeling, but they were good hosts.

'It was in Lake Como – a magnificent expanse. It was like a hotel because their players used to be put in some kind of quarantine from a Thursday to a Sunday match, so they had to have the cinema and the restaurant all there – it was beautiful. The game at White Hart Lane had gone live back to Italy and all the people working at this place were Inter Milan fans, so they were quite happy with me scoring two goals. When we walked into the hotel to book in, it was all "Where's Perryman? Where's Perryman?" You've got to remember I'd travelled all over the country and probably half of Europe with this team and I'd never had that kind of acclaim. It was always Chivers and Jennings and England and Gilzean – and rightly so. But because of those two goals it was suddenly "Where's Perryman?" '

What were you? 20? 21? Did it go to your head?

'No, no. It didn't go to my head or anything like that – I was too much of a defender for that.'

You're Steve Perryman, you're in Japan and someone you don't know phones you up from the other side of the world and asks you what your greatest game was. How long, do you think, would it take you to answer? It's already taken you longer than it took Steve. I expected that it would be that way. I just knew that it was going to be very straight down the line.

'AC Milan, semi-final of the UEFA Cup, first leg.'

Tottenham Hotspur 2 (Perryman 2)
AC Milan 1 (Benetti)

UEFA Cup, semi-final, first leg
5 April 1972

Tottenham Hotspur: Jennings, Kinnear, Knowles, Coates, England, Naylor, Gilzean, Perryman, Chivers, Peters, Mullery (Sub: Neighbour).
AC Milan: Cudicini, Sabadini, Zignoli, Anquilletti, Schnellinger, Rosato, Sogliano, Benetti, Bignon, Rivera, Golin (Sub: Zazzaro).
Attendance: 42,064

'It was a cold, windy evening at White Hart Lane. The pitch had been ravaged a bit by the winter and it hadn't really recovered and, as it used to be said in those days, you needed a couple of goals advantage to take back to Italy for the second leg. They were giants, Milan, and I think something like eight of this team were in the team that won the European Cup two or three years later. The Italians being the Italians, they defended stoutly; they backed off you, they defended their 18-yard box, so I suppose if we were going to score against them it was going to be from outside the box. Unfortunately, after the first twenty minutes when we were really piling on the pressure, they got a breakaway and we went a goal down. This was going to make it very hard, because at that time the Italians were supposed to be the masters of the clean sheet, so the fact that I eventually scored a goal before half-time to make it level was vital for us. But they'd got their away goal, so we faced the prospect of going back to Italy effectively 0–0, and that's good enough for them. Then I scored another goal in the second half and that won the game for us.

'They were a very good team. Rivera did some magnificent things in the game. I remember he got the ball from a throw-in, I went in to close him down and he nonchalantly kneed it over my head. Before

I knew it, he was gone. You know, I still don't really like to watch that – but even at the time, there was an appreciation of the skill.'

Was Rivera your responsibility?

'Yes, he would have been. There was Rivera and Benetti in midfield. Benetti was nicknamed "The Englishman" because of the way he played. There was actually a blocked tackle in the game where I went for the ball and I tackled with my laces – I remember when I was younger one of the trainers saying, "If you keep doing that, you'll break your leg." It was tackling as if you're going to shoot for goal. This big, strong, well-made Italian just put his foot there as a normal side-foot tackle and there's no way you can win the tackle the way I was doing it. It was quite a bone-crunching affair, but it was the same technique that got me my two goals as well.

'Both of my goals were from outside the box, and people said afterwards that that was the only way we were going to score against them. I think the second one was from a corner which got cleared. I was patrolling half way in the opposing half. The ball was obviously coming to me and I touched it out with my feet very well. It was sitting up nicely so I hit it and it ended up in the corner of the net.'

The ball came out and, in a split second, you controlled it, evaluated the situation, saw the keeper off his line and went for the gap like you're William Tell and it's an apple?

'Goals like that, you like to think that you meant it, but really, you throw it up and see what happens.'

It's a curious admission, that one. It's all very well, the old post-match, sweat on the brow, milk bottle in the hand interview cliché – 'Stevie knocked it to Stevie and the ball broke loose and I just hit it' – but, really, no one believes it. That's the stuff we do on Sunday mornings, me and you, we hit it. The ball comes and we hit it. Surely when Spurs play AC Milan in the UEFA Cup semi-final there's a little bit more geometry involved?

'No. You've got to understand this, because there's a defensive aspect to it as well. If you do the wrong thing from there, they get the chance to break at you and from there they could score. So you're concentrating on the ball. You've got to get it right. You're concentrating on the ball that's coming towards you and it's really the way that you control the ball and the way that it sits up or doesn't sit up that makes your mind up what to do next.

'I mean, sometimes you get a decent touch of the ball but it's at an angle and it encourages you to play it straight out to the corner kicker where the ball's come from. That was Bill Nick's favourite piece of advice. You know, when you're in a position that I was in, you smack it out to the wide player, which means that you're not going to concede anything as a team, because he'll cross it and you'll get a second chance. But this sat up so nicely that it had to be volleyed – it was a sort of dipping volley really, and it was a nice feeling. But still, I was thinking more of what my defensive responsibilities were. I never used to congratulate people when they scored goals because I was always worried about us conceding one from the kick-off.

'It was one of those games that turns the corner for you because I wasn't having the greatest of seasons. My first two seasons, things had gone extremely well in a weird sort of way. I would just clear balls from the edge of the box, put Jimmy Greaves in for the goal, he'd beat five players and I'd be acclaimed for the pass, and all it was was a clearance. But this game opened up my career again. After the game, our doctor kindly told me that Bill Nick was thinking of not picking me during that spell and leaving me out for that particular match. Good job he didn't.

'It was a magnificent game. Most people remember it as Alan Mullery's game. Mullery was just on his way out. We'd loaned him to Fulham, but because of our injury problems they'd cut his loan short and we'd taken him back and put him straight back in to captain the team in the UEFA Cup semi-final. So he played it and was his normal sort of storming self.'

Time for a brief recap. Alan Mullery, club captain and England stalwart, was having what might be considered a bad season. What had started out full of optimism had turned into big-time disappointment. A strained pelvic muscle had taken him out of the first team, but by the time he was fit again the team had moved on. That's the problem with getting injured. There are plenty of vultures waiting to feed on the carcasses of the injured, ready to take their place. Ralph Coates had moved, with some success, back into midfield from the wing. John Pratt, a hard-running, hard-working, faithful servant type of vulture, had come in and done reasonably well.

John Pratt – how might his career have gone had he changed his name? How can we best describe John Pratt? If we say Pratt was a Perryman minus the charisma you may get the idea. Steve Perryman was loved, needed, admired and respected – a hard-working pro appreciated by his fellow pros. But charismatic? No. Not even his mother would call him charismatic. Steve himself would probably consider it a veiled insult, figuring you meant dilettante. There he'd be, with his shirtsleeves carefully folded up – not rolled, folded – to just above his elbow, running around with a deceptively short-paced staccato step, his arms bent, a little scuttlebug. And he'd run. In football parlance, he was honest, a 100 per cent geezer, a 90-minute player, a good pro. Perryman was all those things, but charismatic? No. Alfie Conn was charismatic. And what did Perryman think of Alfie Conn?

'A will-o'-the-wisp. He did it only when he wanted to do it; if he didn't fancy it or he couldn't do it, he never delivered.' Dishonest. Talking to Perryman later, I said that he seemed like the earth wire of the team. 'Yes, I suppose I was.' This was a compliment.

John Pratt was, like Perryman, 100 per cent honest. He played like him and he looked like him. Same age, same haircut, same height (5 foot 8 inches), same sleeves carefully folded up – not rolled, folded – same scuttlebug running style. He joined the professional ranks in 1965 and by the time he left the scene in 1980, Pratt was Spurs' longest-serving pro. Always thereabouts if not quite there, Pratt was the quintessentially useful squad player, great to have around but not really a star – maybe if he'd changed his name.

Mullery, at 30, should have had a bit of life left in him. Okay, in the football world, 30 might be the time to start thinking about pension plans and life assurance schemes, but it isn't the end. So, rather than play in the reserves, Mullery asked to be loaned out. Much to his surprise (and, no doubt, to his chagrin) he was on the next bus to Fulham. It was a bit like one of those cry-for-help suicide bids where everyone says, 'We don't want you to top yourself, but if you must . . . and please, don't make a mess on the carpet.'

It was not so long ago that he played so well and to such acclaim in the 1970 World Cup, particularly against Pelé in the Brazil match. Pelé seemed a long way from Craven Cottage.

To the footballing gods, this was a particularly dull way to end a sparkling career. No disrespect to Fulham, but something had to be done. Now, as fate would have it, in the build-up to the Milan match over the Easter period, Spurs had a game at Ipswich, two days before the big one. Everyone played badly. No one did well. Maybe it was a question of too many games in too few days. Maybe it was a question of players not wanting to over-extend themselves and risk injury only two days before the big match. The star players, the probables, knew they were in for the Milan match and didn't have to try too hard. For the possibles, the opposite was true. Maybe because of that, they froze. Some, like Ray Evans, froze over and cracked.

But it wasn't bad form that came to Mullery's rescue – again, too dull. John Pratt, ironically one of the few players who had been playing well, broke his nose and had to be rushed to hospital. What to do? This was Monday. Milan was Wednesday. What to do? Time to send up a puff of smoke. 'Calling International Rescue. Come in International Rescue.' Nigel joins David on stage for one last Japanese tour. It had that air to it.

That was Mullery.

However pleased Spurs, and Perryman in particular, were feeling with themselves, it must have paled in comparison to how Milan were feeling. Only a single-goal deficit, and the vital away goal that's a 'get out of jail free' card in Europe. Away goals count double in the event of a draw. A single-goal win would do it for Milan, and next to coffee, there's very little that Italians do better than the single-goal win.

Going over to the San Siro must have been like walking into the lion's den; a mixture of rabid anticipation and dread. It really doesn't matter that you're Spurs and you've got a 2–1 lead. This is Milan. It doesn't matter that you've got the inspirational Mullery back, it doesn't even matter that Gilzean is out injured, though, God knows, it doesn't help. John Pratt's all well and good, but he's not Gilly. This is Milan. There's going to be the crowd, the noise, the referee . . . What's the feeling going to Milan for the return match?

'Excitement. Pure excitement. You get that simply because of never having played in that stadium before. The crowd was amazing. At our place, you could understand what the crowd were chanting. I can't remember what I could hear on the night, but watching the video, and the cameras are right by the main Tottenham Shelf, you can hear them chanting about Mullery, and my name for goals. You could hear everything and you could relate to it.

'At the San Siro, the crowd were higher up and further away from the pitch. There was more noise, but you couldn't understand what was being shouted, except that it was against you. They certainly made it tough for us. On the ride through to the ground, they were whacking the coach with sticks. They tested your nerves, let's put it that way. There were firecrackers going off when we looked at the pitch before the game. It's difficult to explain the difference. I remember going to St James' Park as a 15-year-old with Dave Mackay and it made a huge impression. I couldn't say it was vicious or angry or what it was, but it was full and there was this black hum above the crowd, a hum of expectancy. The Milan crowd has fervour and excitement and laughs and firecrackers. The English feel is there but it's more cutting.'

In *The Glory Game*, Hunter Davies relates the experience.

> I went out with the team onto the pitch to inspect the turf and immediately ducked for cover. Fire-crackers and smoke bombs were let off the minute the crowd caught sight of the Spurs players. I'd never expected them and thought it was gunfire. I made a quick retreat back to the dressing-room, my ears blocked and my head reeling.

The crowd's one thing, but the team . . .?

'However good Rivera was at our ground, you probably expected him to be better. He did something on the ball against John Pratt – the ball came to him, Pratt closed him down, Rivera stubbed his toe into the ball and played a one-two, but without another player, he did it with the ground. He stubbed the ball and spun it past John Pratt – it was an incredible piece of skill, incredible. But you can overdo it with this feeling of, "Well, they're better than us. They've got more ability and more skill." But I think that was the era when the English heart and drive was still able to overcome that bit of extra technique. We were still very much in that post-Ramsey time.'

As theatre, this was the one that the football gods had been waiting for. If Mullery had made the prodigal's return at White Hart Lane, in Milan he rescued the townsfolk, married the beautiful girl and saved the world from Martian attack. After seven minutes of intense Italian pressure, Spurs got a break. The ball broke to Perryman and, as everyone expected him just to hit it (while remembering his defensive duties), he side-stepped and passed it square to the advancing Mullery. With a shot straight out of the comic books, Mullery hit a perfect volley that curved and cut and flew through the air into the net. Spurs were now 3–1 up and, even for Milan, pulling that back was too much to ask. A late penalty wasn't much consolation.

'The return match we drew 1–1. Mullery scored – it was a very, very good volley and that put us in the final, which I suppose was a little bit of a comedown. When we got back to the dressing-room we found out that Wolves had beaten Dynamo Dresden or whoever it was [Ferencvaros of Hungary] so it was going to be an all-England final.

'We were happy to be in the final to justify the season. But really the AC Milan game was our final. In fairness, we did think that playing Wolves in the final gave us a better chance of winning it, but there was nothing different about it. It was a European final but it could have been a League game.'

Did that feeling go through the whole team?

'Yes. It was an anti-climax, that final. The club had promised to take all the players' wives or girlfriends abroad if we got to the final, and there we were, going to Wolverhampton.'

'Darling. We beat Milan. We're through to the final. At last we can go away together.'

'Oh wonderful, darling. Where are we going. Is it somewhere like Dresden or Ferencvaros in Hungary?'

'No, we're going to Wolverhampton.'

Who'd be a footballer's wife?

Watching film of the game now, it's amazing how it looks just like a regular Sunday afternoon big match; Spurs v Wolves, Brian Moore commentating. At least the first leg at Molineux had the romance of being played at night. There's something about big European ties that says they should be played at night, under floodlights. Fittingly, Spurs scored two cracking goals, both from the enigma that was Chivers. The first came from a set-piece, a flicked header that would have looked easy and straightforward to anyone who has never tried a flicked header from a set-piece. It's testament to the mood that Chivers was in that it looked so easy. The second – the second was the stuff of legend. The ball came to him just over the half-way line. He turned, took a few heroic, muscular paces and then hit the ball from about 500 yards out with a ferocity that made Peter Lorimer look like my mother. It was a wonderful strike, a Cup-winning strike.

The second leg at Spurs, played in the daylight, was a huge anti-climax; like getting married in your local newsagent's. It was a 1–1 draw; Mullery, of course, scored the winner. Sometimes the gods are just so predictable. They mean well, but it's strictly last-reel stuff. As a postscript, Perryman ended the season by getting called up to the England Under-23 squad. Mullery, his work done, was sold to Fulham.

'Looking back, the final was good in itself but it was very normal – too normal, you know, even though we won it at home and collected the Cup in front of our own supporters, which is unusual.'

Still, surroundings are just surroundings.

Spurs had won the Cup. Trebles and win bonuses all round, then? 'I think Bill Nick was always disappointed with it, after the teams that he'd had previously. We always had this feeling that we weren't good enough. The double team was always on top of you, of course. Bill Nick came in after the final and said, "You didn't deserve that." You actually didn't feel like you'd won the trophy. He said, "I've been in there and told them they were the best team." Bill was coming to the end of his days and maybe he was getting a bit over-critical.'

On the face of it, that's a ridiculous attitude, a terrible slap in the face. You enter the UEFA Cup, you win the UEFA Cup – and no one can ask for more from you than that – and you get greeted by your boss who tells you that you didn't deserve to win it. You were expecting a pat on the back, a bottle of champagne, a well done, and what do you get? 'You didn't deserve to win it.' Yet you've got to feel something for both Bill Nick and the Spurs players. Bill Nick: 'As a European final, it was nothing like our 1963 win. That really was a wonderful occasion. I'd say that was the best Cup victory I've known. Winning by five goals to one against Atletico Madrid and winning in style.' As a statement, it's beyond challenge – the first European trophy – and in such style. For such a dour, pragmatic Yorkshireman, Bill Nick has an almost unholy belief in doing things with style. Yet for the players, how can it feel? Doing everything they can, winning one of only three European trophies on offer, yet still being told it wasn't good enough; style and insensitivity in equal part.

Still, we are here to praise Bill Nick, not to bury him. It was difficult for him. He was coming to the end of his time. He knew it. Everybody knew it. He'd had a difficult season. Good as the team was, it relied heavily on a man who shared only one thing with Nicholson – and we're not breaking any confidences here – an intense mutual loathing. It must have been gutting for Bill Nick. You win in a sloppy game; you don't play particularly well despite the fact that you're wearing the beloved all-white strip; the second leg in front of your own people which should have been the triumph, the one where you turn it on for your fans, you can only draw 1–1, and the goals that clinch the Cup are both classics scored by that skulking manatee of a striker who you can't stand. The price of success is sometimes strained.

There are a million ways you can ask someone like Perryman if Chivers was as much a pain in the arse as history has painted him. Was he a difficult man? Was he an overly sensitive man? A man who relied perhaps a little too heavily on his emotions? Was he particularly close to his mother? It doesn't matter what you say, how you put it, there's going to be a straight bat response; wouldn't have it any other way.

'That 1972 team relied heavily on Chivers' goals. Every top team does that. Chivers was the top man in Europe at the time – he had two years when he was phenomenal and, after a time, people never used to follow him up. If we got him away from the half-way line, you said to yourself, "It's a goal" and more often than not, it was.

'The people who go on an ego trip – like Chivers did in his day – get surrounded by all the wrong people; the lawyer, the solicitor, the accountant and the new-found friends. Those people were around even in that era. He lost his way a bit, Chivers. We were probably too reliant on him and all of a sudden he wasn't forthcoming. He wasn't the greatest at handling it. He was living an unreal life as footballers can sometimes do, especially goalscorers.'

Isn't it a necessary part of the striker's armoury to be an ego monster? Don't you have to be more than a little selfish?

Garth Crooks: 'Yes. I'd not thought about it like that before, but you may well be right. Yes.'

Epilogue

Why did you leave Spurs? John Duncan: 'I'd been left out a couple of times and really all it was was a little bit of ego – stupidity.'

Was it a kind of ego madness?

'Yes, beyond what was real and what should've been.'

Steve Perryman: '[Steve Archibald] was a . . . Well, goalscorers have got to be what goalscorers have got to be – self-motivated. They've got to be selfish types and that's fine when you're on the pitch, but off the pitch that's ridiculous. But I don't know. Can you separate the two? If they become less selfish then maybe they won't be able to play so good.'

Garth Crooks: 'I do think the early 80s team broke up prematurely. That was because of ego, ambition . . .'

Ambition?

'Players wanted to earn more money, get on a bigger stage and use their success to better advantage – which was what the game is based on.'

Bigger stage than Spurs? What stage is bigger than Spurs?

'Barcelona.'

Discovered by Spurs in 1966, Steve Perryman, MBE, played 655 league games over a period of 17 years from 1969 to 1986. He saw

– and survived – Jimmy Greaves and Alan Gilzean, Pat Jennings, Glenn and Ossie, Keith Osgood and Ian Moores. Every year, it was the same number of games, the same number of goals. This is Perryman, not a game of chance. With a perspective gained from a record like that, Perryman is perhaps the person best positioned to answer that most trainspottery of all fans ' questions: what was the best Spurs team?

'Definitely the 1982 team, no question. We had the confidence of having won the 1981 FA Cup final, against Manchester City, and to that we added Clemence and a couple of squad players like Gary Stevens, Danny Thomas and Paul Price. None of them except for Clemence did fantastically well for Tottenham, but winning the Cup gave the already good players there a new confidence. All of a sudden by having won something we'd got a standard. There was Hoddle, myself, Ardiles, Roberts and Miller . . . you know a lot of people rated them as hard-working, hard-hitters, but they gained a new status with the Cup win. It took us from being a nearly team to being a very, very nearly team. We jumped a couple of rungs.'

What would have made you a 'there' team? A 'made it' team?

'Maybe if we'd all been together. But that's hindsight. That's hindsight.'

The 1982 team was the classic Spurs team, emerging from the dark years of the mid to late 1970s to dazzle and shine. Playing, so the memory has it, in the all-white, they got to Wembley seven times in eighteen months – okay, so there were a couple of replays in there – winning the FA Cup twice and the UEFA Cup in 1984; Hoddle, Ardiles and Villa creating, Galvin charging, Archibald and Crooks scoring. Archibald; with his ragged facial growth and surly one-man-against-the-world image, Archibald was a wonderful cartoon striker, a cut-out-and-keep bad boy. But he was also as sharp as a cutlass, coldly efficient; a born fans' favourite. The only trouble was, it wasn't a gag.

Perryman again: 'For the crowd Archibald was always popular, but he split the team. He was doing great things while he was proving that he was a great player and, when he thought he was, he went the other way. He was one of the reasons why the team broke up. Half of the team were with him and half were against him – it was that black and white, without a doubt. I was the captain, so I couldn't be seen to be in either camp, but privately I thought he was an awful pro.'

I'm not sure that it's relevant here, seeing that Perryman was captain and not in either camp, but his son's name is Glenn.

'It was a big thing between Hoddle and Archibald. If the crowd chanted one name in front of the other – and this was more from Archibald than from Hoddle – there was jealousy. It was incredible. Keith had big, big problems with Archibald – this is well documented.

'People like Ardiles who came to us from abroad – World Cup players – used to thrive on making other people better players with their down-to-earth approach and friendly advice. Archibald's attitude was, "I'm a good player and you're here to serve me. I scored a goal, so I don't come back and take corners – you do that." We'd say, "Come on Ossie, have a word with him because he's your mate," and he'd say "Yes, but he's a special type of character" – he'd talk round it. But it wasn't right.

'Others in the team didn't justify it, but they were his friends and they thought he was trying to do the right thing. Players do lose sight of what's happening and where they are. It's all very well to say, "I'm a good player and I'm having a purple patch and these people are providing the ball for me." Well, rather than turning those people off, you should nurture them so they help make sure you keep doing it.

'He and Crooks were both good players when they were striving to prove their worth. When the likes of Hoddle picked the ball up, they ran forward to make the best out of his passes. But as soon as they thought they were good players, Glenn would knock it through, and they'd say, "No, I want it at my feet." We had loads of meetings saying, "You can't play if you want it at the feet – you are about pace." They protected each other in the end. They convinced each other that they were both right and in truth they were both wrong.'

Keith Burkinshaw: 'Steve Archibald? I still like the fella and I think at the bottom of him he's not that much anti-me. I remember someone telling me that they'd seen an article up in Scotland where he said that he'd played under three great managers: Alex Ferguson, myself and Venables in Barcelona. So that proved a point somewhere along the way. What happened with Stevie was I took him from Aberdeen and he came down with Garth Crooks and they were magnificent, the pair of them. And then financially he got a bit unstuck. He bought a pub for his father and this was distracting him.

'We played against Coventry in an evening match in September. We were beating them 1–0 with about 20 minutes to go when Stevie started complaining of an injury. I sent a physio on who said that there was nothing wrong with him. Stevie came back and said that he'd still got an injury and he wanted to come off. I was getting absolutely fed up with it, so I sent another physio on who also said there was nothing wrong with him. He didn't look as though he had much wrong with him, but he kept coming back to the bench saying "I want to come off." The thing was, we would only have had ten men if he came off. He did come off with about ten minutes to go and they got a goal in that last ten minutes. We drew 1–1 and I was absolutely . . . I don't know. He said he'd got this knee injury. That incident pointed out to me one of his weaknesses. He wasn't the best team player – it was about Steve Archibald rather than Tottenham Hotspur.

'Anyway, the following morning he came to the training ground. The first team were off that day because they'd played the night before. He came in, had a bit of treatment and said, "I want to go out." We were having a practice game with the reserves and the youth team and he said, "I want to play in the reserve team in the practice match." I said, "You've come off because you say you've got a bad injury and we've lost a bloody point because you've come off the field." I was absolutely seething. I said to the press, "This fella was cheating last night," and I meant it. I meant to humiliate him. Anyway he never spoke to me after that till I finished. I didn't mind it because he was still playing good football. We spoke when we'd got to about team affairs, but apart from that – socially – we didn't speak. I was fairly close to the players in those days. I was close to them all except for Stevie. It was something that didn't worry me. He was a strange character. When he was at odds with people, he played his best and he was always at odds with me. He says he was always at odds with Alex Ferguson up at Aberdeen – they were always arguing you know. When he'd got an argument with somebody it got the best out of him – that was his way.'

Archibald's playmate Garth Crooks: 'Steve's an amazing character, a lovely man if you can get close to him. For those who can't, they find him intolerable. Many of the Spurs players found him intolerable. He didn't allow them to get too close for his own reasons. I don't know why but Steve was the sort of character who was best motivated by conflict.

'It took me the best part of three to four months to cement a relationship with him, but when it was cemented, he was extremely loyal. It was important that we understood and respected each other and we worked hard to establish that. I saw him as the key to my success – wrongly, but yes I did. I say wrongly because it wasn't about me and Archibald – we weren't the engine room, we were simply the people who finished the hard work that others had done. We felt that the whole team hinged on how successful we were at scoring goals, and to an extent that was right, but the real heart of the team was Ardiles, Hoddle and Villa.'

Was there resentment in the ranks because of you two?

'Resentment is the wrong word. I think it produced professional jealousies which Steve did not respond to very well.'

Did you feel yourselves separated from the rest of the team?

'Only in so far as we were the strikers and once it got into the last third we would have to dictate how things went. Steve and I were aware that Spurs had recently gone through a period where their strikers weren't scoring that many goals. We thought that much as we liked playing football and enjoyed decorating the game, our job as seen by the management and the fans was to score goals and if that was going to happen, then Hoddle and Ardiles would have to allow us to say to them in the last third, "Hang on a second – this is what we want. Up to that point though, we'll do what you want." '

Balls played to feet?

'Yes and we'd discuss it as well – I mean, Hoddle and Ardiles and those people they were never – and this is where the genius of Hoddle, Ardiles and Villa really stands out above everyone else – they were never too big to listen to their team-mates and perhaps to forego their own way for the benefit of all. They were capable of going their own way, saying stuff it and putting two fingers up to everyone else. But they didn't and I think that's true humility and I think it's a sign of greatness in football terms.'

So it was a question of respecting each other's space?

'Yes, but there was a time when that respect broke down, unfortunately, and that's when the team wanted to break up.'

Keith Burkinshaw: 'I got Garth Crooks from Stoke City, as you know, and it was tremendous when he and Steve got together. That first season there was something magical about them. They never had as good a season as that afterwards. The thing with Garth was he wanted to be a footballer, which was fine, but I bought him to be a striker. We'd got probably the best midfield players in the country with Ardiles, Hoddle and Villa, and Garth wanted to come off into midfield like Sheringham does these days and be the one that's laying them in for people. I said, "Garth, we've got three players who are probably as good as any players in the world playing balls through. I'd like you to be on the end of them because you're better at scoring goals than they are; and you want to come back and knock them back for other people." He said, "But I'm good at that – I'm a terrific footballer." I asked, "Where do you think you come in the pecking order, technically, in our team?" He said, "I must be right at the top." I said, "You're probably about twelfth or something like that." I was knocking him down deliberately, but he'd got this wrong idea about himself, you know. He was terrific up front. If those balls came into the box, I wanted him in there. If he had to come 20 to 30 yards, other people were going to be coming in there and he'd be standing watching. I didn't want that.'

Steve Perryman: 'Losing sight of what gives you success normally breaks people up. That's why I think the Liverpool players who did it for ten years showed fantastic management. Fantastic. Rather than break it up, it made them stronger, it made them harder to beat the next year. We had limited success with the FA Cup, the UEFA Cup, but it destroyed us. It was lovely, but it could have been so much better. Why couldn't we be like Liverpool and do it for ten years, with the talent we had? With Hoddle and Ardiles and Archibald at his strength in the team, Clemence in goal and my experience and leadership, why weren't we better? Why didn't we win more, why weren't we genuine League people?'

For the first time, Perryman betrays real anger in his voice, and it's not hard to understand why or to sympathise. Nearly 20 years at the same club and, finally you get a team that's going to do it. Why couldn't they just fold their sleeves up carefully just above their elbows and get on with it?

Why we weren't genuine League people is something Perryman knows better than anyone else. David Pleat knew: 'Anybody who manages that club has to play in a certain way, with good passing, preferably with one or two individualistic characters in the team. Any other way is unacceptable.' Keith Burkinshaw knew too: 'You can have all the ideas that you want as manager, but if you came here with defensive ones you would have to change them in a month because of the pressure that would be on. You have to play the Tottenham way.'

Just before we hung up, I asked Steve about the other matches that players chose for this book. When we came to John Duncan's choice, the home victory over Hull that secured promotion from Division Two, he related the story of the game and then got to the goal. Time was running out. Minutes were left. It was 0–0 and Spurs needed to win. The whole season depended on a win. One goal would do it.

'. . . I pushed up front and I think that I went for a cross with the goalkeeper, and the ball fell down to Duncan to score.'

'Curiously it happened the other way round, Steve. Duncan went up for the goalie, and you scored.'

'I scored? That says something about me then, telling it that way. Incredible.'

7

THE MAN WITH NO NAME

Pat Jennings

> Normally, when you meet someone, you shake his hand. It's a curious greeting, wagging someone's hand, but there you go. Meeting Pat Jennings, I waved, well, flapped. I couldn't do it. All during our interview, I felt like a young adolescent boy who's confronted by an older girl. It's summertime and she's in that no bra, loose-fitting low-cut top that both boys and girls (for their different reasons) like so much. You can't help but look. You want to look, but you don't want them to see you looking. It's embarrassing, but you want to look, so you look. They know you're looking; and you know they know. But you look anyway. What the hell. You'd both be disappointed if you didn't.

I was recently in a group of about six people, all of whom were aged between 30 and 35. For reasons that are irrelevant here, a situation arose that I found perplexing. Scratching my head, I said to no one in particular: 'Where do we go from here?' As one, they replied, 'It is down to the lake I fear.' It was a kind of reflex response, which drew upon the vast reservoir of the subconscious. If you're outside that age-bracket, this will mean absolutely nothing and don't worry about it.

Things like that live in the dark recesses of your brain for no reason other than to prove your membership of a certain club. This shared-knowledge idea came to mind recently when I went to a friend's wedding in Northern Ireland. The day after the event, a few of us took a car and went off for a drive, looking for somewhere interesting; a bar, maybe. We drove a bit, went through towns, drove a bit more, went through more towns. After a few towns more we passed a sign which said, 'Newry welcomes safe drivers'. Of the four people in the car, my friend Peter and I suddenly stopped rabbiting and stared out of the window, saying nothing, just staring at the people passing by. After a few minutes we caught sight of each other and laughed. It was a curious feeling because we both knew what the other was doing and why he was doing it. We started to try to explain to the others, but gave that up. It was the shared deal. If you didn't know, you wouldn't know.

We were, of course, looking for people with big hands. Pat Jennings comes from Newry and Pat Jennings, as everybody must know, has big hands: Pat Jennings, big hands and a haircut that never changed or moved, moving purposefully across his goal, rising at corners and free kicks, catching the ball with one hand.

Jennings is one of those rare creatures: a true icon. Legend has it that when Clint Eastwood was first researching the role of The Man With No Name, he went to White Hart Lane to check out Pat Jennings. Whether that's where he got the idea for the poncho isn't recorded, but certainly there's more than a passing resemblance between Our Pat and TMWNN. Tall, dark and imposing, he rode into town, intent on doing his job – no more, no less – and moving on once his work was done. It's surely no coincidence that in all the Eastwood films he starts off facing the enemy backed with pledges of support from the locals. He doesn't say anything. He doesn't have to. He knows that when the going gets tough, they'll disappear, leaving him to do the job. Maybe they disappear because they're cowards or maybe – and let's be generous here – they go because they have such faith in The Man that they know they'll not be needed. He knows this and they know he knows it, but it's okay. It's his fate.

It's uncanny. You could have as many Terry Naylors as you liked, it didn't matter. They always had to get past Jennings, saying nothing, just being there.

The curious thing about Jennings is that a drama was never a drama when he was around, a crisis never a crisis. Yet when he left Spurs . . . bang. It was Krakatoa: East of Java all over again. He was 31, in goalkeeping terms he was barely into short trousers. He'd just set a new club appearance record of 449 League games, passing Ted Ditchburn's total of 418. He'd been voted the writers' Player of the Year in 1973 and the players' Player of the Year in 1976; he was an MBE, and was Northern Ireland's most capped international with 59 caps. It was obviously best to get rid of a player like that.

'I reported back for pre-season training,' says Jennings. 'I think it was three weeks into pre-season training, and I took it for granted that they wanted me to stay. I'd played in a few build-up, warm-up games, so I thought, "I'm obviously starting off in the Second Division next year." I remember one Thursday morning I went in and Keith Burkinshaw pulled me to one side and said, "Right. Now that we've decided that you can go, the team are leaving for Sweden tomorrow and I don't want to take you because you'll be an embarrassment to Barry Daines."'

It's too good a story to let slip by. We'll come back to it.

Tottenham Hotspur 4 (Knowles 2 (1 pen), Chivers, Conn)
Leeds United 2 (Jordan, Lorimer)

28 April 1975

Tottenham Hotspur: Jennings, Kinnear, Knowles, Beal, Osgood, Naylor, Conn, Perryman, Chivers, Jones, Pratt.
Leeds United: Stewart, Reaney, Cherry, Bremner, Madeley, Hunter, Lorimer, F. Gray, Jordan, Yorath, E. Gray.
Attendance: 49,886

Before we go any further, there are two remarks worth bearing in mind. The first, by Pat Jennings, is a measure of how bad things had got. The second, by Terry Neill, is a measure of how sad things had got.

> After the game it was better than any of the Cup wins we had – it was just a carnival atmosphere. I got more satisfaction out of staying up that year than I did out of any of the Cup wins because you just didn't want to be part of the team that went down.

> It was as if we'd won the Cup, but I'd worked 24 hours a day, seven days a week to keep Spurs in the First Division and I'd taken a lot of stick from the fans for my trouble. Yet here they all were chanting my name and calling for me to go out on to the pitch and acknowledge their cheers. Did I go? I went straight home. I'd paid my dues.

By the end of April 1975, things had got bad. Spurs were like your best friend after a relationship break-up. Moany and lacking in a certain grace, no fun, no style. You kept going to see them – that's what friends are for – but it wasn't an enjoyment, it was a duty. Watching them, you couldn't help but feel that they felt the same way. When you give off bad energy, that's what you get back. In Spurs' case this meant no points.

Pat Jennings: 'With three games to go at the end of the season, we beat Chelsea at home on the Saturday 2–0. We went to the Arsenal the following week and lost 1–0. They were both really difficult games as well as being local derbies. We had to win against Leeds on the Monday to keep up, so that was more or less three games over seven or eight days. Basically my worry was that I didn't want to go down in the history of Tottenham as one of the team – and it was a great team – that went down to the Second Division, you know? I don't think that anyone wanted to be part of that.'

It's just what you need. You've got to get a result in the last match of the season to stay in the First Division and who are you playing? Coventry? The Orient? Stenhousemuir? No, Leeds. You're playing Leeds. The reigning League champions and possibly the last team you'd want to play in this situation. How shall we say this? You know the football expression 'hard but fair'? Leeds were hard. If Pat Jennings was Clint Eastwood, Leeds were Lee Van Cleef, only not as good-looking. The only thing faintly humorous about Leeds was that they played in white; obviously a tailor with a keen sense of irony.

On a different day, it might have all been a bit Hamilton, but this was an evening match at White Hart Lane, and some traditions are sacrosanct. It was Leeds's final League game too, but they had nothing to play for. They eventually finished ninth, and even if they had beaten Spurs they'd have only gone one better. It's not a great incentive and in those pre-Sky days, when teams weren't awarded a huge placings-dependent chunk of post-season wedge for finishing, there was even less incentive. Also, Allan Clarke, Johnny Giles, Gordon McQueen and Duncan McKenzie were all out injured. There was one other thing that the cynical Luton fan (Luton were the team relegated instead of Spurs) could perhaps point to. Less than a month later, Leeds were down to play in the European Cup final . . .

Do you think Leeds might have been coasting, Pat?

'Leeds were very much like Don Revie and I can't imagine Don Revie saying to them, "Look, take it easy boys." You know, it doesn't happen in football. We've seen similar situations arise over the last couple of years – Blackburn going to Liverpool needing to win and Liverpool beating them, Manchester United going to West Ham. Nobody does you any favours in football – certainly not in professional football. You always want to go out and finish the season with a blast. You're thinking, "Right. End of the season, might be nice winning and start again next season."

'I think the Leeds players were pleased for us at the end of the day. I don't know who would have come up in our place, but it's to everyone's benefit to have a club like Tottenham in the top division. Nobody ever wants to see the Manchester Uniteds or the Tottenhams going into the Second Division. But nothing like that matters – anyone who plays football will tell you that there's never any favours done.'

Perhaps realising that they needed to call upon the Spirit of the Past, Spurs recalled Chivers who'd been out in exile since February. As soon as he appeared, it was obvious that he hadn't been idle. He'd grown a beard. Things started at a frenetic pace – well, from one end, anyway – with Alfie Conn firing a volley inches wide after only a few minutes. After five minutes Reaney brought down the up-for-it Conn on the edge of the box. Knowles spun the free kick in. 1–0. Spurs were firing; Leeds weren't. For someone who didn't know what the story was, it would have been difficult to tell which was the struggling team on the verge of relegation. For someone who did know what the story was, a different truth seemed clearly obvious.

There was one thing that fired up the Leeds team. Steve Perryman tells it: 'There was big pressure from the house. Alfie Conn got all carried away with getting a result and had a great night – we avoided relegation, but let's temper it. This is Tottenham Hotspur and we're one game away from relegation, so, yes, let's enjoy it, but let's not get too strong. We'd had a very bad season. Anyway, he sat on the ball and against Leeds, you just don't do that sort of thing. I remember Billy Bremner said to me, "Steve, tell him, tell him. You're going to win the game, but I'm not sure he's going to finish it." So I told him and he said, "Yeah, yeah, yeah, yeah, we're going to win, we're going to win." I just looked at him and thought, "And there's another season next year." But it was a great game. Great atmosphere.'

It's one of those typical instances where fans have a completely different perspective from the players. To the paying punters, Alfie Conn was one of the few bright spots in an otherwise dull team, one of the few individual sparks. So sometimes he played and sometimes he didn't. He was, in one of those great football clichés, a character. And sitting on the ball? Top entertainment for a group of punters who'd been starved of that elusive quality all season. It's a release, a 'thank God, we're safe', a hoot. Unless, of course, you're Billy Bremner, in which case you'd break the bastard's legs. There's no point getting sanctimonious. We've all been Conn and probably – and sadly more often – we've all been Bremner.

Pat Jennings: 'He was a good little player, Alfie Conn. He would have been a good player in a good team, but unfortunately we weren't a good team at the time. He was a skilful lad, scored a lot of good goals. Had he been in a good team he could probably have done a lot better, which we all could have done. Those sort of players, they need people around them. When he sat on the ball, you can imagine from our point of view, we thought, "Bloody hell, don't take the piss, just get on and play." I mean, we're coasting the game and all of a sudden . . . that's the last thing you want to do to experienced players like Leeds had, get their backs up. From having a nice game which you're quite capable of winning, all of a sudden you've got a war on your hands.'

So Leeds were below par, and Spurs were above par. Maybe that cynical Luton fan was being a little too cynical. Maybe both teams were really trying as hard as they possibly could. Maybe it was just that Spurs couldn't lose.

We don't thank Terry Neill for much these days, but if we're honest and decent, there are three reasons why we should be grateful. First, it was he who brought Keith Burkinshaw to the club. Second, he used to illustrate his team talks using model cowboys and Indians. Just thinking about this . . . it's an extraordinarily funny idea. 'Okay, lads. The boy Lorimer's good from distance and he'll pick you off one by one. Terry Naylor and Keith Osgood, you take the rest of the lads and form a circle, and you, Perryman, you get on top of the wagon with the rifle.' It's almost as good as Graham Taylor telling Nigel Clough about his 'hole'. Third, he was mates with, and brought in, a showbiz hypnotist who went by the name of Romark. Up until that point in the season, it looked as though the players had been going to a hypnotist who stopped after the words 'You are feeling sleepy'.

Pat Jennings: 'Cyril had been to Romark on the Sunday, the day before the game, and he was one of his best subjects. It was Terry's idea. Terry wanted to take everybody to the hotel – I think it was the West Park Lodge where we usually stayed – so that we could all be together on the Sunday ready for the Leeds match on Monday, and I suppose that he looked round and saw that most of the lads were panicking a bit. He knew this Romark – I don't know how – he'd done a few things with him, but they were both into positive thinking – hypnotism. So anyway, Terry invited him up to the hotel on the Sunday, and for us it was a laugh as well.

'Part of it was that you went to him for an individual session. Only myself and John Pratt opted out. I didn't go because, to be honest, I was frightened. I thought, "Whatever I can do, I'll do it on my own. I'm not going to depend on somebody else." I wasn't curious – I was more frightened of what he might do to me. I was confident in my own ability. But all the other lads went and they had a laugh.

'His technique was to get you to think about your best game, whenever you've done well, think about the feelings in your mind. You can imagine the crack with the lads: "When was the last game you played well?" "It was so long ago I can't remember."

'We had good fun, it probably lifted the tension. Knowlesy was a fantastic subject. He had Knowlsey asleep just like that, in a trance. He told Knowlesy that he'd score two goals and he did. I don't know if that's coincidence, but he did. I remember he'd got Cyril over the back of two chairs and he put his neck over the edge of one of them and his feet over the other one and he kept saying to him "Imagine you're a steel girder" and Cyril was lying there stretched from toe to neck on the back of these chairs. I got up and sat on him and he never moved. I mean, you've seen levitation, well, this must be the same. But it worked. We had a good bit of crack in the afternoon, so maybe from that it did take the tension out of it.'

If Spurs had shown the fire they showed against Leeds earlier in the season, they wouldn't have been in the position they were in. But they hadn't and they didn't and they were. But now they were safe and the nonsense was behind them.

'We got out of trouble that year certainly, and we celebrated on the night, but that should have been the writing on the wall. Unfortunately nothing was done about it. Spurs missed the drop that year. The next year we finished pretty reasonably, sixth or seventh or something. With the same players the next year, we went down.'

Epilogue

There are some words and phrases that somehow seem to strike against the natural order of things, the unwritten constitution that is the Universal Law: the Tories have been re-elected, the Adverts have reformed, Spurs sold Pat Jennings to the Arsenal.

Perhaps Pat should have seen it coming: 'Bill had moved on. We saw him now and again. It was such a disappointment to all of us, the way he left, particularly to go on to another club. I mean, we thought he'd retire, but Bill had taught us loyalty over the years. That was all we ever got out of him – loyalty, loyalty, loyalty. At the end of the day the club would look after you. So it was such a kick in the teeth for all of us when this man who was preaching loyalty . . . what happened to him.'

To say that perhaps Pat should have seen it coming is like saying that Bill should have seen it coming. These things just didn't happen. If it happened once . . . well, maybe that was a cosmic blip, a far-off meteor causing a momentary reversal of the natural laws, God sneezing. These things are possible, but not twice in a couple of years. There's even a four-year gap between Tory re-elections.

'I mean, I was part of the furniture for fourteen years and I'm sure that I was just taken for granted when I was there. People don't realise how good a job you're doing until all of a sudden they haven't got you.

'I'd missed 21 games that year with an ankle injury. I knew from a player at Ipswich that they'd made a bid for me, round about Easter time. I know for a fact that Spurs thought about selling me at that time, but because of the situation the club was in – relegation trouble – they'd have been slaughtered had they sold me before the Easter programme. You can pick up a lot of points then, you've a chance of getting yourself out of bother.

'Although Ipswich had made an approach, Spurs must have said no. There was a lot of talk about it in the papers. I can remember going to Keith Burkinshaw at the end of the season and saying, "What's happening next year re the goalkeeper?" Barry Daines had played half the games because of my injury, and done well, to be fair to him. Keith said to me, "Why? Do you want to go?" If you want somebody to stay, you don't say "Do you want to leave?" His next words were, "Well, there have been one or two clubs looking for you. I'll have a word with them." There was no use in me saying, "Well hold on, I don't want to go." I knew from that minute on that they were still seriously thinking about selling.

'I was coming up for my 32nd birthday, and the length of time I'd been at the club meant that I would have had a free transfer at the end of the next season. I could have walked out without them receiving any fee for me. I know from the papers that the fee mentioned for Ipswich was £85,000 or £90,000. I eventually went for £45,000 or something.

'Normally you wouldn't take much notice of the papers, but I knew that there was an interest and then it was confirmed by the newspaper reports. It was true at the end of the day. It was the end of the season, and I knew that my time was up at Tottenham. I thought that if he wants me to stay, he's going to say, "Well, yes. We want you for another two to three years. We'll give you a new contract and we'll talk about it." But my contract was up and there was no mention of a new one.

'There was no animosity between Keith and me. That's not just me, that's football. I play golf with Keith now. We're the best of mates. But I'm just saying that he could have made it a lot easier for me at the time. If he'd said that the club is making a decision to sell – which it did – whether you like it or not, it would have been so much easier for me. A lot of people thought that I had walked out because we were going to the Second Division. Instead I wasn't even offered a contract. My contract was up and there was no talk about a transfer.

'There were all sorts of stories about, some attributed to the directors saying that I'd asked for a massive signing-on fee. But I never even got asked to sign a contract. That was how big a load of rubbish that was. Having said that, I was so disappointed with the way the club was going. There you are thinking for so many years that you are going to be part of a championship-winning team – and it was always my ambition to win the championship – and all of a sudden, you're fighting off relegation and ending up being relegated. What with the writing being on the wall two years earlier with the Leeds match and nothing really being done about it – or not enough being done about it – it was disappointing.'

So you went into the summer holiday not knowing where you were going to be playing or, come to think of it, living this time next year.

'That's right. I reported back for pre-season training, I think it was three weeks into pre-season training, and I took it for granted that they wanted me to stay. I'd played in a few build-up games so I thought, "So I'm obviously starting off in the Second Division next year." I remember one Thursday morning I went in and Keith pulled me to one side and said, "Right. We've decided that you can go. The team are leaving for Sweden tomorrow and I don't want to take you because you'll be an embarrassment to Barry Daines." You can imagine what my reaction to that was – "Do you want me to apologise for being a good player all these years?" He said, "Bobby Robson is ringing me" – Ipswich were on a pre-season tour of Holland at the time – "Bobby Robson is ringing me at six o'clock tonight, and I'm ringing you at six thirty and I want you to know where you're going before we leave for Sweden tomorrow." So here was a manager asking me to make a decision about my future in half an hour.

'You can imagine what my reaction was. I told him, "I'll tell you in my time where I want to go." Bobby Robson rang me that night and I said, "Right, if you come up with a deal, I'll go to Ipswich." They had a great side at the time, they were within a fraction of winning the championship. Bobby Robson said to me many times, had he signed me, Ipswich would have won it. I mean, they went on to beat Arsenal in the Cup in 1977. The lad [Paul] Cooper had a lot of good seasons, but maybe Bobby thought that with my experience, they may have been good enough to carry it through to the championship. He said it to me many times.

'But that night in the match in Holland, Trevor Whymark got his leg bust. Bobby Robson rang back and said, "Look, I've got to go out now and buy a centre-forward." The money that he was going to spend on me, he had to go and spend on a forward. So my move was off.

'Meanwhile, Terry Neill had been in touch with me. He obviously knew that Ipswich were in for me, and I said to Terry that I'd given Bobby Robson my word. I said, "If it doesn't come up, Terry, I'll ring you in the morning." I don't think anything happened then for three or four days. I went to Bill Nick who was back by then, and you can imagine what Bill said. Imagine what Bill thought about me moving to Arsenal . . . Any other club in the country but Arsenal. But as I say, I'd done everything that they wanted for fourteen years, and now it semed to me that I was being thrown out, shown the door. It was an opportunity for me to create the biggest embarrassment for whoever was responsible in the club for letting me go. I hope I did that. I was that angry. Also I knew that I was joining a great club in Arsenal. I felt sorry for the supporters and I have done so many times since, but I didn't want to move house nearly 100 miles to suit someone else. There was no way I wanted to pull the kids out of school and disrupt them for the sake of a couple of years. I didn't know at that time that it would be another eight years.

'The day I left, I went to the ground to pick up my boots and things. The lads were leaving the next morning to go to Sweden. The directors completely ignored me. This was before news of the Arsenal move. That hurt me more than anything. I could only think that the right messages weren't getting through. With hindsight it seems ridiculous that they let me go, when I went on to play for another eight years at Arsenal, and when you look at the money Tottenham spent trying to replace me. Even Terry Venables reckoned he had a goalkeeper for every day of the week bar Saturday. He had a load of them there – none of them any good. I'm Tottenham through and through; I mean, I haven't missed a home match in the last ten years. You've just got to look at the fact that I still went back even in 1985 . . .'

But the Arsenal? What about the rivalries between the clubs? Surely you feel that, too.

'Bloomin' hell. I was caught up in it, year in year out. If we never won a game all year, that was the one game we had to win, Arsenal v Tottenham. It didn't matter what else you did . . . the rivalry was unbelievable between the two. Most of that came from Bill Nick.

'But from my point of view, I knew that I was joining a great side at Arsenal, with all the Irish lads – Liam Brady, Frank Stapleton, David O'Leary, Sammy Nelson, Pat Rice, John Devine and Terry Neill – plus the fact that Willie Young had gone over from Tottenham. It was home from home for me. I'd already got a great reception from the Arsenal fans over the years and not many people can claim that. I've always been made welcome and got a great ovation at Arsenal.

'Playing against Tottenham was horrible, horrible. One of the worst games of the year. Thankfully my first game back we won 5–0.'

We, in this instance, is the Arsenal.

'It wasn't a nice situation from my point of view. I'd rather have played anyone else but on the day I had to play against them. Whatever I'd done, I couldn't do right. I was kicking the Tottenham fans who'd been so good to me over the years – but I was playing for Arsenal and there was no way I wouldn't give blood for them. They were paying me and that was it, you know.'

In days of old, when knights were bold . . . Brave and fearless, a warrior among infantrymen, Cliff Jones was like four Power Rangers bound together in one classic white shirt. Was it all a dream?

In days of old, when knights were bold . . . Like two playful young boys going for an afternoo kick-around, Ron Henry and Dave Mackay delight in the happy knowledge that there really i nothing to worry about. Was it all a dream?

In days of old, when knights were bold . . . Pure white shirts, v-necks, just the right amount o bag on the sleeves. Effortless style, consummate grace. The double team. Was it all a dream?

LEFT: Where it all began and (who's going to argue?) where it all ended. Bill Nicholson with his trusty wife Darkie, once and forever Mr Spurs

BELOW LEFT: When Clint Eastwood was researching his *Man With No Name* character, he came to White Hart Lane and saw Pat Jennings. Strong and silent, defiant in the face of insurmountable odds and abandoned by his people, left alone to face the enemy hordes. It can't be a coincidence

BELOW RIGHT: Tearing down the wing, hair flying in his wake like Isadora Duncan's scarf, and in one motion he'd look up, deliver the perfect cross and sweep his locks back across his naked scalp. The thrilling Ralph Coates experience

Emerging like a cygnet in an era of Canada geese, Our Glenn was derided as a maverick, a luxury, a fanny merchant. But the truth is (all together now) it's the bad players who are a luxury. So now he's the England manager. Any wonder he's a believer?

Level-headed, straight as a die and spirited: if Steve Perryman hadn't been a footballer, he could have made a living helping people put up bookshelves

Compare and contrast . . . One of these teams turned in the greatest performance ever seen by a British club side in Europe, beating Atletico Madrid in the Cup-Winners Cup in 1963. The other team took part in a bizarre social experiment in the late 1970s to see if Spurs could turn into Leyton Orient. Can you guess which is which?

1984 UEFA Cup. There's nothing quite like winning a major European trophy for putting a smile on the face. But somewhere, deep in the heart of White Hart Lane, a man in a wheelcha waits with a bottle of champagne. Nothing will be quite the same again

A wage slave. A cog in the system of capitalist oppression. Garth Crooks discovered Marx anc Burkinshaw at more or less the same time (LEFT); John Duncan (RIGHT): Many years ago, lon, before you were born, Spurs were lost, stuck in a dark, dank place. One man stood alone. 'Wh scored?' asked my sister. 'Duncan,' I replied wearily

1991 FA Cup final. Happy, smiling faces. But wait! There's someone missing. Wonder who it could be? He started the game but he doesn't seem to be here. It must be a mystery

After a disallowed goal, a missed penalty, a Forest goal that was . . . let's call it a 'ploy' . . . ootball's coming home. The Boy Lineker watches in wonderment as Paul Stewart scores for the good guys

In days of old, when knights were bold . . . After making more of an impact in one season tha most players manage in three careers, dashing Jürgen flew away as quickly as he came. Was it a a dream? (photo: Richard Sellars/Sportsphoto)

8

WHO SCORED? John Duncan

> I suppose I was Terry Neill's man – but I never thought about it in that way. Other players came at that time. It never actually dawned on me that I was the first of them so it never became an issue. I think that he must have upset the old stagers. Those players of the older Spurs who'd done well for Spurs . . . he was the one who, in their eyes, made changes too quickly and they went to pastures new. A manager is never loved if he moves people on. And then he committed the unpardonable crime. Coming from Arsenal was one thing, but then moving back there . . . It wasn't the done thing, was it?
>
> John Duncan

Consider this evolutionary equation. At one end, you've got the Tyrannosaurus Rex, huge, darkly efficient eating machine – huge legs for running, huge tail for balance and huge teeth for chewing. It didn't really have much else, but then it didn't really need to. At the other end of the same equation, you've got the albatross, a graceful, virgin-white glissando bliss-bird, soaring and gliding on the breath of angels, flying thousands of miles, searching for food, then flying thousands of miles back to take it to the life-partner. Both, in their very different ways, are beautiful creatures.

Somewhere in the middle of this timeless evolutionary line lies the archaeoptyrex; the first bird or the last dinosaur. It doesn't matter. The archaeoptyrex was a flying dinosaur. It had scales, not feathers and it spluttered along like a learner driver with no sense of clutch control. It was inefficient and ugly, but without it there could be no albatross. Without it, we'd still have the T-Rex.

Spurs in the mid 1970s were inefficient and ugly, lost between the successes of the Chivers era and the glitter of the Ardiles/Hoddle boom-time. Maybe they just reflected the times – and the times were crashingly dull. It was the Callaghan era, nothing to take the mickey out of, like Heath and Wilson, and nothing to hate, like Thatcher. It was just genial Jim, shining like a diamond among the fungal moral cut-outs who ran off to form the SDP. Musically, things weren't much better. We were post-Glitter, but pre-punk. Supertramp, that's what we were. In desperation, some of us children of the bong hung on with Hawkwind and sang along with Gong . . .

When considering the mighty Spurs in the mid to late 1970s, there's one inescapable truth: they were rubbish. They were devoid of style, class and grace. They were dour and dull, and Spurs – as we know – can only succeed when they're being dashing and flash. Not only did the football stink, the politics of the place stank too. But in the true Spurs tradition, the fall from grace was accomplished wholeheartedly. It was embraced, pursued with a Mackay-like tenacity.

Bill Nicholson left and was replaced by former Arsenal stalwart Terry Neill. This whole sorry episode is really a story for a different place, but that one sentence is worth repeating because, as any Spurs fan knows, it is the second worst sentence in the history of this illustrious club. Bill Nicholson left and was replaced by former Arsenal stalwart Terry Neill.

The thing with history is this. Once it is written, there's very little you can, or indeed should, do to change it. So Terry Neill came to Spurs as an Arsenal Trojan horse, deliberately set out to undermine their greater rivals, lumbered us with Willie Young, took us into the Second Division and stole Pat Jennings for them. Typical of the Arsenal. All the style of a constipated goat and the morals of a can of tomatoes. That's the way history is written and woe betide you, you fact-seeking blasphemers.

Bill Nicholson was, as he himself now admits, 'tired'. Maybe he was getting old. Maybe the constant fighting with the skulking manatee Chivers took too much out of him. Whatever the reason, when Spurs needed the Nicholson of old, he was found to be just that – old. The Nicholson who sneaked up the motorway in the dead of night to sign Dave Mackay, the Nicholson who sniffed out John White, the Nicholson who recognised Pat Jennings, that Nicholson was gone. Wale and the Tottenham board dumped him. That they refused to consider Blanchflower – a candidate so obvious it hurts – just because Nick had recommended him is tantamount to criminal negligence.

Okay, they wanted to show Nick that he was a mere employee, that they paid his wages, but to do it to the detriment of the club . . . ? Liverpool, for example, treated Bill Shankly just as badly and with just as little respect, but at least they had the sense to replace him with one of their own. They didn't go and appoint Brian Labone as manager. And Terry Neill? He never stood a chance. He shouldn't have been there; but once there, he never stood a chance.

'To be honest, Terry Neill is a friend of mine. Terry took me from Tottenham to Arsenal with him, but certainly, with experience, I wouldn't have wanted Terry as manager at Tottenham,' says Big Pat now. 'I would never have thought he was good enough at the job at that time; possibly later on, when he went higher. I think that Arsenal was a good team. But certainly when Terry came to Tottenham, I was looking for a bit more, somebody with a bit more experience. The fact that Bill went showed that things weren't right at the club. I mean, the fact that he was allowed to leave . . .'

The way that Jennings's voice trailed off provided one of those rare but reassuring moments when a professional sportsman's viewpoint aligns perfectly with that of a fan. Someone as experienced and long in the tooth as Jennings can, even now, betray such emotion.

'I got a bit tired actually and I thought I've had a long time as a manager,' says Bill Nicholson himself. 'It's not usual for a manager to last as long as that, is it? So I thought, I've had enough of this. I decided to pack it in and let someone else do the job. I suppose you do that when things are not going too well, when some of the players don't react in the way that you'd like them to, and, of course, when the results don't go for you. I knew some of the teams we were playing and I knew that we should have won, but we didn't. So on an occasion like that, if the manager feels that way, the manager should realise that it's not working, and if he can't put it right right away then the best thing for him is to let someone else have a go.

'Through the years, you do similar sorts of things and you have a belief about the game and the way you coach and train your players. A lot of it is repeated from one year to the next, and it all becomes a little bit old hat in the end. And if you feel that way about it, you should seriously think about packing it in, or at least taking a break from it all. Those things happen.

'I had no say in it at all. I thought our directors would have asked me who I thought could take over, and why. I tried to suggest that Danny Blanchflower could take over for a while to see how he got on even though he didn't have any experience. I don't know if he applied or not. No, it wasn't hurtful. It was me who resigned and put the club in trouble so they had to find a manager. Eddie Bailey could have taken over as manager for the rest of the season, but they never even asked him. For them to appoint Terry Neill, who was an Arsenal man, I thought Christ, what's happening to this club? It was bad enough me packing it in, but I didn't mean to upset the club.

'I was curious, but I never asked them why. It was one of those things. I'd resigned and I felt that they were probably expecting it. They probably thought, "Well, that's your look out; leave us to get on with our business," which was typical of our directors of the time. And I suppose that it was their responsibility. I would have put my foot in it – although after all that time I'd spent at the club, I would have thought I could go out giving them a bit of good advice.

'Maybe there were a couple of directors who were thinking, "He's not doing too good, let's get him out." There are lots of directors who think that way. I mean, there were lots of things said at the time that they were not treating me the way I should have been treated after all the success we'd had at Tottenham, and I was just going out like that; saying "Ta ta".'

'We couldn't believe it,' says Jennings. 'I mean, it was all the talk at the time. He wanted to bring in Johnny Giles and Danny Blanchflower as a double management team and it wasn't even considered. He wasn't even asked his opinion. He'd been in the game . . . Bill Nicholson was Tottenham, to be honest. He was the Bill Shankly of Tottenham. You just didn't question his opinions. With his beliefs in football and his experience of football, not even being asked . . . It was being left, I suppose, to board members and, with the greatest respect, you can't compare opinions of theirs with Bill Nicholson's.

'Under Bill Nicholson, whenever top players became available, he was in for them – Mike England, Alan Mullery, Jimmy Greaves, people like that. Anyone who had any ambition, who wanted to win something, thought that Tottenham was the club that was going to do it. But then the standards went down, and we started to buy players who were smashing players, but who – with the greatest respect – were not Tottenham players. We were slowly going down and they were doing nothing about it.'

Steve Perryman who, with Jennings and Ralph Coates, was the only remaining link with the early 1970s team, identified the same problem.

'The fact was that we just didn't replace in good enough style.

Terry told me once, "If you want a centre-half, you make a list of ten, and you make the phone calls until you get one and it might have to be the tenth." Well, I'm not sure that was Bill Nick's ethics. Maybe Bill was able to buy the best because of who he was or because of the image of the club at the time, the name of Tottenham, the carry-over from the double, the aura surrounding the club. Maybe people wanted to join the club. But in the 1970s, that stopped. People didn't want to join the club.'

'It was a huge frustration,' says Jennings. 'Considering that only a few years before we were within stepping distance of winning the title and, I mean, you're busting your gut, day in day out thinking, "Well, next year we're going to do it," and then, all of a sudden, you start going from the top to the bottom.'

Was there an arrogance about the club? A feeling that 'We're Spurs, this can't happen to us'?

'No, certainly not. Not from me anyway – there might have been at director level. I wouldn't have thought there was at manager level. Terry wouldn't have been that stupid. It could happen to us.' And so it did.

Step aside for a minute and consider John Major – dull, grey, monospatial John Major. A case could be made for the argument that John Major was 'given' the Tory leadership because it was felt that whoever took over from Thatcher was going to feel the weight come tumbling down faster than you can say, 'Listen. I've got a great idea. Let's privatise it.' To nick one of her favourite images, it was like someone who'd been borrowing madly without having any idea of how to pay it off. So the idea was that John Major would get the red bill and would be disposed of, and her memory would be safe. By the time Spurs received their red bill, Terry Neill was back where he belonged. The record books show that it was Keith Burkinshaw who took Spurs down, but that didn't matter. Burkinshaw was a Spurs man. It's as simple as that.

In retrospect, Neill's tenure looks better than it did at the time. Three things make it stand out. One, he wasn't the one who boldly led us into the Second Division, nor did he sell Pat Jennings. Two, one of the main reasons he left was because he wanted to give the players a bonus after doing well on a particularly gruelling post-season tour to Canada, New Zealand, Fiji and Australia. Three, he signed John Duncan. Hard-line cynics could add a fourth, he lasted less than two years, but I think that's harsh. After all, it was Neill who tried to sign Johan Cruyff. (The board vetoed the move.)

John Duncan scored 53 goals in 103 games for Spurs, a figure which compares more than favourably with Martin Chivers's 118 in 278 appearances. But who's the Spurs legend? For three seasons, Duncan was the hope, the one we all relied on and the story of those three seasons tells you everything you need to know about that hope. Season one: Duncan arrives and scores 20 goals in 37 appearances. His two striking partners are rather less prolific. Chivers gets seven in 35 games, Chris Jones gets five in 34 games. Spurs finish a respectable ninth. Season two: Duncan does his back in and plays only nine games. Spurs are relegated. Season three: Duncan returns half-way through the season and scores 16 goals in 27 games. Spurs are promoted.

Together with the emerging cygnet, Glenn Hoddle, John Duncan was the light in the dark. When you bought a programme, the first thing you did was check if Duncan was playing. When the team changes were announced over the tannoy you'd hold your breath and hope. If Duncan was playing, you stood a chance. The performances would be garbage, but you might win. With Jennings in charge of the sieve at the other end, you might get away with it. You'd get a goal anyway. When Spurs played away, I'd sit and watch *Grandstand* waiting for the bobbing head of the teleprinter to tell me the news. Invariably the news was bad. 'Crapski Athletic 4, Tottenham Hotspur 1'. I'd sit there looking glum and my sister would walk by.

'Who scored? Duncan?' I'd nod, she'd smile and that was that. A weekly ritual.

'I was 25 when I came to Spurs in 1974. I was whisked off from training at Dundee by my manager who said, "You're going to a team that's bottom of the League," and I didn't fancy that too much. I didn't think that it would be at the bottom of the English League. It turned out that it was Spurs and obviously it didn't take long to make the decision and I was delighted to go. I wasn't aware of the politics, though I was aware that a lot of the big names were leaving. Mullery had left, Gilzean was just finishing. Coates was still there and Alfie Conn, although he didn't stay that long. As soon as I got there, I realised what was going on.

'But it wouldn't have mattered to me because, as it happened, Tottenham was one of the teams I followed anyway. I was 12 at the time of the double team. Players like Greaves and Gilzean captured my imagination. Gilzean was my hero as a player at Dundee:

I watched Dundee win the League in 1960–61. My nickname at Dundee was Gilly after Gilzean. He went to Spurs so obviously there was a big link there, there was a connection. Great guy. He knew my wife's family when he was playing for Dundee and she was a kiddie.'

Did you feel a lot of pressure, knowing that you were the hope?

'When I came down, Scottish players weren't having a good time. They were more likely to be failures at that stage; the pressure was on there. I did well and got goals when goals were scarce. Goals were really hard to come by in those days. In the early 1970s it was really hard going, everything was work rate. I mean, Alf Ramsey was keen on work rate and it was still the aftermath of that. I got 20 goals in the First Division and the next season I injured my back and the team got relegated. I only played in about six games. We came straight back up next season and I was top goalscorer that year as well. That's where the whole bit comes from that if I had played, they wouldn't have gone down.'

Well, maybe so, and maybe not. As we've already established, it was all Terry Neill's fault. Having Duncan around, though, would've helped. Irrespective of his not inconsiderable talents as a striker, he was worth a place in the team for his talismanic value alone.

Duncan again: 'Our team was in the shadow of the team before. They won the FA Cup twice and the UEFA Cup which was great. Funnily enough, after I left, with Ardiles and people like that, I don't think they felt in the shadow anymore. But I don't know. Our team wasn't as good as that but it was a good team unit. It was close to success but it wasn't anything like other Spurs teams. It was in transition – a new Spurs being built – and it was never going to be as big as those other teams because it wasn't competing financially at the levels it is now or as it was before. But there was a new spirit building up, and we actually had a couple of good years.'

How did the relegation affect you?

'A lot of people didn't associate it with me. I wasn't as tarred with the brush as other people because we came back up again and I got a lot of the goals. But with the injury year and then the relegation, it meant really that I was going to spend at least two years out of the First Division. It was bad for the club, but personally I felt it because I didn't want to be a Second Division player. I don't feel it separated me from the other players. I felt right in it and as determined as anyone that we should get back up there as quickly as we could, and fortunately we did it.'

Tottenham Hotspur 1 (Perryman)
Hull City 0

26 April 1978

Tottenham Hotspur: Daines, Naylor, Holmes, Hoddle, McAllister, Perryman, Pratt, McNab, Jones, Duncan, Taylor.
Hull City: Blackburn, Daniel, De Vries, Nisbet, Croft, Roberts, Hood, Haigh, Warboys, Bannister, Stewart.
Attendance: 36,913

> I always remember Sid Wale coming to me and saying, 'Keith, we appointed you last year because we thought you were going to be a very good manager. We still think that. Just take us up. That's all you've got to do.'
>
> Keith Burkinshaw

When Spurs fell out of the First Division (the first time they'd done so in over four decades), manager Keith Burkinshaw resolved that his team would play their way back into the top flight. The board continued to back him. Maybe Wale and his cronies felt that they owed it to the Spurs faithful after the Neill nonsense. Maybe they stuck with Burkinshaw as a mark of respect to Bill Nick. One of the first things that Burkinshaw did after being appointed manager was to insist that Bill Nick be brought back to Spurs.

There are few absolutes in football, but one that everybody knows is that you can play yourself out of the Second Division, but only down into the Third Division. In the Second, pragmatism is the order of the day. No fannying around.

Two of the problems that Duncan identified – 'In midfield we didn't have as much craft as we needed. And we also had problems at the back' – were immediately addressed.

'Steve Perryman, who'd been in that good team before us, slipped back to play at the back and was outstanding, unbelievable. He was a very spirited player, a good captain, and he had better technique than people probably thought he had because he did so much running and had such a good work rate. He was a very good player.'

Perryman was a revelation to everyone, including himself: 'Your brain gets better as you get older, but your legs give out. You can't handle the pace of it. My change started in the Second Division. I was playing against a centre-back, Keith Osgood, and every time we played out, the ball went through me. Every time the keeper had the ball, it went through me and it was that year the game became clear to me. After all that closing down and hustle and bustle of midfield and tackling, all of a sudden I had the ball and I could spend ten seconds on it if I wanted to. I could run at someone and lure him on to me before passing it on to Hoddle or the full-back, that was nice. Before it was just "win it and give it, win it and give it".'

Full-backs Terry Naylor and Jimmy Holmes were encouraged to overlap and make the team movement much more fluid. 'You'll never get out of the Second Division playing like that,' the cynics said, and it was nearly true. After a bright start that culminated in a 9–0 home win over Bristol Rovers, Spurs reverted to classic type and fell away. What were once habits are now vices, as they say. It could have been easy, but it wasn't. Between winning at home to Stoke on 22 March and the Hull match on 26 April, Spurs played six League games – two draws, one win, three defeats. Like a tennis player choking in the fifth set, Spurs twitched. The last game in that sequence – a 3–2 home defeat by Sunderland – left things looking decidedly iffy.

Although promotion was actually clinched three days later with a 0–0 draw at Southampton (a curiously anodyne affair which, in a more cynical world, might be explained away by noting that both teams needed a draw to ensure promotion), it was the Hull match that was the key.

'It was very tense,' says Perryman. 'We needed to win it. It was a night game, a full house – 36,000 in the Second Division. It was a struggle though. I think I found out afterwards that there was some extra meaning in the game for them as well. I'm not suggesting a bribe or anything, but we noted to each other afterwards, "Christ, for a team that was playing out the season, they didn't half have a go." And they did. They defended like tigers, if you'll forgive the pun. They threw everything in the way of the ball, and made it very difficult for us to win the game.'

Curious thing to say. 'I'm not suggesting a bribe.' Who had?

So, John, everything to gain, everything to lose. The big occasion. That Spurs moment. Atletico Madrid. AC Milan. Hull City. It was at night, too.

John Duncan: 'We were poor and I played terrible. A poor game – we didn't create much at all. It was getting closer and closer in the last minutes. A cross came in to the end of the box. There was no way I was going to get it. It was the keeper's ball all the way. I knew it was the last minutes, and I said to myself, "Look, I'm just going to go for it as hard as I can," and I smacked the keeper as he went up – there was no way I could get the ball.'

What? You shoulder-charged him?

'Yes, shoulder, yes. I just took my chance that it wouldn't be given; it was a free kick. But the goalie bungled it down and the ball fell to Steve Perryman. He strikes it in and I can't believe it. I thought it deserved to be given as a free kick, but we won 1–0, went to Southampton, got the draw and that's what took us up. I remember that Hull incident as clear as day. It was not like it's a great goal, but it was important.'

So it was illegal?

'Yes, I just went hard in and felt that there was a chance there. It was a free kick. I couldn't get the ball. I didn't go in high or anything – it was a straight challenge. But illegal? I never thought about it in those terms. You know, breaks go one way and then go the other way and I never felt that I shouldn't have done it. But out of all the goals that I scored, strange for that to be a vivid memory . . . We were doing really well and slipped quite badly. If we hadn't won that game we wouldn't have gone up. Simple as that.'

Epilogue

The curious thing about John Duncan was that for a couple of years he had been the hero of the terraces. He'd got the Spurs back where they belonged, saw the arrival of Ardiles and Villa and witnessed the dawn of a new era and then . . . he disappeared. Why did he go?

'Well, I had the chance to go to Derby. I'd been left out a couple of times and all it was was a little bit of ego – stupidity. When you're a striker at a club like Spurs, you shouldn't really be guaranteed a place every week and I suppose I acted wrongly to think that.'

You must have been 28 or 29?

'Yes. I was just insecure at the time. I should have stayed. I might not have been in every week, but I think at the end of the day I was going to get in most weeks. At the time they had Colin Lee, Chris Jones, Ian Moores, Peter Taylor, Gerry Armstrong. I really shouldn't have moved, but I did and that was a mistake, but . . .'

You were the best striker in that lot.

'That's what I mean. I knew that and that's what annoyed me. I wasn't 100 per cent fit at that stage and maybe I wasn't playing as well as I could have done. I just needed to get myself fighting fit and

I would probably have been okay.'

I don't know if I'd be too happy with the prospect of playing second fiddle to Colin Lee, Chris Jones, Ian Moores, Peter Taylor and Gerry Armstrong, and I really can't imagine it's a decision Duncan would have had to make. But there is another idea. It wasn't anything to do with Keith Burkinshaw wanting new blood?

'No, really. Not at all. It was me. I got along okay with Keith. Everyone has their crosses with their managers, and I suppose I wasn't too happy about being left out, but I thought he was a decent guy.'

Was it a kind of ego madness?

'Yes, beyond what was real and what should've been. That's what happens in football.'

It happens everywhere.

'Yes. I would say that.'

It's that old head on young shoulders deal. If I knew then what I know now . . . It's a game we can all play and it is to Duncan's credit that he's now ready to accept that the monster came to stay. But if his acceptance is a testament to his honesty, his monster was a testament to his talent. When the same thing happened to Chivers and Archibald, the explosion was so loud that it engulfed and destroyed the team. When it happened to Duncan, his Achilles tendon snapped.

What must it be like to grow up in Alan Gilzean's shadow, follow him to the best club in the land and then find yourself playing alongside Don McAllister and Ian Moores in the Second Division? A couple of years either side and you could have been clutching silver.

'It would have been nice to win something, but you've got to be thankful for what you get. Maybe if I hadn't missed so many games, maybe if I hadn't missed that whole year which was a killer for me because I was at my peak then, I don't know. Yes, it was terribly frustrating, but I can't complain. I had such a good spell at Dundee and at Spurs; I could very easily not have had any of that.'

Your last game?

'A 2–2 draw with Chelsea. It was the first game for Ardiles and Villa. It was fantastic when they joined. It was a real coup for Keith Burkinshaw and good luck to him. They didn't settle immediately. They had a hard time. First there was the World Cup celebrations, and then they weren't 100 per cent fit. It took them a while to get into the English game. Ardiles got hit. I think it was Tommy Smith.

It was the worst tackle I've seen in my life. It shook Ardiles up and at that stage I thought, "He's got to be thinking, I fancy Argentina," but full credit to him. Villa did well too.

'I scored the first goal that they made at White Hart Lane. Ardiles dribbled the ball down to the touchline, Villa back-heeled it and I knocked it in. But I got injured again and left about a month later.' The Argentinians first game, the dawn of a new era. Irony abounds.

'They brought in Archibald and Crooks just after I left, decent players and that might have been a harder year to get in the team. Maybe my Scottish character came in. I wasn't too happy at the idea of playing second fiddle which I should have been able to do.'

It's very noble of you to say so.

'That's exactly the truth of it.'

9

THOUGHTS OF A MANAGER

Keith Burkinshaw

Keith Burkinshaw: 'I think the best game we played was when Cloughy had his best side at Nottingham Forest and we went up there and beat them 3–0; we absolutely paralysed them. We just ran them ragged for 90 minutes. Glenn and Ossie and Ricky were superb; Tony Galvin and all the others had terrific games. I mean, we had a terrific side then, and when we did hit form, we could wallop anybody. We were super in every position that day and it was probably the best ever performance by that team. Nobody ever remembers it, you know, and I can't even remember what year it was [15 November 1980] but I can remember that it was the only time Cloughy came into the dressing-room. Well, he didn't come in – he saw me in the corridor and he said, "That was absolutely fantastic. You gave us a real hammering there." That was the only time he spoke to me after a match. He just went. He didn't stay about, especially if we beat them.

'In terms of pure football, the finest half we ever played was against the Rotterdam team, Feyenoord [19 October 1983]. We had Glenn at his best in those days and Cruyff was playing for Feyenoord.

'The first hurdle we had to overcome when I was a manager was to beat Southampton. We had to get at least a point from Southampton in the final match of the season to get promoted back out of the Second Division. I don't think I slept for about four or five days before that match because I knew that the whole future of the club rested on getting those one or two points. It was really traumatic as far as I was concerned. I don't think that I've been put through the wringer as much as I was that week. Sunderland had just beaten us at home and we left ourselves with this bloody task. Southampton were already up and so they were playing freely, without any problems, and we had this massive game ahead of us. So from a psychological point of view, that was one that we really had to get something out of.

'But the one that gave me real satisfaction was the FA Cup final against Manchester City, the culmination of what we'd been building up to from 1976 till 1981 – five years.'

Tottenham Hotspur 3 (Villa 2, Crooks)
Manchester City 2 (Mackenzie, Reeves (pen))

FA Cup final replay
14 May 1981

Tottenham Hotspur: Aleksic, Hughton, Miller, Roberts, Perryman, Villa, Ardiles, Archibald, Galvin, Hoddle, Crooks.
Manchester City: Corrigan, Ranson, McDonald, Reid, Power, Caton, Bennett, Gow, Mackenzie, Hutchison, Reeves (Sub: Tueart for McDonald).
Attendance: 92,000

In the end, the 100th FA Cup final produced the game of the century... and the winning goal, scored by Ricky Villa, will always belong in football history.

The Guardian

'People think that you can just change things round in football, but with a club like Tottenham in those days, it was like a juggernaut; you know you've got to do it slowly rather than quickly. It took us five years to get to where we were in '81. Winning that replay against Manchester City was a tremendous thing for me and I think it gave the lads immense satisfaction. It was good to peak at a vital time and we played some of the best football I'd seen at the club. That was the first final that we won. We won three while I was there – the two Cup finals and the UEFA Cup. I'm sure that if I'd stayed there we would have gone on to win more stuff.

'I was watching that Cup replay recently, and what amazed me was how well everybody played, what a good football match it was. We played exceptionally well – the passing was very, very good. Do you remember when we played them on the Saturday? We had a disappointing game, lucky really to come away with a 1–1 draw.

They'd set about us. They had this fella who did all the kicking – Gerry Gow – and they kicked hell out of us. It had upset us and we hadn't played our normal game. Afterwards I said, "Look, the thing that's struck me is that they played at their best – they couldn't play any better than that. We've played about 50 per cent of our capacity. We've only got to play our normal game so that we're going to be, say, 20 per cent better than what we were in that game on Saturday, and they can't hold us. They're not as good as us."

'Ricky, who I'd taken off, was crying in the dressing-room after the half an hour extra time; he thought he was out of it. I think the reason he was so down was that his parents were watching him from Argentina and in their culture, unless you're seen to be doing well they're right down in their own country. I mean, he was devastated. I've never seen a fella as devastated. I said, "Lift your head up – you're playing on Thursday." I don't know what made me say it – it was just instinctive. I knew I'd got to say that, and it worked out. He played tremendously on that Thursday. As soon as I said, "Lift your head up – you're no worse a player now because you've had a poor game today. Go out and show us what you can do on Thursday," he just opened up like a flower and he was beaming, you know. I think that that's one of the best decisions I've ever made. I knew that it was the right thing to do. I wasn't doing it for Ricky, I was doing it for the team. If I'd thought that he couldn't do it on the Thursday, he would have been out. That's the way you had to be as a manager. But I knew that it was the right thing to do and the right time to do it.

'The build-up to that game on the Saturday had got out of all proportion. It became as much an Argentinian Cup final as it was Tottenham's, you know what I mean? I think that got to the players a little bit and they didn't play at their best; but we were free on the Thursday and we really did play well.

'From my point of view, Ricky was a bit of a nightmare because I was never sure what he was going to do. For instance, I felt that we would have beaten Liverpool in the 1982 League Cup final at Wembley but for Ricky. I'm not putting all the blame on Ricky, but, with only five minutes to go, he had the ball at a sort of left-back, left-half position and he knocked a square pass across the face of our penalty area. Ronnie Whelan – now the manager of Southend – knocked it in the net. Now if Ricky had kicked the ball up the field, we'd have been able to regroup, but we couldn't do anything about the square ball – we couldn't defend it. We were five minutes away from winning that Cup final. Ricky was one of those lads who could do the mercurial, glory things but, by golly, he could also do the things that put the team in trouble.

'Ossie, I thought when he came to us, was the most accurate passer of a ball in the world. If he misplaced a ball a couple of times in 90 minutes, I was amazed. He was so accurate it was unbelievable.

'I hadn't been to the Argentine for the World Cup, but I'd watched it on television and I was enough of a judge to see that Ardiles was the best player in that Cup final. When the manager of Sheffield United, Harry Haslam, came on the phone to me and said, "If you fancy Ardiles, you can get him", and he stated about £300,000, I couldn't believe it. I thought he was having me on. "Well, even if it's not genuine," I thought to myself, "I'm willing to give it a go, and if I don't get him, I don't get him." The board knew what was going on – that's the way I was with the directors. As long as there was money in the kitty, they used to say, "Go ahead and do it." That was the way we worked in those days. The secretary and I ran the club really. We used to have a budget and it was left to us to work within the budget. Now budgets have gone out the window with all that money being thrown about.

'I mean, it was a big thing, but it was fantastic from my point of view. I always remember talking about buying and selling players; all that big money. There was a fella I wanted – David Johnson, the centre-forward from Ipswich. He was available. I said to Sid Wale, "Look, Johnson from Ipswich is available. I would like to bring him here if it's possible. It's going to cost us around about £400,000." He said, "Yes, fine." It was the first big transfer deal that I had done so I asked him if he wanted to be with me while I was talking to them. He said, "Look, Keith. You are our manager and our managers do the transfer deals themselves. Get on with it. We've got confidence in you." That's fantastic for a young manager who nobody ever knew about, starting off at a club like Tottenham. Sid Wale was fantastic for me – the old-style chairman who would have 20 minutes with you on a Friday and that was all you saw of him all week. "Get on with the job, Keith. You run the club."

'Johnson never came because he wanted a lot of money – it was a bad business deal. But with Ardiles, I went to Argentina and it was one of the simplest deals I ever did. It was all done in 20 minutes. We left on a Friday and arrived on the Saturday morning. We were met by the big fella who was sent off while playing against England in 1966 – Rattin. He knew the Sheffield United manager and escorted us while we were there for about three or four days. I thought he was a magnificent bloke – a real gentleman. It shows what misconceptions you can have about people.

'On the Sunday or the Monday, I met Ossie and his wife, Sylvia, I took Ossie up to my bedroom and within twenty minutes we'd signed forms. It was so simple. I think that the crux of the thing was that he must have liked me immediately and I immediately liked him. He wanted to come to England to prove something and there was no problem. I got him for just over £300,000.

'And Ricky? Ossie just said, "My friend is available. Would you like to sign Ricardo Villa?" I knew about Ricky so I rang Sid Wale and said, "Look, I've just signed Ossie Ardiles, just like that – probably the best player in the world." We'd just come out of the Second Division, and he said, "Oh, fine." I carried on, "I can sign another one out of the World Cup side, but it's going to cost about the same money. What do you think?" He said, "Give me 20 minutes to get round the other board members," and then he said, "Go ahead, Keith, if you want him." He only came on as substitute in the World Cup, but I liked what I'd seen.

'I thought that two of them coming together would be much better than one coming on his own because it was an alien culture – we'd never had anyone in England from South America. I think they were the first ones who came. I signed Ricky in five minutes – it was so simple it was unbelievable. There was no problem with work visas. I mean they were World Cup stars – they were going to enhance our football, weren't they? It's not like some of them who have come recently. They were fantastic names. They lifted Tottenham from being a mediocre club – it lifted them up here. When those two came, I had invitations to play all over the world immediately. We became a world club. When we had free time, pre-season, we played football all over the place. Everyone wanted to see us. There were always massive crowds. It was exciting.'

10

DIAMOND LIGHT

Glenn Hoddle

Glenn Hoddle is possibly the most divisive personality in English football. Managers, coaches and critics either love him or revile him, while supporters give a positive vote with their feet by putting extra thousands on the gate every time his name appears on the Tottenham team sheet. In a real sense, he is one of the golden oldies – men like Danny Blanchflower, Johnny Haynes and Bobby Charlton – whose mere presence was a guarantee of something special.

The Guardian, 16 May 1987

He's a fanny merchant.

Anonymous

A luxury? It's the bad players who are a luxury.

Danny Blanchflower

He was a great player who I had liked but it was only on the pitch that I realised how good he really was. I was a shadow without any presence.

Johan Cruyff

A few years back there was a television documentary about the great jazz pianist Theolonius Monk. Now Monk was a pianist like no other, he played like no one else and, even to someone who knows nothing about the mysteries of the keyboard, it was clear he was different. His contemporaries talked about him finding new notes, of playing in the spaces between the chords. They said his left hand and his right hand weren't even related. Monk's appearance also marked him out as being special. Zoot suit, dark glasses, beret, a neckerchief above his shirt collar, sparkling painted tie . . . this was someone who knew exactly what he was doing. The documentary was made as if Monk was dead for there was no presence of the man. Then, about two-thirds of the way through, he appeared. The interviewer asked him a question, probably something simple about *Round Midnight* or something. Monk listened to the question, but made no reply. Then, after a few seconds had passed, he got up and very slowly stretched his arms out and started to spin around, rather like a young child would if pretending to be an aeroplane.

As an answer, it was perfect, if a little unorthodox. Words are fine if you want to have a chat or buy a meal, but how are you going to explain the workings of the artist? More to the point, why should you? By seeking to rationalise it, you must necessarily demystify it and suddenly it's ordinary. What a dull process, to make the extraordinary ordinary. Where's the fun, the joy? How much better, how much more eloquent Monk's answer was – 'I don't know how I wrote *Round Midnight*, but here's a quick impersonation of an aeroplane.'

Glenn Hoddle: 'There have been highlighted goals and there've been performances like Cup finals, but for a one-off game, if there's a single memory, one game that really takes me back and gives me a nice buzz, it was the game against Feyenoord in the UEFA Cup. It was 4–0 up after about twenty-five minutes, and I'd created all four goals, and everything I seemed to touch that night, you know, went in the back of the net. We seemed to gel on an evening which was magical. I think we won 4–2 in the end. Johan Cruyff was at Feyenoord at the time and I believe that a young Gullit was at the back as well. So it was a very, very good evening all round for us and I think that's the one that sticks in my mind.'

When was it?

'Oh, I don't know. I don't even remember my wedding anniversary.'

Talking to Glenn Hoddle about his favourite game for Spurs, it was impossible not to be drawn back to Monk. The similarities between the two are inescapable. Both were artists, both operated outside the accepted notional norms of their field, both did things that others thought impossible, both inspired an alien suspicion; Monk toyed with a goatee while Glenn flirted with a moustache . . .

Keith Burkinshaw: 'I think Glenn was at his absolute best – I don't think I've ever seen Glenn play better than that.'

Tottenham Hotspur 4 (Archibald 2, Galvin 2)
Feyenoord 2 (Cruyff, Neilsen)

UEFA Cup, second round, first leg
19 October 1983

Tottenham Hotspur: Clemence, Hughton, Galvin, Roberts, Stevens, Perryman, Mabbutt, Archibald, Falco, Hoddle, Brooke.
Feyenoord:Hiele,Neilsen,Troost,Duut,Wijnstekers,Hoek-Stra, Gullit, Jeliazkov, Houtman, Cruyff, Vermeulen.
Attendance: 35,404

There are very few things that you'll ever see – in any field – that make you think, 'Well, that was absolutely brilliant. That was about as perfect as perfect could be. I really don't know what to say': the flashback scenes in *Once upon a Time in America,* seeing the Fall play at The Nashville in 1978, waking up for the first time on the beach in Goa, seeing Elly smile her first smile . . . and the first half of the Spurs against Feyenoord match.

Steve Perryman: 'It was a great game, the first half was perfection. It flowed. Sometimes you have good performances and the ball hits the bar, or goes over the bar, or inches wide, or the keeper makes a great save. But that night it all happened. All the finest football worked and had a great finish. I had a team feeling that night the same as the personal feeling I had in my game at AC Milan. But it was something special. Glenn was the man that game.'

Such sweet understatement: 'So it was a very, very good evening all round for us.' 'Glenn was the man that game.' Let's get to the point. It was a great game, the first half was perfection. It was the finest half Spurs ever played. Hoddle aside, it was a classic Spurs performance – a dance of delight up front almost thrown away by sloppy defending and careless mistakes. But the end . . . we can wait for the end. The beginning is what we came here for. Spurs were everything, everywhere. It was a classic white-strip, floodlit, evening European performance, toasting the spirit of Atletico Madrid and laying the ghost of Benfica to rest. Feyenoord were so shell-shocked, that after only 35 minutes they made two substitutions, taking off the Dutch international Houtman and a pre-dread, ugly duckling called Ruud Gullit.

Maybe it's because football is such a simple thing, but it's undeniably curious how it continues to throw coincidences to the wind like so much confetti. After so many years in the international wilderness, the match that Spurs chose to announce their return – loud and proud – was against Feyenoord. It was ten years earlier, on 30 May 1974, that Spurs blew their reputation (or rather, had their reputation blown for them) when their fans rioted in Rotterdam at the final of the UEFA Cup against Feyenoord. In a strange way, if Spurs were going to be internationally rehabilitated, the Dutch were the perfect opponents.

There was another reason for it being a quite remarkable night. On the field were three generations of 'The Best Footballer in the World'. Not only was there Johan Cruyff, the ghost of glories past, and Glenn Hoddle, the very tangible now, but there was also Ruud Gullit, the ghost of triumphs to come.

Keith Burkinshaw: 'I'd been to watch Holland play Ireland, in Ireland, and when I came back I said to all the lads, "We've got a big game on here, I tell you, because there's a fella called Gullit who's a really, really good player. We're going to have to be at our best to beat this lot." They had Cruyff and they had some good players in the side in those days. But after the two games, the lads said, "You're not much of a judge – he can't play, this Gullit. He's a poor player." He'd just had two poor games.'

Did you put someone on him? Make some special contingency plan?

'No, we never did that at Tottenham. I made the players aware of him, you see, and he did have two poor games. But there was no contest really; we were superb.'

No disrespect intended to the other two – and certainly no club bias – but it's entirely fitting that Glenn should have, that night, reigned supreme. The king is dead, long live the king. (And don't worry about the prince; his day will come.) Feyenoord may have had both ends of the spectrum, the past and the future, but Spurs had the now. 'It was one of those special nights,' says Hoddle, 'where within 20 minutes we were 4–0 up, you know, against a side that had a good reputation. I think I created all the goals. It was a performance that was up there with the best.'

It couldn't last. It wouldn't be Spurs if it did. If you want to read about a team that shut the gates, you should be reading a book called something like *The Day I Stayed Awake at Highbury*. In the second half, Spurs fell apart – and don't moan, we both know we wouldn't have it any other way. Two goals in the last fifteen minutes and Feyenoord coach Thijs Libregts was smiling. 'We are back in the race now.' But maybe Cruyff knew better: 'We slipped away into the night and I had to admit to the other players that it was all down to me.'

Somehow that night all roads led to Cruyff. Thinking about it, I couldn't help but be reminded of that scene in Woody Allen's *Annie Hall* when they're standing in a cinema queue and the lecturer type starts pontificating about Marshall McLuhan. Allen, who disagrees with everything he's been saying, finally snaps and walks over to the camera to complain to us that the lecturer type knows nothing of McLuhan's work and is, essentially, an idiot. The lecturer notices this and says, well, that's okay for you to say, but I happen to teach a course blah blah blah. Allen gives him a killing look and moves aside a nearby billboard to reveal McLuhan himself who's looking aghast. 'You know nothing about me or my work,' says the venerable cultural critic. Allen looks back to the camera and says, 'If only life could really be like this . . .'

It's a great fantasy and it's one that probably everyone has indulged in at one time or another, playing God to manipulate a situation, not nastily but just enough to prove a point.

Glenn Hoddle: 'I remember feeling very good on the night. They were very special nights at Tottenham. Every European game was special and I think with any club it is. There's a difference there for supporters, the atmosphere seems electric. Maybe Cruyff playing on the opposing side made it more so.'

Was that personal?

'I don't think so. I just got on with doing the job for Tottenham. It was just one of those games that I can really remember. I take a lot of pride in that performance.'

Keith Burkinshaw: 'We had Glenn at his best in those days and Cruyff was playing for Feyenoord. He said he didn't believe all the hype about Glenn Hoddle. "Wait until we come there," he said, "and then see what a team can do." He thought Glenn Hoddle would probably not get a kick in the game. He was that vocal that day, he really didn't hold Glenn in high esteem and, of course, it worked for me because I didn't have to say anything to the players. They were seething, and we went out, and we were 4–0 up at half-time.'

Johan Cruyff: 'Glenn Hoddle was a great player in my book. He played football the way that I wanted to see it played. He could make great passes and was the best player for Tottenham. I wanted to test myself against the young star of the present. I knew I could play. I wanted to see what level I was at.' In the press, Cruyff was rather more vocal, mouthing off about what he was going to do and who was this kid anyway. The papers, especially *The Guardian*, fell for it hook, line and sinker, and created the type of buzz that precedes a heavyweight boxing fight.

In retrospect, it seems bizarre that someone as experienced as Cruyff should have gone down this road. Like an ageing gunslinger who's heard that there's a new kid in town, Cruyff went looking for Glenn Hoddle. Really. You'd think they never show westerns in Holland. Does everyone not know that the only thing ageing gunslingers have got going for them is that they wont age for long; and, before your popcorn's dry, the new kid is an ageing gunslinger.

Keith Burkinshaw: 'I can't remember Glenn saying too much about the Cruyff thing – all I can remember is that Glenn was fired up and he was magnificent in that game. There was no contest because of that. I think that Johan Cruyff had done the job for me by coming out with all these stupid things before the match, saying that Glenn wasn't a good player. I remember another fella that had a go at Glenn before, when we played Bayern Munich – what d'you call 'im? The fella they've got now? Beckenbauer – and it worked the same way. He said: "This Hoddle's not what they crack him up to be, and Tottenham's not the side that people say they are. It's going to be fairly easy for us." We lost in Germany, but we beat them 2–0 at home. What Beckenbauer said fired us up, and they had a strong side in those days.

'I used to love it when people came out with things like that. The psychology of football. Liverpool were past masters at it – they just used to get on with things. If they won, fantastic. If they lost the occasional game, they never said anything about it. They didn't fire other people up by shouting their mouths off about what they were going to do before a match; I think that I learnt a bit from that. That's the way that Liverpool were in those days. Secretly behind the scenes though, they weren't very good losers. You know the record of Tottenham against Liverpool; up to me finishing we'd never won there in 70-odd years. The following year Peter Shreeve went up there and Spurs beat Liverpool in the League for the first time in about 76 years. Every time I went up there I had to move with grace. I always went into the boot room and had a chat with the staff, you know. I remember the chairman – a man called Smith – would come up and say, "The game is not about taking part – it's about winning." Oh, very nice, and I had to smile and take it. On the occasions when they come down to our place and we beat them, they just used to slink away on the bus and never say a word. Maybe they were such bad losers because they didn't lose very often, I don't know.'

Despite the pleas of Libregts, Cruyff insisted that he marked Hoddle; and if Cruyff insisted that something happened then, odds-on, it would happen. Apart from being Johan Cruyff, professional living legend, he was also Johan Cruyff, technical director of Feyenoord. It's rather like the editor of a newspaper saying to the features editor, 'That's a good idea for an article. I think I should write it. What do you think? Do you think that's a good idea?'

Johan Cruyff: 'It was a bad error of judgement. I thought that I could mark him and keep him quiet, but the result showed that I couldn't.'

Spurs, or Keith Burkinshaw anyway, weren't that stupid or egocentric. Gary Mabbutt was given the job of marking Cruyff. So, of the three players, there were two winners and one left looking rather silly. The irony is that it was the most experienced of the three who lost out. While Cruyff wasted his energies and his talents marking Hoddle, Mabbutt did what he was good at; and Hoddle played.

After eight minutes, Hoddle sliced the Dutch defence open to leave Steve Archibald with the easiest of chances: 1–0. Ten minutes later, a 30-yard cross/pass dropped onto the head of Tony Galvin: 2–0. Just after the half-hour, Mark Falco struck a fierce shot which the Feyenoord keeper did well to block. Gary Mabbutt was the first to react, setting up Steve Archibald: 3–0. Three minutes before half-time came the *pièce de résistance*, only there wasn't that much resistance. How could there be? Hoddle – as if we needed to say – hit an inch-perfect 40-yard pass exactly into the stride of the on-rushing Galvin, who did what had to be done: 4–0.

If there's one overriding memory of that night, it is of Hoddle lording it around and *pinging* these huge long balls into the path of Tony Galvin, BA (Linguistics); socks down, head down, ball comes flying over, '*Spaseeba* very much'.

Keith Burkinshaw: 'It was Glenn and Tony Galvin, if I remember . . . The thing that struck me that day was that Glenn and Tony were magnificent in that first period. You'll remember Tony as that big, strong, powerful runner. Glenn was hitting balls in behind their full-back and Tony was galloping in. He seemed to be on the end of every ball that Glenn was passing and he was getting balls across. I think that Tony Galvin actually scored a goal that game.'

Let's just go back to that idea of football clubs having distinct personalities for a minute. Apart from the familiar flash and flamboyant angle, there's something else distinct to the Spurs character; something else that has remained a constant. The stars. The club demands its stars, the fans demand them. It's essential that the players who perform for Spurs are highly paid stars, preferably bought for a huge transfer fee. It's a glamour thing. From Cliff Jones in the double team and Ralph Coates in the early 1970s to people like Lineker, Gascoigne and even Chris Armstrong, Spurs have to have their big-money heroes. It's a tradition, and while it's no doubt hugely frustrating to any number of talented youth players who've seen their dreams trashed as yet another cheque takes their place, they cannot argue. They know, as we all know, that you cannot mess with tradition. It's a question of universal balance. Ask Mark Falco. Honest as the day is long and a very effective striker, Falco did everything that could have been asked of him. He ran himself into the ground, he scored goals, he supported his team-mates, he tried his best. Yet he never really won the hearts of the Spurs crowd. He was appreciated, yes, and his goals were welcomed. But loved? No. The crowd loved Steve Archibald. Stroppy, selfish, egocentric Steve Archibald. Expensive Steve Archibald. Consider it this way: if the tradition did not exist, what would become of Norwich City?

In the Spurs team of the early 1980s, Tony Galvin was a footprint on Sunset Strip. Ardiles, Villa, Hoddle, Archibald, Crooks, Thomas, Stevens . . . Tony Galvin. He didn't come from anyone and he didn't go anywhere; from Goole Town to Spurs to life. There was no big-money move to Monaco or Marseilles. Tony Galvin was just there at the right time – perfect – and then he wasn't. Money, talent and immense presence aside, there was something about Galvin that set him apart, that singled him out from any number of cheapo journeymen. Galvin is responsible for a wonderful piece of football trivia, a priceless trivial pursuit. He has a degree in Russian from Hull University.

Keith Burkinshaw: 'Tony was a very down-to-earth Yorkshireman, like myself. You could rely on him. He would work his bollocks off for the team week in week out, he was as fit as a log. He wasn't a drinker or a smoker, he was just a great team player. I bought him from Goole Town. He was a university student, up at Hull I think it was, and a fella I knew in Scunthorpe said to me, "There's a boy playing for Goole. I'm sure that he would be terrific for you down at Tottenham." He said: "I've heard so much about him, but I haven't actually seen him." So I said: "Well, go and have a look at him." And he went and had a look at him, and he said: "He's a good player, come and have a look." I think I sent Bill Nick up to see him, and then I went up myself, and I bought him for £3,000. Three thousand quid . . . and once he was in the side I don't think he was ever out of it. He was one of our most consistent members; an unsung hero really, but a very effective part of the team. I mean, not only was he good at going forward, but he was good at getting back and giving assistance to Chrissie Hughton. The pair of them had a terrific understanding. They were big mates, and they seemed to be almost telepathic.'

There are so many clichés about footballers' feet – cultured, educated, could open a tin-can, could turn the pages of a book. Talking about Hoddle in the first half of this match, your John Motsons or Barry Davies could rabbit on about size 8 PhDs and they still wouldn't be half-way there. It was Elly smiling at the Fall in Goa.

If that was what it was like to watch, then what was it like for Glenn Hoddle to do?

'The adrenalin was flowing and that's a wonderful feeling: to have those moments of magic was wonderful. It gives you an extra boost – and confidence is three-quarters of being a footballer. A bit of adrenalin gives you an extra buzz that some people think they have to find in other ways. I can remember getting that buzz when I was playing well and when the team was playing well, when everything was going to plan. The motivation factor with a European tie is that the supporters are a little less forgiving than on a normal Saturday. In that game, certainly at the beginning and then going 4–0 up, you knew it wasn't going to be a night when they were going to be too critical.

'At the time, we were unstoppable, but you can't play football like that for 90 minutes. It's always harder to create than to destroy, but when something comes together, it's a moment. The rest is average, it's pretty mundane. We might have played rubbish the previous Saturday. But it's that moment that you play for.'

Epilogue

> In Hungary we make love to the ball and we sleep with it. The English eat it.
>
> Florian Albert, former European Footballer of the Year

Back in the early 1950s, Spurs had a great team. Led by their visionary manager, Arthur Rowe, they revolutionised English football, playing in a fast and fluid style that came to be known as 'push and run'. Rowe was fortunate in that he had the players who could take advantage of his radical ideas – one without the other would have been useless. Of all Spurs' stars, none shone brighter than their flying winger, Alf Ramsey. A quicksilver butterfly, Ramsey had feet like mercury and the balance of a ballet dancer. He could beat players on either wing, with either foot and was equally adept at going inside or outside. Though film footage of him is confined to the grainy black-and-white images of the era – funny baggy shorts, flat caps and dinner-suited commentary – you can see clearly the gazelle-like grace of his play. Ramsey's name lives on, fixed in the same sentence as Finney and Matthews, and you can be sure that somewhere a familiar argument still rages. Who was the best?

A bit of football fantasy, that one; a 'what if'. What if Ramsey had been a winger instead of a dull, dour – and, yes, very efficient – full-back? What then? Maybe he'd have built his World Cup team around people like himself, people with flair and the maverick ability to do the unexpected. Maybe if that had happened, that would have been how English football developed. Just think – no Arsenal double team, no Don Revie, an England team that combined the talents of Frank Worthington, Alan Hudson, Stan Bowles and Tony Currie, no barren years of missed international opportunity, no Ron Greenwood, no decades of nothing.

Well, it's possible. After all, in real life Ramsey the full-back created teams that reflected Ramsey the full-back (and executed the final revenge on a career spent getting carved up by flash wingers) and the success of these teams set the standard for the next 25 years.

> If Hoddle had been born in Brazil or West Germany the national team would almost certainly have been built around his unique talents, just as Holland made Johan Cruyff their creative general in the 1970s. But in the muscular work-obsessed world of English football, Hoddle has been regarded with suspicion,

> partly because he makes so many ambitious 40-yard passes, partly because it took him years to learn to fight in order to express his skills.
>
> *The Guardian*, 16 May 1987

Of all the maverick talents that leaked into – and out of – the English game in the Arsenalesque 1970s, none was treated worse than Glenn Hoddle. A curious thing to say, given that our Glenn got over 50 caps, while the likes of Hudson, Bowles and Currie barely got a fez between them. Even taking away the bar-room question of 'who was the best?', it's not difficult to see why I say what I say. All the others – and you can throw in Osgood, Worthington, George, McKenzie . . . all the usual suspects – were boys with attitude. And whatever you think of that rock'n'roll outsider stance, there comes a point where you must concede that it's got to be difficult if not impossible to harness that attitude into the regimental framework that exists around the world of soccer. The idea of disciplining Stan Bowles – we don't really need to say anymore, do we?

Saying this is not to justify the stultifying Revie-isation that was happening; far from it. Remember, we're Spurs fans here; better to live one day as a tiger and all that. It's just that we accept what is and what isn't.

Glenn Hoddle was treated worse than any of the above because he was a good boy, a nice boy. Didn't drink, didn't smoke . . . he was the sort of boy you'd feel safe taking home to mother. Okay, so he grew the odd iffy moustache, and he released a pop song with Chris Waddle, and he would never tuck his shirt in his shorts, and he saw the Light . . . these things aside, there was no attitude, no rebel yell. And he was still rejected. So you come to the conclusion, the sad shocking conclusion, that he was rejected for one reason: he had quite phenomenal skills.

No wonder he turned to God. He didn't enjoy any of the fruits of attitude – how many pictures are there of Glenn on the dentist's chair with only a ripped T-shirt and a bottle of tequila for company? Yet he didn't get the benefits of mediocrity.

> It might be worth taking a chance with a midfield player whose principal assets are not his lungs.
>
> Peter Shreeve

In a curious way, though, Hoddle had more attitude than a thousand

Hudsons or Bowles, but his wasn't shown by booze, birds and gambling. His was arrogance, an arrogance that friends of Hoddle will call self-belief.

We were talking about Ardiles and Villa and how they settled in. They must have been good players, I said. After all, they'd just won the World Cup.

'I think that you have to have the right temperament. It doesn't matter how talented you are, you have to have a temperament of steel to get over the hurdles that come your way, and they obviously had it, I've obviously had it, and a lot of the players in that Tottenham team had it – Steve Archibald, Perryman, Paul Miller, Graham Roberts, Ray Clemence. It was instilled. It was that kind of team – very talented, but very single-minded, a lot of good hearts, strong hearts.'

Is that the difference between good and bad players?

'Yes. The good players can become very good if they've got a bit of steel. People think that means putting your head in, but it doesn't – it means having the confidence or inner self-belief. It's bordering on arrogance, but the minute you get into that, it slaps you in the face, so you've got to handle it right. It's having a touch of inner steel and knowing that you're in control. If hurdles come your way, you have to know that you can jump them and get on with life.'

Keith Burkinshaw: 'I was watching a tape of the Manchester City FA Cup replay the other day and something struck me that I hadn't noticed before. The best ball winner we had that day was . . . go on, guess.'

Er, Ardiles?

'No. That's who I would have thought. But, no. It was Glenn. Now, he was never renowned for tackling, was he? I mean, I know what Ricky did with the goals and I know that Ossie played a tremendous game, but if you look for someone who influenced the game more than anyone else that day. . . Glenn Hoddle. He was working harder than anyone else and his distribution was immaculate – some of the balls he pushed through for people . . .

'His pass to Garth Crooks was absolutely out of this world. He's got a group of people in front of him and Garth's just trying to make that little move. They're a little bit square, trying to hold us; if we go forward we're going to be offside. I can see Garthy's eyes, he was just waiting, and Glenn just lifts the ball up – virtually just scoops it up and over this group of players and Crooks was there. It would only be Glenn who could have done that.'

He's a fanny merchant. What does that mean?

Glenn's early years are well documented. At the age of eight, he could do almost all the tricks he could do when he was in his mid-20s, except one.

'I couldn't catch the ball on my neck which was too small. It really annoyed me. I had to practise for years.' He was spotted at the age of 11 by Martin Chivers and Ray Evans after the two ex-Spurs players went to Harlow to present a trophy. Ball-control was practised with an assortment of tangerines, apples and oranges because doing it with a ball wasn't really much of a challenge. He scored on his debut at Stoke.

'I'll never forget that day because I was only seventeen and I scored the winner with a 25-yarder that screamed past Peter Shilton. It was a very special day for me and not a bad way to start.'

The footage of that game is a treasure. The ball ricochets out of a crowded penalty area to an incredibly young-looking, skinny malinck. The commentator says: 'He's got to chip it back into the area,' but Hoddle can't hear him . . . and bang! Peter Shilton is on his pants throwing a look that says, 'What was that?'

Glenn Hoddle: 'Of course the runners and tacklers are part of the game but people don't have a go at them if they can't play 40-yard balls or go past three men at a time. They don't expect them to do the things skilful players are good at. For some reason it doesn't apply the other way round, but that is the way we are in England and maybe it's part of the reason why Brazil do a bit more than us at international level.'

On 22 November 1979 he made his debut, aged 22, for England, at Wembley against Bulgaria. He scored, naturally, but maybe a little too naturally for some people's tastes.

'I thought about blasting the ball but there was a defender chasing me so I decided on a side-footed shot from 20 yards. I suppose, technically, that sort of thing isn't done. It's not in the soccer manual. I side-footed the ball because I wanted to make sure the ball was accurate, but it couldn't possibly have been planned. This goal was extra special because it was side-footed on the half-volley. That's a more complex technique.'

Even more naturally, he was left out of the next three matches. It's a curious irony that the England manager of the time was Ron Greenwood, the so-called football purist and high priest of what was laughingly known as the West Ham Academy. This was supposed to be the home of the cultured player, a temple to all that was good and pure. Greenwood should have embraced Hoddle. Instead, he rejected him. Possibly the idea that a Hoddle-inspired England might actually win something frightened him just a little too much. After all, the trophy cabinet down West Ham way isn't exactly creaking under the weight.

When he went to play for Monaco, the team coach, Arsene Wenger, had already decided on the tactic that would best utilise his new acquisition's talents. He told his team, 'Win the ball and give it to Hoddle.' They did. Nine months later, Monaco were the proud new owners of the French Championship.

He's a fanny merchant. God knows what it means, but in this context, it's not a compliment. For years, Hoddle was derided – and not even for the things that he should have been derided for. That's why the game against Feyenoord is important. There was Glenn, rejected again and again by his country, pitted head-to-head against the brightest and the best of Europe, and he answered in the most eloquent way; in a way that would have made Theolonius Monk spin around like a Concorde on fire.

For Hoddle, despite his 'I just got on with doing the job for Tottenham' protestations, it must have been the sweetest of sweet revenges; nothing personal against Cruyff, but something very personal against the British establishment. Now the fanny merchant is the manager of England.

11

ONCE UPON A TIME IN N17

Garth Crooks

> The door bursts open and in comes the chairman elect of Tottenham Hotspur, Irving Scholar, in a wheelchair with a beautiful woman in one hand and a magnum of champagne in the other. 'Keith,' he says. 'This is for you. Congratulations.' Keith looks at Irving Scholar – the entire dressing-room fixes on both protagonists – and does not take the magnum. And so Irving Scholar says, 'Keith, this is for you.' I'm looking at Peter Shreeve now, the players are looking at them, and the whole thing's frozen. Keith hasn't said anything but he's refused to take the bottle of champagne. So Irving Scholar asks him a third time and I think, if I'm not mistaken, Peter said, 'Go on, Keith,' and I think a few of the lads said, 'Come on boss, crack open the bottle of champagne,' and he takes the bottle. Keith was too much of a man to have glossed over the situation. He wasn't a politician, Keith. He was a dour Yorkshireman and he wouldn't have betrayed the very things that had made him.
>
> Garth Crooks

It's a lovely scenario.

When I started researching this book, I had a fair idea of what matches each player would choose: Mackay and the Leicester FA Cup final, Hoddle and Feyenoord, Perryman and AC Milan. Others were a complete surprise: Pat Jennings' choice of the 1975 league game against Leeds, for example. I would have bet a very large wedge against a player choosing a match that he didn't actually play in. Yet, just as the 1991 FA Cup final was a match that had more plots than a dozen cemeteries, so the 1984 UEFA Cup final against Anderlecht had a resonance and a symbolism that far outweighed the highly charged, ridiculously dramatic events that took place on the pitch: it's the manager's last game, the captain is suspended and the latest big-money striker has decided he's no longer a part of the club. The one before that – the one who still scores all the goals – has said that he'll play for the club, he just won't talk to the manager ever again. His striking partner is a bit lost to football, gaining a perspective by doing a social sciences degree and an ego by presenting *Top of the Pops*. Meanwhile, deep in the bowels of White Hart Lane, a magnum of champagne is sitting on ice, waiting . . .

As the 1970s turned into the 1980s, Spurs became a spiritual barometer of the times. Maybe there's a karmic symbolism behind it, and maybe it's simply a reflection of the worth of their value systems, I don't know. But, looking back, there are just too many crashing points of reference, too many coincidences.

As the decade opened, the country was being led by Margaret Thatcher – the personification of shallow, amoral monetary values – and was going down the pan, while Tottenham Hotspur's manager, Keith Burkinshaw – an honest Yorkshireman who knew the price of a pint of milk – was turning them into a serious thing. Where the former sold style as a superficial distraction from the grim actuality, the latter added style as a bonus to his solid, underlying values.

There were similarities, though. Bizarrely, both sought to gain popularity and success by turning to the Argentinians. Okay, so he embraced them and she attacked them, but that's a picky detail. Each chose tactics that suited their circumstances and, in truth, both tactics were successful. It's a further irony that Burkinshaw's Spurs climaxed with a triumphant, if ultimately implosive, European victory. In marked contrast, Thatcher spent all her energy taking on the Europeans yet never got so much as an away goal. There used to be a football club here. That's what Keith said, isn't it, Garth?

'Exactly. That's exactly what he said. He left because he saw the monster well before anyone else, the monster being Tottenham Hotspur plc, and he felt that it was beyond him to shackle that monster. There was a new entrepreneurship coming into the game. Today we see it all around, it's become very much a part of the game, it's mainstream; but in 1984 it was a new phenomenon.'

There's something about this whole period of Spurs' history that's incredibly *zeitgeist*: they were so much of the moment, a reflection of the time, that it was almost comical. You half expected the players to come out with mobile phones strapped to their waists for those vital 'Man on! Man on!' moments.

'Er, I've got a window at 4.10 p.m., I can pass to you then.'

'Let me check my filo. Er, yeah. I can do that. Let's do it.'

Would it be fair to say that your era was the start of the proper money?

'Uh huh.'

And the start of the real head-turn stuff?

'Uh huh.'

Which is what the club should have been aware of?

'Yes. What's the question?'

Garth Crooks came to Spurs in 1980, just as the sun was rising and the dark years were receding into the distance. This was the era of Ardiles and Villa, Hoddle and Archibald, and Ossie's trembly knees. There was a vibrancy at the club, a feeling of hope and optimism. In 1981, Spurs won the FA Cup, beating Manchester City 3–2 in a replay. In 1982 they repeated the trick, beating Queen's Park Rangers 1–0, again in a replay. They were cooking. Aleksic, Hughton, Miller, Roberts, Perryman, Villa, Ardiles, Archibald, Galvin, Hoddle, Crooks. It was, in Steve Perryman's esteemed view, the best Spurs team since the double years.

Now, two years later and bolstered by the likes of Ray Clemence, Gary Stevens and Danny Thomas, the team had reached its zenith, a moment of wonderful drama caught in time at White Hart Lane; a night-time match, a European final, the all-white strip, the expectations, the shoot-out, the managerial fall-out . . .

Garth Crooks: 'For the first time in my career I was looking at the game from the outside, I was able to assess things from a different perspective. It made quite an impression because I suddenly started to see the club in a different light.'

Slow down. You're still a big-money star striker, but now you're on the bench. What happened?

'I'd lost form. I was 24, 25 and I'd lost my way, which was probably more the point. I'd lost my focus. I'd become distracted by other things in life that young men discover – it's a big world out there. You've been wrapped up in a very insular profession and suddenly you think, "Hang on a second, I come into work, I play football, I go home, I got to bed and I play football. There's got to be more to life than this," and there is. If you go looking for it, you often find it. I was excited by other interests, I was excited about what was happening in sport and sporting politics, I was excited by the media and the way that it worked, I was excited about aspects of the good life. These were things I'd never explored before. It is absolutely essential for a player who wants to reach the top of his career to keep his focus, and that's very difficult, particularly when you're in the midst of success. To keep it, you've got to work even harder; and that's when I started doing *Top of the Pops*.'

So what are you saying here? You were 25 and you were getting bored with football?

'I hate to use those terms, but I was a bit, yes. I didn't want to give it up, not at all; I just didn't think that there was anything wrong with wanting to explore other things. Maybe I was a bit naive to think I could just bolt things onto what I did. Doing that breeds resentment. Football takes up all your time and all your effort, especially if you want to be the best, and if you want to play for Tottenham. People in football don't take kindly to footballers doing things other than football.'

Keith Burkinshaw: 'I didn't object to people doing other things like that because I think that life's a fabric and the more rich they make that fabric, the better you are as a person, and I like people to be expansive.'

Without dipping into politics too much (as if), it's classic capitalism to keep the workers stupid so they won't question anything, and won't rock the boat. A stupid worker is a happy worker.

Garth again: 'I would say the football clubs accept that the good players and bright players might have to suffer for the not so bright players. They club you all together and for the sake of engendering team camaraderie and focus, you've got to go for the lowest common denominator.'

It's got to be said, it's good management tactics. What level of mayhem would be caused if you've got a squad of, say, twenty-five players and they're all running around pressing buttons. 'How does that work?' But for the bright button-presser, isn't this frustrating?

'It was extremely frustrating. If I hadn't been given the opportunity to present *Top of the Pops* or to share a platform for a quiz show with the emerging Rory Bremner . . . It was wonderful and I thought "Should I be on this platform?" But then I thought, "It's fantastic. Take it, grab it – it may never come along again." To meet all those people who were either fans of Tottenham Hotspur or of mine was ludicrous – you wouldn't have had that at Stoke-on-Trent. Four years on from signing, I suddenly found myself in a situation where I was dealing with all these household names. I remember bumping into Charlie Watts in the car-park at Spurs once and he wanted to come over and talk to me about the game – this was a member of the Rolling Stones. It was phenomenal as far as I was concerned. It blew my mind.'

There's another classic situation at work here, isn't there? The young provincial lad comes down to the big city, gets dazzled by the bright lights. He's got fresh folding in his pocket and it's burning. You've got to remember that Crooks joined Spurs in 1980. In 1984 Irving Scholar took over. Sometime in between, Charlie Watts said hello. Now consider this. In 1977, the highest paid player at Manchester United was on £300 a week. Crooks's time was boom-time, with proper money. You're a young lad; it's fun time.

'It is phenomenal. It's something that has escalated out of all proportion. The problems will become greater, I just hope that professional footballers equip themselves with the skills to retain it all and keep their sense of purpose and values.'

All this is so obvious, so logical. Was there no guidance from the club? No help or support structure?

'It's not the club's job to give guidance. Their job is to turn out professional footballers to the very best of their ability.'

Okay, but what about protecting their investment?

'In an ideal world, that would be a logical and sensible statement. However, they're in the winning business and there's too much work to do and too little time. They're not nannies. They're professional coaches – that's how they see themselves. From your position, I think you're entitled to be surprised, but once you're in there . . . you know, it's a fascinating environment. It's not always a pleasant environment to be in, professional soccer, but you're dealing with an environment which is cut-throat. It is very, very highly motivated and structured. To them, winning the Championship or the FA Cup or the European Cup is like a million-pound deal to Alan Sugar or Rupert Murdoch. Everything gets left behind if it languishes.'

And you're just a cog.

'Absolutely. When I decided to study social sciences, one of the most horrific things that I discovered was that in the classic management structure, professional footballers are labourers. I remember saying to my lecturer one day, "So what you're saying is that footballers like myself at White Hart Lane are glorified employees." And he smiled and nodded his head and said, "Yes, you're right." All the rest of the class hadn't the foggiest idea what I was talking about, but he knew. Well, they knew, but they didn't understand the impact it had on me. It did shock me because then I understood where the directors sat, I understood where the chairman sat, where the management sat – middle management. I thought, "Hang on a second," and suddenly my life had been transformed into a whole different world and it was quite frightening.'

Was this was before you came to Spurs?

'No. I was doing that course at Tottenham Tech while I was playing for them. I knew that my academic skills had stood still – even gone backwards – due to the footballing environment. I just wanted to equip myself to deal with the media better, to talk to people, to communicate. Being able to communicate is something I've always enjoyed. I may not be brilliant at it, but I enjoy it and I want to do it better. If there was a glimmer of something for me after football, then this was where it was going to be.'

I bet that impressed the other players – Garth with his Max Weber essays; as Engels said about the 4–4–2 system in . . .

'I think they always saw me as a bit of a maverick, inasmuch as "football's not enough for him". They would do it collectively. They weren't particularly vicious about it.'

Did it frighten them?

'I don't know. Once one player made it quite clear why he thought I did it.'

Why?

'Because he thought I wanted to be a star. It hurt me, but I think that at the time I did. I wanted to be involved in more things than football. He had a certain point. But I didn't want to do it to the detriment of anybody else.'

Hardly to the detriment of anybody else. You were the big-money, star striker, but you were on the bench for a UEFA Cup final.

'I spent most of the early evening convinced that I would actually get on at some stage, get on the pitch and be part of the occasion. I'd never been omitted from a major football event, this was the first one I'd been left on the sidelines for, and as we got ready and changed, it was rather strange not to be at the centre of what was going on. To talk in general terms about what it was like is very difficult, but it was as detached as I'd ever like to get. I didn't cut the subs out when I was a prominent member of any team, and it didn't happen to me on this occasion. In that situation, you have to remain a part of what's going on. You can be called upon at any time and still be a central part of the team's success or, indeed, its failure. So you've got to remain very attached and feel very much a part of it. It was a new phenomenon for me and I had to work very hard to keep my concentration.'

Was it a dreadful ego blow?

'I wouldn't say it was a dreadful ego blow, but it's not something I'd like to go through again. No, it wasn't an ego blow – you don't realise that you've got an ego until someone treads on it. I'd been out for most of that year, and I was quite relieved to be on the bench. I was far more concerned with getting on the pitch and having a more important role to play. There was doubt that I'd even make the bench. In my mind, it was only because Alan Brazil had decided not to be a part of the club, so his omission meant that I would certainly be on the bench.'

Tottenham Hotspur 1 (Roberts) Anderlecht 1 (Czerniatinski)

Spurs won 4–3 on penalties

UEFA Cup final, second leg
23 May 1984

Tottenham Hotspur: Parks, Thomas, Hughton, Roberts, Miller, Mabbutt, Hazard, Archibald, Falco, Stevens, Galvin.
Anderlecht: Munaron, Grun, De Greef, Czerniatinski, De Groote, Vercauteren, Brylle, Scifo, Arnesen, Olsen, Holkens.
Tottenham Hotspur penalty-scorers: Roberts, Falco, Stevens, Archibald
Anderlecht penalty-scorers: Brylle, Scifo, Vercauteren
Attendance: 46,258

The story so far . . . Both teams had crawled under the wire to get to the final: Spurs beat the eternal Hajduk Split on the iffy away-goal rule, while Anderlecht (the holders) beat Nottingham Forest thanks to an incredibly dodgy last-minute penalty. Anderlecht, armed with international singing stars like Morten Olsen, Enzo Scifo and Frankie Vercauteren, looked a good side; good enough to beat Spurs who were drawn to play the first leg over at their place.

Before the game, Spurs would have settled happily for a 1–1 draw – neither side ahead through actual goals, but with that vital away goal to tip the scales in Spurs' favour. As it turned out, up until the eighty-fourth minute, things were looking rather better than a mere 1–1 draw. Away goals? That's not the Spurs way. We win in style or not at all.

A stunning performance laced with balletic elegance and delicate, silky skills (read: a gritty, stoical performance) was capped by a 58th minute Paul Miller goal – a typically forceful set-piece header – and it looked as if victory was ours.

Keith Burkinshaw: 'Now Paul Miller, he was an unsung hero. He played his best games in all our top matches. I mean, whilst I was there I made it clear to Paul, I used to say, "I'm going to get someone in who's better than you because I'm not sure that you're a good enough player." You know, I used to be hard with him. I was serious to an extent, but I was winding him up as well. And I did. I brought a lad in who used to play for England. He came from Brighton, Gary Stevens, because I always had this thing that we had to be as good at football at the back as we were at the front. And we should be just as good as the Continentals, and Paul was never that kind of player. So I brought Gary Stevens in and I was looking at other people, but this fella Paul Miller just kept coming through, kept proving me wrong. And in the UEFA Cup final he was tremendous – and he loved it.'

But then, six minutes from the end, a hopeful long Belgian-type shot snaked its way through a crowded Spurs penalty area. Keeper Tony Parks seemed to have it covered and he did . . . The ball bounced off his legs and . . . a 1–1 draw, but with that vital away goal for Spurs.

Poor old Parks. Standing in for the out-of-form Ray Clemence, he must have wanted the ground to swallow him up. Little did he know . . .

There's one other detail to include in this 'story so far' section. Keith Burkinshaw had announced that it was to be his last match as Spurs manager. For Burkinshaw, the second most successful manager in Spurs' history, the final was to be the final. 'There used to be a football club here,' Burkinshaw said as he closed the door. Wonder why?

Anyway, it's Garth Crooks's match, best let him speak.

'It started off that Anderlecht were really very good, in particular Scifo and Olsen at the back. He was outstanding. I remember Peter Shreeve turning to me and saying, "I bet he's never had a drink in his life or seen the inside of a nightclub." It was something that never left me. A beautifully gifted, balanced player, he seemed to be able to cope with everything. I just wanted the opportunity to get on and ruffle his feathers a little bit. But that never happened.

'We were having difficulty, especially in the first half, coming to terms with their passing and their ability to control the ball; and therefore the game. We never seemed to be able to return to the game which we'd become famous for, which again was a passing game. Instead we'd become too consumed in the event itself – the final at White Hart Lane – and we got carried away with the fans and a kind of expectation that we would win the game in the first 35 minutes. And, of course, that wasn't the case.'

Inexperience?

'No, it wasn't so much inexperience . . . Well, I suppose so, but not so much on the players' side. I think it was the entire management. I can look back now with the benefit of ten years' hindsight and I can see where we went wrong. But at the time, we all got too carried away with going out there and putting on a good show, smashing the opposition. They were far better than that.

'I think they were far more composed. They were far more focused on what they had to do to win the trophy and, indeed, the tournament away from Bruges. It showed in their playing. I think they were more tactically aware.'

Is this that old roasted chestnut that European football is somehow more intelligent, more sophisticated? You know that this cliché is at the traffic lights waiting for them to turn green as soon as you hear those dread words 'the Continentals'. It's curious how footballers are apt to call Europeans (or anyone non-British) 'the Continentals', as if they were aliens, as if the desire to shave every morning and read a newspaper were somehow suspicious. The Continentals – curious beasts who talk to each other in fifteen different languages simultaneously and who know exactly what type of stitching to have on their loafers.

'No, it's not that they were more intelligent or more sophisticated. It's like the British diet – it's what they prefer. I think it's less to do with sophistication, it's just what they [the British] prefer and if what they prefer is more sophisticated, they would search for something more sophisticated.'

More composed, more tactically aware – shall we just call it a greater professionalism?

'I think that's a bit harsh. I think we were as professional as we could have been, but sometimes in a given situation, footballers get carried away with all sorts of things for all sorts of reasons.'

Okay, they had a greater respect for the moment than you had.

'Exactly. We suddenly thought that because we were at home – it was one of those wonderful European nights, we'd played very well and we were worthy finalists – that it was only a matter of performing the way we could perform and we'd win the game. It was as though Anderlecht knew that and had gone to great lengths to make sure that it wouldn't happen. We hit a brick wall and spent a lot of the game searching for different routes around that wall, but we just kept on hitting different brick walls. It was at that point that I was convinced I'd get on.

'I remember both Ossie Ardiles and Alistair Dick going on about 20 minutes from time – which was a great shock to me because Ali was a winger and a young player and I thought we needed to score goals. It was goals we were lacking. There was a wonderful chance as Ossie came on. He hit the bar and I sank back into my seat; the final for me was effectively over now. I was a spectator. I remember thinking I could have put that chance away, particularly in the mood I was in. I was very keen, very hungry to re-establish my career at White Hart Lane, and I saw this as the event to do it.'

In Eamon Dunphy's brutal and honest account of life at Millwall, *Only A Game*, he describes his time as a substitute in very stark, human terms. How, at times, he sat there on the bench outwardly cheering for his team and doing the right thing while inside hoping that the player in his position – the player keeping him out of the team – had a bad game and effectively failed. That way, he, Dunphy, would get back in the side. After all, how many times have we heard a manager justify his selection by saying, 'I couldn't change a winning side'? It's not a very noble thought, but it's real.

So, Garth, what did you think when you were watching those two stripping their tracksuits off?

'You're sitting there thinking all sorts of things, but the most important thing is that you still have a role to play; even as a fan you've a role to play. I was a part of the team, I'd scored goals in that tournament, I was a part of that squad and it was my intention to go up on that rostrum and pick up my winner's medal. But as they stripped off, I resigned myself to the fact that it was over for me. That side of the game was over for me, and that's not a pleasant feeling.'

And what Dunphy said?

'It's a very human thing and I've experienced something like that, but I never wanted them to fail. I always assessed their performance with a very jaundiced view. Everything they did I thought "I can do better than that". It was very strange but I remember thinking that I wanted to do it, but I only wanted to do it my way. But really, it depends on the situation. I remember seeing Alan Brazil in one of his early games scoring an excellent goal, and I was thinking, "That's a super goal, that." Now I would have scored a goal just as good, but differently, which I suppose was a great compliment to Alan because I hadn't relegated him. It sounds complex, but I'm trying to be honest. I hadn't dismissed him as being of no threat.'

Alan Brazil – there's two forgotten words from the Spurs dictionary. Curly, blond hair which had started to attain that older, more dignified look, Alan Brazil was actually a top player. Skilful, precise and at once delicate and strong, when Brazil was at Ipswich he looked the business. A goalscorer who could play. But the road from Ipswich to Spurs is a difficult one and it's not always easy to drive down it. One minute you're in a tractor chugging down a dirt track, chewing a bit of straw, admiring the local longhorn, and the next you're in a soft-top Porsche, Ray-Bans on and there's a Britt Ekland asking what you want on the tape player.

'I don't know why he didn't crack it at Spurs because he's one of the most gifted strikers that I've ever set eyes on. But Spurs are rather like Man United, and I use that example because he went to both of them – in that if you can't handle the pressure, forget your talent. It would appear that the demands placed on Alan were incompatible with the way that he thought football should be played.'

What a lovely way of putting it. The demands placed on Alan were incompatible with the way that he thought football should be played – a sentence that defies questioning. In a display of salesmanship worthy of a market trader selling genuine Ming vases, Spurs later sold Brazil to Manchester United for £1.75 million.

Actually, it was Brazil that Crooks had to thank for his place on the bench.

'Alan Brazil by this time had found himself more offside than I'd become. He'd completely fallen out with Keith Burkinshaw and made it clear that he wanted to leave, so it was decided that Garth's attitude wasn't half as bad as Alan's, so we'll use him.'

It's a bizarre scenario. Consider yourself Burkinshaw. Your number one striker (Steve Archibald) has publicly stated that he'll play for the club on the proviso that he doesn't speak to you. The number two striker (Brazil) doesn't speak to you either. And he won't play for the club. The striker that you bought number two striker to replace (Crooks) is sitting on the subs bench wondering who's going to be on *Top of the Pops* that week.

What were the crowd like at this point? The Spurs crowd are not, you'll remember, renowned for their patience. What was it Terry Venables said about the crowd not being that bad; that they'd give you three games before the barracking started?

Garth Crooks: 'I think the fans at this juncture were tense. They could sense that this was a good team. They could sense that the final was anything other than academic and that it was possibly drifting away. I think we all sensed that because they were starting to create chances, they were looking dangerous, and one goal could win it. I remember settling for a draw and thinking it would go to penalties. I distinctly remember at the time thinking "I'll take a chance on penalties", because at one stage they were passing us to death.'

Did you all sit there on the bench fretting about this? Did you talk about it? Did anyone say anything?

'No, I never articulated this to the manager – it wasn't my place. The manager and the coach were astute enough to see what was going on. They'd have seen it five minutes before I'd seen it.'

After an hour the hugely impressive Morten Olsen picked up the ball and passed it sweetly through to the Pole, Alex Czerniatinski. Skip, skip, flick: 1–0 to Anderlecht on the night, 2–1 on aggregate. And all the time, Spurs kept hitting the wall. Even the introduction of Burkinshaw's Argentinian talisman had made very little difference. Looking back, it seems a curious decision to send on Alistair Dick instead of Crooks. Form and an extremely dodgy haircut notwithstanding, Dick was young and inexperienced; Crooks wasn't. He was an FA Cup final winner, a man used to the big occasion. It says much for Burkinshaw's opinion of each player's attitude that he chose as he did. Time was running out and it looked as though Spurs were done, beaten by a very polished goal.

In many ways, Graham Roberts wasn't like a traditional Spurs player. He fought. He got stuck in. But then again, you could draw a line starting with Dave Mackay and, somewhere, run into Graham Roberts. In terms of finesse, Roberts lacked ingredient 'X' – call it what you will, skill maybe. But Roberts wanted it. Tonight he wanted it more than ever.

Steve 'Mr Tottenham' Perryman had been booked in the first leg and would now miss the second: 'I am very, very sad but at least I have the consolation of being part of a very good performance and a very good result. I suppose it is a little ironic that I am likely to be the only player from the squad Keith took over who is fit to play in his last game, and now I will miss it.'

For Roberts, though, it meant something else: 'It was an honour I had only dreamt about. Captaining a side is something really different and I decided to play it the only way I know. I wanted to lead the lads by example.'

And so he did.

'Hazard normally liked to beat a player before crossing, but this time he crossed early and the ball cannoned off my chest. There were two Anderlecht defenders close by, but by taking the ball on the chest I went away from them. That I think was the hard part. I simply hit the ball then and hoped. It was an incredible feeling of ecstasy and pain. As soon as I ran to the crowd my legs went. The noise was terrific. I was in a total daze.'

That was that and that was extra time. And 44 knackered legs ensured that extra time was soon penalties.

Garth Crooks: 'I was almost relieved that I wasn't on the pitch to get involved with the penalty shoot-out. I remember thinking that we didn't seem as prepared for this as we might have been. I know we practised penalties the morning of the game when training, so maybe I only thought this when the people who were taking the penalties were selected.'

It's the final of a major European trophy. You've got dossiers and free kicks signalled by a scratch of the head and God knows what. Surely it's not a question of 'Hands up who wants to take a penalty?'. Are the five runners and riders not pre-selected?

'Well, they are, but a lot of things can happen in 90 minutes – substitutions, injuries, lack of confidence. It's too vague to say now how different the original five were, but I think it did change. I remember thinking that there were at least two players who I was not confident about – Danny Thomas was one, and to this day I don't understand why he took a penalty because he wasn't one of the best penalty-takers we ever had. But circumstances might have dictated that he was perhaps more willing than anyone else – I don't know that. I didn't get close enough. We weren't allowed on the pitch when the selection took place. I remember thinking "Danny – it's a huge event, it isn't a practice game, it isn't a league game – phew." Then I remember thinking, "Oh, it's probably me – I must be wrong. He'll be all right." And he turned away and walked to the edge of the box and, of course, the rest you know. He looked unconvincing. Some players, you put the ball there and no problem. Then someone else missed. Who was it? Paul Miller? No, Maxie was pretty sound on penalties.'

Maxie? Of course Paul Miller was Maxie. It was only ever going to be Maxie or Windy.

'It was one of those nights where even with the penalties it was nip and tuck; it was high-wire stuff.'

No one else missed for Spurs, only Danny Thomas. Roberts scored, then Mark Falco, Gary Stevens and Steve Archibald. Then Danny Thomas missed. Poor Danny Thomas. Watching as a punter that night, I can remember thinking how small he looked.

'There was a feeling of desperation when Danny missed the penalty. I felt it for him because not only was he a fine player, but he was an honest player – what you saw was what you got – he wouldn't have cheated anybody. He was very well liked and I think everyone felt desperately sorry for him. I remember hearing the fans chanting his name and thinking that that really is wonderful – that they don't hold him responsible. It's happened, it's happened, that's life. But Danny sat on his own, detached from everybody else, his head in his hands. I imagined him thinking, "My entire career hinged on that penalty." That's what you would think, but, of course, it's not true. For those few seconds, a lot of the players were with him; but then it was on to Tony Parks and it was, "Can he pull us out of it? Can he make a name for himself?" He was reserve keeper. He was a good keeper but he was never, ever going to be a star; he was never going to be an Ian Walker, or a Ray Clemence, or a top international goalkeeper, but he was a good competent keeper nonetheless. This was his night.'

It was fairy-tale stuff. Up strode Morten Olsen for Anderlecht's first penalty. If he'd never had a drink in his life, I bet he had a few that night. Parks saved his penalty. Then, in true fairy-tale style, it all came down to the last penalty. If Parks saved from Arnor Gudjohnsen, Spurs won. Burkinshaw won.

'It came at me at the right height, a lovely height to make it look a spectacular save. We all like a bit of glory and I must admit that I made it look a better save than it was,' said Parks.

So, was it job done, back on board the Stringfellows express?

Garth Crooks: 'I remember being massively part of the celebrations when he saved the final penalty. We'd won the trophy. It seemed like our whole season depended on that last second. But even picking my medal up and being part of the celebrations, I felt hollow. I hadn't played. I hadn't kicked a ball. I was fresh. I had all this energy. I'd trained, I'd rested, I was up for this game, I'd saved all this energy for this game. It was the weirdest sensation and I thought, "What am I going to do with it? All these guys are tired, elated – all sorts of emotions." I went to the bar and thought, "I'm as fresh now as when I came to the club at six o'clock."

'I remember not going to bed at all. I remember spending the night with Danny Thomas and Chris Hughton. Danny couldn't concentrate at all on anything other than the penalty. The penalty miss had robbed him of his success and his achievement. I can understand that. You could see him mentally wandering off. It wasn't a big night-club night. We just went off to a local club, sat together and had a meal. These lads weren't going to settle down till three o'clock in the morning anyway. They were too up, the adrenalin was still flowing. It was just the three of us and wives and girlfriends. I think for the girlfriends it was a time to relax – they were going to get their husbands back. But for us, it was analysing the game, over-analysing the game.'

So Crooks, Thomas and Hughton went out together to celebrate, three Spurs players, nothing wrong with that. But there's something else that those three have in common, something that football has a particularly bad reputation about.

'For a little time, I suppose, we were three black players who got on. Secondly, away from the ground and football, culturally we got on, and in a way we had our little idiosyncrasies and sub-cultures, and that was quite fun away from the ground. Chris and Danny were particularly close and their wives were very pally – and anyone who plays football knows that if the wives are pally, invariably the players will be pally.'

There was no racism?

'Before I came to Spurs, I was still a little bit afraid of it because I was completely submerged with the indigenous population. I was isolated. But when I came to London I wasn't so isolated. I was actually moving out of my youth and starting to read more and study more and become a little more aware, and I was less intimidated and less afraid and more prepared to step out into the areas which I believed in and which started to mean something to me.'

Keith Burkinshaw: 'I'll tell you a story about Garth Crooks. He and my wife got on like a house on fire. She thought Garth was fantastic, and always the first person he'd come up and chat to was my missus. And I always remember; I'm at home one day and the phone rings, and Joyce answered it and it's Garth. He says, "I'm wanting some help here, Keith" – they all called me Keith, never Boss. It was always Bill when Bill was manager, that was Tottenham in those days – and he said, "I've got a problem, I've been abducted on the street. The police have taken me in and I've got to have a character reference. I've got to have someone talking to them." I got on to the police and I said, "This is absolutely stupid. You've got to let him go because you're going to be in trouble, you lot, you know." What happened was he was walking down the King's Road or somewhere like that and because he was black the police had nabbed him. A black guy had gone into a shop and taken some goods. And because Garth was well dressed, they pounced on him and wouldn't listen to a word he was saying. Whether or not that was something that influenced him, I don't know.'

Epilogue

Gareth Crooks: 'One of the things that really sticks in my mind is that this was the beginning of a whole new era – that's why I chose this game. When you asked me, I remember thinking that it's because it was the beginning of the Scholar era, in effect the beginning of Tottenham Hotspur plc. And this is where the whole story began. Exit the Richardsons, enter Tottenham Hotspur plc. This was crucial for me.

'When I arrived, the Richardson family were in charge of the club. It was very much a family operation, and Spurs, while being a very famous old club, was a club that seemed to be in need of some fundamental changes in the way they designed their infrastructure. Things were done on a rather . . . not on the most professional footing. I'm talking in terms of the way people bought and sold tickets; the sophistication that the club has now has been greatly enhanced in a very short space of time. Having come from Stoke City, I was a bit surprised to see the inside of White Hart Lane as rather basic, somewhat amateurish. I'm not saying that Stoke was more sophisticated, but that Tottenham was not more sophisticated than Stoke. It was, in a sense, simply a bigger Stoke. I was a bit surprised. The offices were not particularly grand, the players' lounge wasn't anything special. I just expected everything to be so much bigger and so much better.

'And within the space of four years, what I'd identified when I first arrived was all going to change. It needed a coup d'état at the very, very top and that's exactly what happened. For me to sit outside, it wasn't just what was happening on the field, but how that related directly to what was happening off it – that was quite fascinating. '

We're in the dressing-room at White Hart Lane on 23 May 1984.

'I remember seeing Irving Scholar coming in with this beautiful lady, who we'd seen about a year before in Monte Carlo on one of our trips, wheeling him in. His leg was in plaster, and he had a magnum of champagne that he was going to hand to Keith Burkinshaw, who had already decided that he was going to leave. The decision had been made. He would be leaving Tottenham at the end of the season.

'As a player, it was fascinating; absolutely fascinating. It was in that moment that you actually saw the exchange of power. Out goes the old, in comes the new. And we were told then that Alex Ferguson was taking over. Strangely enough, the very man who encouraged Keith to take the champagne actually became the one who took over from him as manager – Peter Shreeve. Word has it that Alex did say yes, but then Manchester United came in and he changed his mind.'

As a player, do you get much of an insight into the background of what's going on? It's all very well seeing this scene out of *Carry on up the OK Corral*, but at the time did you know what was happening?

'The players talked about it at great length.'

But did anyone tell you anything? Was there any communication between you and, say, the club executives?

'No, no. Nobody tells you anything. You surmise and you assess and you pick bits up in the papers. The players at Spurs at that time were quite a sophisticated and intelligent bunch and they made it their business to be a part of the business, if you know what I mean. That was one of the biggest influences I ever had, the players at Spurs when I arrived – they were a special bunch. I'd never come across such a bright bunch, frankly.

'Much of what I'm expressing to you may have been discussed with the players, but I've tried to rationalise it in my own mind. Time has gone on, more things have happened and you look back with hindsight. I started with the Richardsons, talking about the club and how it was, and how it lacked that little bit of professionalism. And here we are finishing with us winning the UEFA Cup, the Richardsons going, and someone coming in who was going to transform the club into this huge money-making machine.'

For the non-business-minded fan, there's a curious irony at work here. The intrinsic nature of the club, the essence of Spurs, remained. It was flash, it was inconsistent, it was stylish, it was vainglorious, it was loud and it was individualistic. It didn't matter who owned what or whose name was on the letterhead, the spirit of Spurs survived. It's curious, no?

'You can rewrite history, but with a great deal of difficulty. Irving Scholar could never take that brick out of the history of Tottenham Hotspur FC that's been there since 1961, '62. He can't remove that brick. It's there, there's nothing he can do about it, but what he can do is build on it. I just sense that the Scholar era could have been a magnificent era and you'll look back and you'll see it as the era that almost crashed the club.'

Of course it almost crashed the club. What was going to happen? Spurs were going to get a solid defence and win the League? Of course it almost crashed the club. This is Spurs: all flash attack and no defence.

In retrospect, it can be reasonably argued that Scholar did nothing wrong. Whatever you or I might think of the moral climate of the time, he did the only thing he could. His aim – to make Spurs self-sufficient outside of the gate – was laudable if a touch Martin Peters (ten years ahead of its time): the travel business . . . the Hummel fiasco . . . especially the Hummel fiasco. Let's see. Can you think of a top club, a top double-winning club perhaps, which does quite well out of a lucrative sideline in shirts? Not so stupid, the boy Scholar.

'He's a Spurs fanatic and wants the best for the club. Sometimes I would say he's a little misguided in how to get it but nobody can say he's not got the best interests of Tottenham at heart.' So said Steve Perryman. That was possibly Scholar's error. He loved the club. He was originally, after all, just a fan.

And Keith Burkinshaw? Perhaps the best way to put it was that he was just another victim of Thatcher's Britain. The second most successful manager in Spurs' history, he'd brought home silverware in style, he'd forged a very good, potentially great, team. The wind direction changed and, through no fault of his own, he found himself a man out of time. Scholar knew that if you made a pop record, you didn't get in the back of a Ford Transit and go driving up and down the motorway. You got on the plane to Rio, made a video and surrounded yourself with lots of bikini-clad flesh. Glamour, that was the deal. That was why he was a Spurs fan in the first place. 'I liked the club so much, I bought it', as they used to say.

Keith Burkinshaw: 'The board then were fantastic and that's why I couldn't stay. Changing from that to how Irving Scholar wanted things to be done . . . Me and him couldn't work together because Irving wanted to do a lot of the things that I'd done at the club. I was virtually running the place. Well, when Irving came in, he felt that the board should buy and sell players, for instance. They should be the ones who should decide how much a player was earning, which had always been my domain. Obviously things have gone the way that he was thinking then, but I was running it right in those days and he wanted to take over. He was getting on to players behind my back and saying to them, "Look, when your contract runs out, this is what we'll probably offer you," and I couldn't tolerate that. Of course, we had big rows about it. In the end, I said, "Look, there's only one way that we can do this and that's for me to finish because it's just ridiculous what you're trying to do here," and we were in the final of the UEFA Cup when this was going on. He also interviewed Alex Ferguson for the job behind my back while I was still there. I'd just won the Cup twice and we were winning the UEFA Cup.

'He wanted me out of it because he knew I was too strong for him to operate as he wanted to operate. I wouldn't allow that because I thought managers should go out and . . . He lived out in Monaco and he had ideas about international players he wanted to bring personally to Tottenham. But he found a manager who didn't want those players, so then there's a clash, isn't there? He didn't want that clash. He wanted to decide when players came, and I said, "Well, it can't work out that way because I'm the manager and whilst I'm the manager, I'll manage them." And he said, "Well, there's only one thing for it. You're going to have to leave." And so I did.'

It could have all been so different had it not been for Heysel, had Spurs beaten Coventry in the 1987 FA Cup final, had David Pleat stayed . . . And, really, even then, what were the options? To become the ego-massaging plaything of some (invariably) Northern feudal moneyman? To struggle? Or, worse, to be small? No, in a curious way, Scholar played the game in a very Spurs way. Flamboyant and risk-taking, big and bold. It was the business equivalent of a five-man attack. Like Jack Kerouac and Neal Cassady, he did nothing wrong, he just did it first.

History has condemned him because of what? He wasn't a 'football man'? Perhaps his biggest 'crime' was to have been operating during the days of Thatcherite monetarist madness. You and I and every other idiot in town bought a house. He bought Spurs.

Garth Crooks: 'He took risks that a conservative businessman just wouldn't take, and he did it with his prize possession – which was Spurs football club. I'm talking now as a fan. He loved the club, he worshipped the club, but he played roulette with his most prized possession.'

12

A SPOONFUL OF SUGAR

Gary Mabbutt

> So I was extremely happy at half-time looking up at the score board seeing Tottenham 2, Coventry 1 and Mabbutt's name on the scoreboard. Little did I know.
>
> Gary Mabbutt

David Pleat's time at Spurs was, in every way, perfect. If someone was making one of those *A Year in the Life of* . . documentaries about Tottenham Hotspur, they couldn't do better than pick the year 1986–87. Bolstered by a couple of glamorous signings, one of which was a dashing European, they played wonderfully entertaining football, using a radical attacking tactic that was as stylish as it was successful. They were heading for success on three fronts, but failed – gloriously, of course – inside the final furlong. It all fell apart – well, imploded – controversially after scandal had hit, and that was that.

Pleat had taken over from Spurs loyalist Peter Shreeve who had taken over from Keith Burkinshaw. Brought to Spurs initially by Terry Neill as youth team coach in 1975, Shreeve was a football man who was thrust into the spotlight, maybe unwillingly, maybe unfairly; but only maybe. Everyone has their ego. Like Burkinshaw before him, Shreeve was a coach, an ideas man. He went into the game primarily because he was interested in that small round thing. To him, it held rather more interest than Des Lynam asking him for his opinion at half-time.

He was never a Scholar man, but he grew into the job, creating an attractive team, signing players like Chris Waddle, Clive Allen, Paul Allen – Spurs players – carrying the torch. But he was never a Scholar man. That Shreeve was taken out and shot was due largely to two things, both of which were beyond his control. In his first season in charge, Spurs played like a dream and finished third. Heysel, however, ensured that there would be no European reward. The next season, long-term injuries to Clive Allen, Ardiles and John Chiedozie wrecked his plans. Maybe if he could have given good soundbites . . .

If you look at the managerial line of succession during the Scholar era, it's easy to see the logic. From Burkinshaw to Shreeve to Pleat to Venables. From the dour Yorkshireman to the compliant (but essentially invisible) to the media literate to the multi-media carnivore. At each step of the way, Scholar got nearer and nearer his ideal; and then it ate him. There's more than a touch of Frankenstein's monster about the Venables/Scholar relationship. Garth Crooks: 'When David Pleat had Hoddle, Ardiles, Gough and Waddle, this is the nearest thing I've seen to the synergy that Spurs need to provide entertainment and the championship. Potentially it was a stronger team than our team. You can't say it was because it didn't achieve what our team did, but potentially, yes, it could have been a better team.'

Great Spurs word, potentially.

Inspired by the great French team of the 1984 European Championship, Pleat took an already continental-looking team and pressed the button marked 'Further', de-Anglicising Spurs to the extreme. Former Liverpool stalwart Ray Clemence, Spurs best green jersey since Jennings, was in goal. The back four were all proper footballers: they were all comfortable on the ball and confident of their ability to use it. The full-backs, Gary Stevens, Mitchell Thomas and especially the ill-fated Danny Thomas, were all stylish and polished as well as being good at their jobs. The two centre-backs, Gary Mabbutt and Richard Gough, were not only the most commanding centre-backs (and no disrespect to Graham Roberts here) Spurs had had since the days of Mike England, but they also had the ability and vision to play in midfield when required. There was a five-man midfield, featuring Waddle, Hoddle, Ardiles, Paul Allen and Steve Hodge, and there was arch-predator Clive Allen alone up front. Waiting in reserve was the one famous Belgian, Nico Claesen, a razor-sharp striker.

If you looked at that team and tried to find a weakness, well, you'd still be looking; if you looked with the sensibility of a Spurs fan, that is. If you were an Arsenal fan, you'd be looking for a couple more centre-backs. Anyone else may look for less flair, more solidity, a few more feet on the ground.

It's curious. With some people, it's only when they're not there that you realise what a huge hole they've left. After approximately 17 years and 4,765 games, Steve Perryman had finally packed his bags and taken those first steps down Management Alley. It's tempting to conjure up a mental picture of him going up to Gary Mabbutt and ceremoniously handing him his shirt with its carefully folded up sleeves: 'Here you are. Keep it safe.' In a team full of mercurial heroes, Gary Mabbutt was the constant, the rock. Richard Gough might have been the captain, but Mabbutt was the Perryman; someone to rely on, someone guaranteed not to put their foot in it. Not surprisingly, Liverpool, at various times, tried to steal them both.

Gary Mabbutt: 'The whole season just seemed to fall into place for us. David Pleat was very innovative and Clive Allen had a great season and scored a record number of goals. The whole team seemed to gel very well. I think we just fell into it. The system seemed to sort itself out, really.'

On the night of 22 August 1986, Clive Allen went to bed a happy young man. It was the eve of the new football season and Clive could barely close his eyes, let alone sleep. His team's new manager had told him that he'd be playing in a new system, a new formation where everything depended on him. There were to be five midfielders and just one attacker: him. It was a huge pressure, but it was exciting; and anyway, the five midfielders were some of the best in the country. It's so tempting to say at this juncture: 'At around 3.05 on the afternoon of Saturday, 16 May 1987, Clive Allen woke up.' But let's not get ahead of ourselves.

'The funny thing is,' says Mabbutt, 'he could have had so many more. Clive's a great finisher and we were creating chances for fun, which is difficult at any time, but that year it all seemed to come together for us and Clive benefited the most from the system we were playing. In the middle, we had Chrissie Waddle, Glenn Hoddle, Ossie (who was still at the club), Steve Hodge and Paul Allen. I mean, Hoddle, Waddle, Ardiles – the names we had then, the creative ability we had was phenomenal and, as I say, everyone seemed just to come together perfectly. The partnership I had with Richard Gough was the best I'd had at White Hart Lane. We seemed quite solid and we got the ball going forward.'

In performance terms, the season peaked on 2 February in a League Cup match against West Ham. Playing in a way that would have made Cliff Jones and Danny Blanchflower swell with a rare pride, Spurs won 5–0. Claesen opened the scoring and Glenn Hoddle added a spectacular second before Clive Allen walked off with an almost *de rigueur* hat-trick.

Nico Claesen was a curious Spurs footnote. He first came to the attention of the Brits after Belgium had beaten Scotland in a televised international match. Claesen lacerated the Scottish defence, slicing them apart with quicksilver precision – a Spurs player. Somehow though, it isn't surprising that 'he didn't fulfil his potential'. Claesen's story was typical of many imports. A young married man, his wife found it difficult to settle and this made it difficult for him. The Claesens had no children. They had the next best thing, but, England being England, they couldn't have their pet poodle with them. It's a human story that had a very human resolution. Pleat left him on the subs bench.

That 5–0 West Ham result set off a great sequence: Arsenal 1–0, Southampton 2–0, Newcastle 1–0, Leicester 5–0. It's now you realise that Clive Allen really didn't wake up at around 3.05 on the afternoon of Saturday, 16 May 1987. He, and the rest of the Spurs team, woke up on the evening of 4 March. If only the season could've ended there and then. Great Spurs word, if.

That was the date of the League Cup semi-final replay against the Arsenal. It was a titanic struggle; the Spurs display perfectly fitting that description. They looked imperious and majestic as they swept along with a rare grace; but then they hit a huge, immobile, ugly lump and sank. Everything seemed to be encapsulated in that League Cup semi-final. Spurs started off like ice dancers, skating through the forest that was the Arsenal's defence and gaining victory, courtesy of a Clive Allen goal. But the longer the tie went on, the more it slipped from Spurs' grasp. Allen kept on scoring but the Arsenal kept on running. We won at their place, they won at our place. The die was cast and White Hart Lane it was.

Gary Mabbutt: 'It was disappointing being so close. I think at one stage we were 2–0 up on aggregate with about ten or 15 minutes to go and Arsenal came back and drew level; that's when it went to a replay. We won the toss and had the replay back at White Hart Lane. That was our downfall. We should have had it at Highbury.'

But it didn't matter: the game could have been played on Mars. By now it was a marathon, and marathons aren't Spurs' game. Suffice to say that the Arsenal were ahead for precisely one minute of the entire five-hour tie. Naturally, it was the last minute. (Where was Nayim when he was needed?) Three days later, it all came crashing down.

Danny Thomas went in for a tackle with Queen's Park Rangers' Gavin Maguire and that was that; a sickening thud, and Thomas was left looking for a new job. It's something that can happen to any athlete at any time, but it must be one of those things that everyone thinks will happen to someone else, not them. In Thomas's case it was especially sad, not only because he was hugely talented and was on the cusp of a major career, but also because he seemed a genuinely nice person. He had that smile. And after missing that UEFA Cup final penalty against Anderlecht, he'd been a huge crowd favourite.

From here on in, things took on a familiar glaze. After being up there with Everton and Liverpool, Spurs fell apart in the League with such conclusiveness that it looked as if they'd been falling apart in the League for years. All that was left was the FA Cup. It was ever thus. It's part of the Spurs psyche that, irrespective of their league form, they can get up for the FA Cup. Watford found out at Villa Park in the semi-final. Now this was the Graham Taylor era, a time when he was more Midas than turnip. John Barnes was at his height. Mark Falco was there. It was a good team, but they were brushed aside. Steve Hodge – Spurs' concession to the notion of 'ordinary' and a living example of the ancient football adage: never buy a Forest player – got two, Paul Allen got one and, obviously, Clive Allen scored. Even Watford's goal was scored by one of the Allen clan, Malcolm. When word came through that Coventry had beaten Leeds in the other semi-final, no one cared. There was one consideration: if they played Coventry they could wear the all-white. That would look nice on the steps.

Tottenham Hotspur 2 (C. Allen, Mabbutt)
Coventry City 3 (Bennett, Houchen, Mabbutt og) aet

FA Cup final
16 May 1987

Tottenham Hotspur: Clemence, Hughton, Gough, Mabbutt, M. Thomas, Waddle, P. Allen, Hoddle, Ardiles, Hodge, C. Allen.
Coventry City: Ogrizovic, Phillips, Kilcline, Peake, Downs, Gynn, McGrath, Pickering, Bennett, Regis, Houchen.
Attendance: 98,000

Maybe it was because there wasn't a '1' in the year. It was one of those stupid, footballing, folkloric beliefs that mean nothing, that are less rooted in reality than superstition (don't look at a full moon through a glass window. What type of window are you supposed to look out of? Aluminium? Who knows where these things come from or why they exist, but exist they do) and – more often than not – they work, too. Spurs fans tried to minimise the potential damage of this most ancient of curses. There was a '7' in the year. Spurs beat Chelsea in 1967, the only other time they'd played an FA Cup final in a year with a '7' in it. It was half-hearted at best, but then, as everyone knew, half was probably enough. After all, this was the FA Cup and Spurs didn't lose FA Cup finals. The other thing was, it was Coventry. Lambs to the slaughter, they were probably happy just to be there, to be part of the occasion.

Despite the way that Spurs had been playing that season – with an imperious dash – Coventry had no reason to fear them; they'd already beaten them, 4–3 at Highfield Road. It was a classic Spurs match. David Pleat: 'At half-time we were luckily in front, courtesy of Clive Allen. After twenty minutes of the second half Coventry led 3–2. They didn't try to sit on their lead, but came at us like lunatics trying to make it 4–2. With six minutes to go, Nico Claesen pulled the score back to 3–3 and our players were convinced they could win the game because we'd had them on the rack for 15 minutes. We went at them as they had gone at us, and then Regis scored their winner.'

Cyrille Regis, the old trooper, was a grand player in his day, big, bold and strong; but his day had gone and he was now in his sunset years. His presence was typical of the Coventry team: a rag-bag mixture, a wedding day team – something old, something new, something borrowed, something blue – except that it was mostly just blue.

The other thing Coventry had in their favour was that no one expected anything of them. Spurs were the glory boys, they had the class, the style. The two Spurs subs, Nico Claesen and Gary Stevens, would, you felt, have walked into the Coventry team. No one expected Coventry to win; everyone expected Spurs to. On the day of the final, *The Guardian* wrote: 'Faith can move mountains and Coventry have already found Spurs climbable. That thought will sustain their players and supporters alike.'

At this juncture, it's important not to overdo the 'little Coventry' bit. They weren't some Second Division side, it wasn't some Sunderland-against-Leeds scenario or some Southampton-against-Manchester United. But Spurs had Allen, Waddle, Ardiles, Gough,

Mabbutt. It was Glenn Hoddle's last game for Spurs before heading off to Monaco. Coventry had Cyrille Regis, Brian Kilcline and Keith Houchen. As they say in football circles, on paper it was no contest; but (all together now) they don't play on paper.

The match got off to a bit of an odd start before a ball was even kicked.

Gary Mabbutt: 'The funniest thing was that half of the team didn't have the Holsten logo on their shirts – that caused a bit of an uproar. The kits got sent in for the final and some of the kits got sent to the club without the logo on for some reason. They said that those kits were for our youth team, because the youth team are not allowed to have advertising on their shirts. But they all had the FA Cup final badge on them, and if you think about it, why should the youth team have the FA Cup final badge on their shirts?'

The only other thing that the shirts had – all the shirts, that is – was the name of the manufacturer: Hummel, Irving Scholar's ill-fated sportswear division. Surely they wouldn't have made such a basic error? To omit the name of the club sponsor?

'The kit comes folded with their numbers showing, so you don't see the front of the shirt. In the dressing-room, we put our shirts on and then we put our Cup final track suits straight on. We went out not knowing, and it was only just before the game that anyone noticed. I'd taken my track suit off and Chris Hughton, who was standing next to me, said: "Look at your shirt." When we looked around, there were about five or six of us without Holsten on our shirts. We didn't change. It was a huge thing and it caused a lot of uproar. I think people were sacked because of it. In the end, I don't know what the big deal was because Holsten probably got more publicity out of the situation than they would have done if all the shirts were the same. To us it was so funny. The following day there was a picture in the papers – I think it was me, Glenn Hoddle and Clive Allen and none of us had Holsten on our shirts. If you can imagine this whole page in the paper and the headline above it was "I bet they drink Carling Black Label". Very quick, very sharp.'

It was either a huge cock-up or an incredibly smart piece of advertising. As soon as the Spurs players came out of the tunnel, you just knew that, come Monday morning, someone was either going to be sacked or promoted. At the time, it was another gag which added to the general mood of celebration.

'It was an incredible day. The days leading up to it really were very exciting and the noise as you walk down that tunnel just hits you on Cup final day. It was a great atmosphere.' It was a gorgeous day. The sun was shining, the birds were singing and Spurs were wearing the classicists dream kit, the all-white. Placards around the pitch proclaimed that 'Waddle sells more dummies than Mothercare'. If Bogart had been there, he'd have looked around, snarled and lit up. 'I don't like it. It's too perfect.' He was always right, Bogart. Something had to give.

After two minutes, Chris Waddle raced down the wing, crossed low and hard and there was Clive Allen to head in his 49th goal of the season. Up and down the land, ovens were being turned on, cakes were being baked. Tonight there were going to be street parties like it was the Queen's birthday *and* VE Day. The only thing was, Bogart wasn't baking any cakes. He was still there, still snarling. It *was* too perfect.

It seems so often the way with Cup finals. The so-called good team underperforms while the no-hope underdogs play out of their skins. It's not so much a leveller as complete role-reversal. Spurs–Coventry wasn't the starkest example of this, but it still fits the pattern. It's not something that anyone is ever likely to admit to – it would be downright rude apart from anything else – but could it be as simple, something as human, as arrogance?

Gary, were Spurs arrogant that day?

'No, not really. We'd had a good season but we'd achieved nothing, and that was why we wanted to win the Cup final. We'd just missed out on the League Cup, losing the semi-final after being in a commanding position, and come third in the League, which was not bad, but not close enough. So no, we wanted to have something to show for the season. We thought we deserved to have something to show for the season and that's why we felt the Cup final was going to be our day.'

'No, not really' sounds like 'well, yes, but I shouldn't say so'. Let's put it another way. Do you think it would have made a difference if Spurs had been playing someone like Liverpool rather than Coventry?

'Of course, psychologically it may have made a difference, but on the Cup final day I don't think that going to play Coventry or going to play Nottingham Forest in 1991 was any different. Perhaps in the subconscious there was the feeling that it was Coventry – we should beat them. But it certainly wasn't a conscious thought.

'We had a perfect start with Clive Allen scoring early on in the game. Dave Bennett equalised more or less straight afterwards, and then I got a dubious goal. The ball was crossed in from the wing; Richard Gough's gone up for it with the keeper and Kilcline's marking me from behind. The ball, dropped in between us. I put my foot on the ball, and he's gone for the ball, and as we'd both gone for it, the ball ended up in the back of the net. The ball was coming right between us, so whether he kicked the ball onto my leg or I kicked his leg onto the ball or we both hit the ball and I got the briefest of touches, I've no idea. It certainly wasn't a clear foot on ball. I got in and just lunged for the ball as you do; he tried to clear it and I tried to score. As we both lunged, the ball went over the line.

'We weren't playing particularly well – it wasn't a great performance by us – and Coventry were playing out of their skins in this game. We came out for the second half. Houchen got an equaliser for them and then the game finished normal time two all, and went into extra time. Mitchell Thomas, who was playing at left-back had gone off on an overlap and the ball was put into space by McGrath, I think. I'm playing on the left side of defence. I've gone across to try and close him down, you know, as he's coming down, he's going to cross the ball in. So I go to try to shut him down, and as he crosses the ball, I put my leg out to stop the cross. I'm probably in line with the six-yard box. I put my leg out to stop the cross, it hit me on top of the knee and I just watched it loop right over Ray Clemence and into the far corner of the goal. It was one of those things. You try to block a shot and 99 times out of 100, you'll block it; it'll go out for a corner, or it'll go out for a throw-in, or you'll clear it or something. On that one small occasion when it just hit me on the top of my knee and went straight into the far corner. I mean, as it went in – it was the first half of extra time – I just sank to my haunches and couldn't believe it. It was a fluke – there was nothing I could do about it. I would have felt far worse if I'd had the ball at my feet, tried to pass it to the keeper and it had gone over his head or something.

'I remember at the end, after it had all died down a bit, I was walking down the tunnel and Ray Clemence was walking behind me. I just turned to Clem and said: "D'you realise that that's the first time I've chipped a ball all season?" and he smiled. As I say, I'd have felt much worse if it had been anything other than a fluke, but I still couldn't believe that the game had finished like that. If we'd played to 85 per cent of our capabilities, we'd have won the game. But full credit to Coventry – I've seen the game a number of times since and they deserved to win it. They fought very well and they played extremely well on the day and we just didn't reach the heights we should have done.'

That was the story. Coventry played and Spurs didn't. Lloyd McGrath marked Hoddle out of the game. 'Glenn Hoddle now knows Lloyd McGrath,' said Coventry manager John Sillett after the game. Hoddle couldn't raise himself. The normally rock-like Gough was petrified by the occasion. Just like the League Cup semi-final, Spurs didn't go for the kill when they should have done.

'Certain players didn't quite get to grips with it today,' said Pleat. When the game went into extra time, when it was time for blood and guts, when it was time for the men to come out and play, Spurs were in the toilet. Poor old Mabbutt ended up as only the third man to score for both sides in an FA Cup final – the previous one being Manchester City's Tommy Hutchison, ironically against Spurs in 1981.

After the match it was said that Spurs getting a goal so early worked against them; that it fired up Coventry, made Spurs too relaxed, that it took even more of the pressure off Coventry, forced Coventry on the offensive.

Gary Mabbutt again: 'No, scoring a goal is never too early. You'd have thought that if you scored a goal early on, you'd have taken it on from there and built on that. But the simple truth is that, on the day, we just didn't play to the best of our abilities and, you know, in the end we lost it to a fluke goal. But I wouldn't take anything away from Coventry, because in the end they deserved to win it.' No one had said that Spurs scored too early in the 1982 replay against QPR.

'The thing was, I thoroughly enjoyed the whole day. Of course, I didn't enjoy the result. Afterwards it was very subdued. There was a huge marquee put up at White Hart Lane for a post-Cup final dinner on the evening of the game which the family went to, but it was very subdued. And that was it – that was my first Cup final and we lost it. I scored two goals in my first Cup final and not many players can say that. Unfortunately, one of them was the winning goal for Coventry.'

Epilogue

Gary Mabbutt: 'I really have enjoyed being at the club. It's been great – it's been like *Dallas*, part two. You know, I've probably been through about nine managers in my 14 years here. Keith Burkinshaw, Peter Shreeve, David Pleat, Terry Venables, Ossie Ardiles and Gerry Francis were the main ones. Then there was a period when Ray Clemence and Doug Livermore were in charge. Is that it? I'm sure there were nine. Oh yes, Steve Perryman was manager for a while after Ossie. Good, I thought I'd lost one there for a minute.'

If Spurs had won that final, would everything have changed?

'Well, you don't know. Would it have stopped David being caught doing what he was allegedly doing? It was a strange scenario that went on in those few months, what with rumours and a lot of media attention. In the end, I'm not sure that anything was proved anyway. It's one of those things that happened. It's a shame because I only appreciated David after he left and I realised how good he was technically. David, I thought, was an excellent manager and it was only after he left that you realised what happened in the season before. In the space of one year he turned it all around very quickly. But things happened beyond our control, nothing to do with the players in the team, and David was ousted.'

Ousted. What a great football word that is – ousted.

'I think he was pushed, to some degree. Why? That still remains to be seen. There are still plenty of rumours that are neither here nor there because they're not proven. It's very sad, though, because things were looking very rosy.'

It's no great secret that there was more than a touch of the Terry Neills about David Pleat; not in his footballing pedigree or his coaching ability or his tactical nous. All that was top notch. But he was an outsider, a man from a little club eager to make an impression. A man in a hurry to do things his way. It's an attitude guaranteed to ruffle a few feathers. He upset Glenn Hoddle; not a smart thing to do at Spurs. He sold Graham Roberts and made wholesale changes to the much-loved squad of '84.

But there were rumours. It's been said that Pleat was forced out because Scholar was completely star-struck by Terry Venables. The idea of having Venables managing Spurs, managing his team, was too much to resist. This seems a strange rumour, for it doesn't explain how all those stories about Pleat came to be in the newspapers, stories that were full of nasty allegations that Pleat was unlikely to contest publicly as all that does is drag it out and keep the idea in the public eye. By the time you're acquitted, if you're acquitted, the damage has been done. So I put the rumour to Gary. Now, a curious thing happened just after I asked Gary this question. A shard of sunlight came down from the skies and caused his eyes to squint and his mouth to curl up, just as if he was smiling, which, of course, he wasn't. Bravely, he ignored it.

'No, I'm not going to comment on that.'

Whatever the reasons, it was a pity for Mabbutt. He was on the edge of great things and wanted by everyone.

'My contract ran out in 1987, and I had a chance to go to Madrid in Spain, Lyon in France, Arsenal and Manchester United, but in the end it was a straight choice between staying at Tottenham and joining Liverpool. Kenny Dalglish phoned me up after the 1987 Cup final and said that he wanted to sign three players that summer – myself, Peter Beardsley and John Barnes. Maybe he saw the Cup final and was impressed by my goalscoring abilities. It was incredible. It was the day after the Cup final when I got the phone call from Kenny Dalglish. He was one of my heroes, and there he was phoning me up, asking me if I wanted to come and play for Liverpool – you know, it was a very exciting time. It was very tempting because Liverpool had been the team of the decade; but in the end, after a lot of deliberation, I thought, well, I'd been very happy at Tottenham for the five years I'd been there and the squad we'd put together was capable of at least challenging for the major honours in the next few seasons. I saw no reason for the upheaval.

'Unfortunately, within two or three months of that, David Pleat left the club and about five or six of the squad left the club – the likes of Glenn Hoddle and Richard Gough. I knew about Glenn leaving but I didn't know about the others. We'd formed a good partnership at the back, Richard Gough and me – he was an excellent player, and it was a shame that the squad broke up so quickly.'

It was such a shame that Richard Gough left. Again, the reason for him leaving is shrouded in rumour. Apparently, word has it that he and Pleat had a huge row at the dinner after the Cup final and he stormed out.

'No, as far as I'm aware there wasn't anything. Richard is one of my best friends, I'm godfather to his little boys, so we speak every week. I doubt that there's anything. His whole reason for leaving . . .' Just as Gary was about to continue, that shard of sunlight descended again and the moment was lost. Let's file Richard Gough next to Nico Claesen (minus the poodle).

'You've got to remember that, as footballers, to some degree you're very well-paid pieces of meat – or you're very well-paid slaves. Someone could come in tomorrow and say, "Right. We want to buy you," or "We want to sell you," and really you're left with no option.

This other team that wants you may be 400 miles away, so you have to uproot, move the family, move the kids from their schools, find a new home. It's a huge upheaval.'

Just as we were about to part, I commented to Gary that his cheek looked much better after that accidental clash with John Fashanu.

'I've still got no feeling in the side of my face. It's numb all the time now. And that'll be forever. The biggest worry when it happened was that they thought there was a chance that I would lose my sight in one eye. The cheek was smashed in four places and the eye socket was smashed in three places. The whole thing caved in and they were worried that the broken bones in the eye socket may have damaged the eye. Fortunately that wasn't the case.'

It must have hurt.

'Yes, it was rather painful. But four operations and a good few months later, everything's back in place. The only thing is that I haven't got any feeling in that side of my face. You always want to pull it because you can never really feel it.'

It must make shaving difficult?

'Yes. But it's something you've got to live with now and fortunately it's not as bad as it could have been.'

Do you see much of Fashanu now? I remember reading about it in the papers at the time, how he was saying what good mates you were.

You should have seen the size of the shard of sunlight that one got.

13

THE BOY DONE GOOD

Gary Lineker

> I suppose it is bizarre to choose a game where you miss a penalty and have a perfectly good goal disallowed and not score; but it's a one-off feeling of euphoria, the feeling of winning the FA Cup – especially after all the odds and all the problems – not just on the day with Gazza and everything, but the fact that the club was at that particular time on the point of extinction. I suppose it all culminated in something a little bit special.
>
> Gary Lineker

'Okay, kid. Give me the pitch. And make it good. You've got ten minutes.'

'You'll love this. Really. I know. This isn't like other film scripts, you'll see. It's got everything: drama, violence, tears.'

'Nine-and-a-half minutes.'

'Okay. This is the pitch. Think of it as a cross between *The Great Escape* and *Gone with the Wind*. The setting is a football match. It's the climax to the season, the showcase, the culmination of everything that's gone before.

'The first team is in a real two and eight, a right mess. They've got no money and the game's everything. They've got to win. If they win, they get into Europe and hit the gold trail. If they lose, it could be the end. Everything depends on their two stars – and you'll love these two. They're like Di and Fergie before their divorces. One's good-looking, cool and shyly aloof. The other's a hot-blooded redhead, fun but dangerous.

'Fergie's the best player England has had for maybe 40 years; maybe the best ever. But he's volatile and, like all geniuses, he's mad, a lunatic. Listen, Robin Williams would be perfect. He's a clown, a child, but he's incendiary. He can create or destroy equally, and no one can tell what it's going to be. The people love him because he's brilliant, yet vulnerable. In the semi-final he was in genius mode. Today? No one knows. No one ever knows. There's one other thing about Fergie. There's a deal lined up. If he does well, he's going to be sold to Italy. The money will save the club. If he screws up, they're all down the pan. Either way, it's his last game for the club.

'The other one, he's the complete opposite, a real apple pie merchant; clean cut and perfect in every way. You'd want your daughter to marry him. Listen, you wouldn't even mind so much if your son brought him home. But he's good. He's fast, sharp and deadly accurate; a real clean-teeth, national-hero type, a Tom Cruise cert.

'The manager of the team, he's a wheeler-dealer type. Got a drinking club – private, you know – cashmere coat, well-cut double-breasted suit, Gucci shoes. A man who can, but maybe a little bit iffy round the edges. George Cole would be perfect. Now, behind the scenes, as the club is falling into the financial abyss, the manager is planning a coup. He wants the club. Meanwhile, from the stands, their owner – a rich, City type, maybe Harrison Ford – looks on, impassive yet involved, taking it all in. He knows everything that's going on, but he's playing it cool.

'The other team is a different kind of mess. The manager rules the club like a feudal landlord. He dominates. Everyone lives in fear of him. And he's unpredictable; and a lush. He's never won the FA Cup and it's become something of a quest, a Holy Grail. But he's a burn out. He can't move. While his loyal assistants, aides from a past glorious time, rally round and do the work he should be doing, he sits there, rooted, quietly sipping pure vodka from a mineral water bottle. His team are in stark contrast – young, fresh and sharp, they bristle with vibrant flair and verve. They have two young wingers, the best defender in the land and a prodigious, but fiery young Irish talent running the show. The main hope for victory – and you'll like this one – lies with Quentin, the manager's son. The complete opposite of his father, Quentin is slow, deliberate and shy to the point of being dumb. Everyone tries to get close to him, but his father keeps him under lock and key. As the father slips further into the abyss, the son goes from strength to strength.'

'Yes, kid, it's good. But I know where it's heading. I've seen it before. It looks like the lush is going to get it, but Fergie, who's been dull and anonymous, suddenly bursts into action and, with a flash of genius, sets Di up to snatch a late winner. Quentin fires off and does something. Maybe next time. I'm looking for something a little less obvious. Sorry kid.'

(The above scenario is fictional. All the characters depicted are fictional. Any similarity to any persons living or dead is a complete and utter coincidence.)

Truth, as Burt Young once said, is stranger than shit. Gazza's manic, suicidal tackle, going off with a career-threatening injury, Lineker's missed penalty and (wrongly) disallowed goal, Forest's dubious 'legal' goal, extra time, Clough Snr rooted to his seat, getting up, ignoring his team and chatting to a policeman, a self-confidence-crisis-inducing own goal by the best defender in the land deciding the event – everything about the 1991 FA Cup final was a little bit special.

We could eulogise about the occasion of FA Cup finals, the spirit, the noise, the moment, but who's kidding who? FA Cup finals are, nine times out of ten, crap; dull, tense, tired rubbish. 'We were expecting a classic but, in truth, it was a disappointing final.' How many times do you reckon Barry Davies, John Motson, Brian Moore have said that? The deal is: if you're there, fine. The atmosphere alone is worth the admission. But for those at home, Cup finals rarely provide much opposition for that old Dana Andrews film that always seems to be on, let alone something like *Ice Cold in Alex*. There have been exceptions, of course: 1982, 1981, 1967, 1962, 1961, 1922, 1902 . . . can't think of any others offhand. Maybe it's the occasion . . . so much depends on it, so many eyes looking at you. Just think, if you make one mistake . . . Think of poor old Gary Mabbutt against Coventry in '87, Tommy Hutchison in '81.

The 1991 FA Cup final was never going to be ordinary; there was too much riding on it, too much that wasn't dependent on poor old football, or on fragile human footballers. This was Wembley as the arena of struggle. It was something beyond conflict, it was epochal and it was time. It was as if the Fates got a few cans in, invited their mates the Four Horsemen round and had a bit of a play. Given the background, the financial shenanigans, Clough's ever-decreasing circles, Gazza's last game for Spurs before the waiting Italian vultures whipped him off, El Tel knocking out a few genuine Lacoste polo shirts to raise a bit of extra folding . . . it was a drama before it started. Drama's fine, but an episode of *Casualty*?

Like all the best drama, it straddled that fine line between comedy and tragedy, and, like both, was necessarily dominated by failure. Gazza lost his head and the plot, nearly finished his career and almost wrecked his move to Italy. Seventeen minutes of madness, one minute of insanity, put him out of the game for a year. Golden Wonder Gary Lineker missed a penalty and suffered the indignity of having a perfectly good goal disallowed. Forest took the lead with a goal that was morally reprehensible and legally more than dubious. Spurs won the game through an own goal by the man generally accepted to be the best defender in England. (In a very real sense, the '91 Cup final affected Walker more than anyone. It may be a coincidence, but he never quite played with the same verve or panache again.) But maybe the worst fate befell Brian Clough. Trying to appear cool, enigmatic and detached, he came across as lost and frightened. He looked that saddest of all things, alone. One of the great characters of recent British life was caught frozen, petrified in the glare of a million pairs of watching eyes.

In the first two years of the new decade, everything began and ended with Gazza. Daft as a brush, talented and charismatic, he couldn't have been more ubiquitous if he'd had an affair with Princess Di. Watching Gazza – it seems to suit him better than Paul – in the pre-game warm-up, you just knew it was going to go off. Pulling mock aggressive faces at the television cameras as the teams walked out on to the pitch, playing in goal . . . it was never going to be just knocking the ball around, a quick chorus of *Abide with Me*, a game of football and a bottle of milk. It was always going to be one thing or another; death or glory.

In his defence, the pressure on him was enormous. What with the financial need for Spurs to get into Europe, a reputed bid from Lazio for £8.5 million, and the fans' expectations after the Arsenal semi-final, he really didn't stand a chance. Remember, this is about a year after his World Cup tears in Turin had catapulted him to stardom. He was a legitimate paparazzi target; no longer just a footballer, not an ordinary person. Gazza was subject to pressures which would have tested the sanity of a mature, balanced adult, and, bless him, he was more fragile than that. Walking out of that tunnel, he was like one of those balsa wood planes with a rubber band attached to the propeller, and it was wound tight. Lineker knew.

'It's a very difficult balance between bringing out the best and the worst in you for someone who's as emotionally charged as Gazza could be. And I think in the semi it brought out the best in him. He was equally hyped before the game, almost manic, but he scored that incredible goal with a free kick after about two minutes. In a way, that released the tension. Whereas in the final, he ran around like a headless chicken, flashing at anything, sticking his studs in. The challenge on Gary Parker's chest was just awful. And then he injured himself. I think in that one he really did go just to whack the ball into the 15 row of the stand, but the guy nicked it first. He was totally connected and ended up doing himself serious damage. The rest is history.'

What must it be like for the other players when they see this thing going on? Gazza doing his catherine wheel near the end of its life routine. God knows what a new kid on the block like Justin Edinburgh or a bread-and-butter journeyman like Steve Sedgley thought. But someone like Lineker, a star, someone who'd achieved all that Gazza aspired to, surely he could have a quiet word in the Geordie ear? Relax him. Tell him about the therapeutic powers of the word 'Om'. Encourage him to watch the breath as it enters and exits his body. Can't you talk to him about this kind of thing?

'Not really, no. I mean you can if you get a quiet moment but there wasn't one. It's also difficult to know that that kind of thing is going to happen. Despite the fact that he was over-hyped, it's incredibly bad luck to get an injury as bad as that. Knowing Gazza as I do, he wouldn't have been going out there to hurt anyone – he just got carried away by the occasion, no more than that. I mean, he's not a vicious bloke, he never has been. He'll respond if he's getting constant grief from a defender and he'll retaliate in a mad moment, but he's not the type of player to go out and hurt people. He doesn't have to be with his kind of ability. I think he just lost it a bit. You do need to be hyped, but sports psychologists will tell you that there's a point where you go over the edge, and I think he did that day.'

How did it affect you?

'I think it gets to the point where you need the big games to bring out the best in you. Despite the things that went wrong, the hardest thing for me was having to play after I'd missed the penalty. That has to have an effect on you mentally. I thought we played very well that day, and there have been many, many occasions where we haven't performed and I've scored a goal. On this occasion it was the other way round because the particular role I had in the game – I was up there primarily as a target man – has not always been my great strength. The fact that I managed to contribute and be the link man, and do reasonably well is perhaps one of the reasons why I picked this game. There are occasions when I've been awful and scored a goal and got the headlines, but on this occasion I suppose I was satisfied, although I knew that I wasn't going to be the one hitting the headlines. It proves that the big thing is winning a big team event. But the Gazza episode brought the whole thing to life, for the wrong reasons maybe, but it did have that effect.'

Tottenham Hotspur 2 (Stewart, Walker og)
Nottingham Forest 1 (Pearce) aet

FA Cup final
6 May 1991

Tottenham Hotspur: Thorstvedt, Edinburgh, Van den Hauwe, Sedgley, Howells, Mabbutt, Stewart, Gascoigne, Samways, Lineker, Allen. (Subs: Nayim for Gascoigne, Walsh for Samways.)
Nottingham Forest: Crossley, Charles, Pearce, Walker, Chettle, Keane, Crosby, Parker, Clough, Glover, Woan. (Subs: Hodge for Woan, Laws for Glover.)
Attendance: 80,000

'I felt good. It was one of those days when I felt good in my game. I mean, you never quite know until you go out,' says Lineker.

'Whenever we played Forest, Clough always put Des Walker on me. He pretty much followed me, man for man. In the end, I used to hang about on the wing just to get Des out of the middle, because he was such a great defender, and let other people do the damage, and it often worked. Then we played them in the League about three weeks before the Cup final and he put Steve Chettle on me. I can honestly say that it's the one time in my career when I haven't had to try very hard. I knew he was experimenting for the final and that he wanted to keep Des in more of a free role. I quite fancied Chettle instead of Walker – no offence to Steve Chettle but Des Walker's one of the best defenders in the world – so I didn't really try an arm and a leg. It was a meaningless end of season mid-table League match anyway.

'Clough fell for it and put Chettle on me for the first half of the final and, to be honest, I had a field day. I scored, even though it was disallowed, and I got the penalty and I was just quite comfortable. It didn't work in that I didn't make the most of that penalty, which was due more to Mark Crossley's fantastic save than anything else. I'd actually practised that hit the whole week. I hit it exactly where I wanted to hit it, but – as Crossley has subsequently proved – he's not bad at saving penalties and not bad at saving them against Spurs in the Cup.' [Note to anyone who spent the 1995–96 season in a dark place, Nottingham Forest knocked Spurs out of the FA Cup. The replay went to penalties and Crossley just happened to fall in front of most of Spurs' noble efforts.] 'But I did have a lot of space and Chettle does lack a bit of pace. It suited Spurs the way I was dragging him in and then moving him out. But Clough must have seen what was happening and in the second half he changed things around so that I was marked by Des Walker. It wasn't so easy after that.'

In the BBC's half-time analysis, the venerable Bob Wilson said that Lineker's was 'the perfect penalty for the keeper to save'. Fair comment?

'It was if you went early and took a chance. But I didn't even place it – I struck it sweet straight in the corner. It might have been the perfect height, but it was a fantastic save – I couldn't believe he saved it because I really hit it well. The next time I played against Crossley I thought about it and chipped it a bit. He actually hit his head on the post when it went in.'

Isn't it best to hit a penalty straight at the keeper? (I said that? I'm sitting here telling Gary Lineker how to take a penalty?)

'Sometimes you come unstuck when you do that because you hit it straight against the keeper's legs. But if you just float it gently, it gives them time to get away. I tried it against Brazil, but mis-kicked completely. There we go. But penalties can be saved. It gave me great relief when Paul Stewart equalised because if your team lose 1–0 and you miss a penalty, it's a bit different from winning 2–1 and missing the penalty.'

Lineker's other moment was his goal. It was a good goal, one of those that looked, to outsiders, like he was just standing there, the ball broke and in it went. The sense of position, the speed of thought and action, and the accuracy of touch . . . there's nothing 'just' about Lineker's instincts here. There was nothing just about the linesman's either. It was a great goal; only it wasn't a goal.

'Yes, it was clearly a goal but not according to the linesman. It was one of those days – you get them three or four times a season – when you just know what you're doing and you feel in control of things. It was a difficult finish, but I felt so in control of myself, almost arrogant in a way. You know you're on top of your game when you feel like that – I just flicked it over the keeper. Look, you generally know when you're offside and I didn't even bother looking at the linesman. Then I suddenly caught sight of the flag in the corner of my eye. It was a bit of a shame, really.'

The green lines of the freshly mowed grass clearly show that our Gary was easily a yard onside when the ball was played. It wasn't even doubtful.

'You know when it's close. If there's someone in your line of vision, you know if you're offside, but it's more difficult for linesmen because they're generally watching the ball and by the time he kicks it and they look up – in that fraction of a second, you make a yard and a half . . . that's the difference. So sometimes you know you've beaten it and you get pulled up.

'For me, it was difficult being the sole striker, but I thought about it and talked to Terry about it. We decided that if you're going to play that role, you've got to stay central to be a link man and come short a lot, because if you go the other way, you're going to isolate yourself totally; it was slightly alien to the way I'd been playing, but it was also challenging. It went well in both the semi-final and the final – that was the way I played. The great thing was that they didn't just hump balls up here because that's not much good with me, and we did play it into feet. I suppose in a way you get a bit of satisfaction out of doing something different.

'In the end it was surprising that it went to extra time. We were well on top and were passing the ball around – we were just a very confident side – as confident as any Wembley side I can remember in a Cup final. I can't remember many decent Cup finals. We played well despite all the pressure, and this game meant quite a lot to Tottenham Hotspur; I thought we controlled it quite well.'

Watching the game, Spurs did look a very confident side. How aware were the players of the financial shenanigans going on in the background? How much did that get through? It's a familiar enough scenario. You work in an office and there's a buzz going round that you're going to be bought out by a different company. It's unsettling. You don't know what's going on, whether the company will keep you going, whether you'll still have a job, you don't know what will happen. It disturbs your mind. It invades your dinner-time conversation. Your spouse gets edgy. It's unsettling, the prospect of Company A buying Spurs, asset-stripping the place and making Gazza, Lineker and the rest of our heroes redundant, one month's notice . . .

'You know it's there, but realistically I don't think players go home thinking about it. I don't think we all thought there's not going to be a Tottenham here next season. You think, well, something's got to happen – and, of course, it did. We did realise that it would make a huge difference if the club won this; they'd be in Europe next year. Obviously, the benefits of winning the Cup are there, but there's huge pressure on you to win the Cup anyway. It just made it all the more important.'

Did the team's tactics change to accommodate the loss of Gazza? Surely, if you lose your pivotal playmaker after 17 minutes, you're going to have to have a major rethink.

'Not really, because Nayim came on and, I mean, he's not in the class of Gascoigne, but it was easy to maintain the same system, which we did. It's been said that losing Gazza meant that there was less reliance on that position and more on everyone else pulling together, and I think that there's an element of truth in that. Something like Gazza going off can either inspire the players or make them think; "Oh, now what do we do?" and an element of fear can creep into the game. On this occasion it seemed to inspire them. But who knows what would have happened if he'd stayed on. Maybe it would have gone the other way with the red card. Thankfully at least we had 11 men.'

As the player most likely to do everything and the team's second most senior player, was there an extra pressure, an extra burden?

'I've always been perfectly well aware that I cannot influence a whole team's performance. I'm a box player really. I mean, I can link up and stuff, but I can't take the ball and do what Gazza can do. It didn't occur to me really – I had to rely on the team anyway.

'There was a lot of pressure; it's not a question of getting blasé about it, but you learn how to handle it. I suppose by that stage in my career I'd done everything, and I was quite confident in my ability, which wasn't always the case earlier. By that time I enjoyed the pressure and expectation. I think maybe you need it to motivate yourself. For example, I couldn't play pre-season friendlies. I used to walk around, and I felt a bit embarrassed by my performances – especially after coming back from the 1990 World Cup. About three weeks later we'd be playing somewhere like Cork in a pre-season friendly which would be sold out . . .'

These people will have been looking forward to that all year; Spurs coming, Gary Lineker coming.

'I know, I know, but I just found it impossible. You need that pressure to do well. You can't just turn it on like a tap – it needs to be big. It helps to motivate yourself.'

There was another side effect of Gazza's moment of madness. Not only did he have to sabotage the Cup final, his career and the future of the club, but he decided to do it just outside the Spurs penalty area. Forest were awarded a free kick smack in the middle of that big red danger zone. Of course, they scored. Naturally, they scored. Spurs swapped Gascoigne for a one-goal deficit. Seems reasonable? Well actually, no, it wasn't reasonable.

I can say this because I'm not Gary Lineker. The Forest goal – and, no, this isn't a partisan comment – was, to these eyes, immoral as well as illegal.

If you don't remember, this is what happened. Gazza was alleged to have fouled Gary Charles and a free kick was awarded to Forest just outside the Spurs penalty area. The Spurs players formed a wall as is traditional in these circumstances and, peskily, Forest striker Lee Glover pretended he was a Spurs player and he too stood in the wall. Just as Stuart Pearce was about to strike the free kick, Glover barged into the Spurs player next to him, knocking him over. Glover too fell over. This created a hole in the Spurs wall through which – by a complete coincidence, I'm sure – Pearce's shot flew. The Spurs keeper had placed himself on one side of the goal, happy in the knowledge that the other side of his goal was secure, protected by the wall.

The shocking thing about the goal was that it was so blatant, so obviously worked out. A coincidence that Pearce's shot just happened to be aimed at exactly the spot where Glover had taken out the Spurs player? Hang on a minute, I'll ask that pig that's flying by . . .

What chance is there of getting Gary Lineker to buy this as an idea?

'Mmmm, it was a foul, wasn't it? You could describe it as that, but it was a ploy often used by teams; dragging someone out of a wall to create a space. Clearly it was a foul and, well, a lot of fouls do happen and don't get spotted. That was one of them.'

But he knocked the ball exactly into the spot where the Spurs boy was standing.

'Yes. He does have a knack of doing that against Spurs. It was a fantastic strike and I'm sure whoever was dragged out of the wall would be pleased now because his head would have been where the ball was. Yes, they got away with it, but it's not the first time.'

So 1–0 to Forest. If there was a just God, it would have been 1–0 to Spurs. How difficult must it be knowing that? Gazza's so knackered he's been taken straight to hospital, they score an iffy goal, you get a perfectly good one disallowed and miss a penalty. Oranges and cups of tea all round, then, at half-time.

'People can get stressed, but we knew we were going pretty well. I remember Terry coming in and being very calm. It was one of those situations when you're playing well and even though we were behind, you don't want half-time to come because it can break your rhythm. But we kept it going, and thankfully got the equaliser. I was probably a bit offside when Paul Stewart kicked the shot, but I certainly wasn't interfering.' After Paul Stewart equalised, the unexpected happened – nothing. Before anyone knew where they were, the 90 minutes were up and we were looking at extra time.

As the players gathered their thoughts and prepared for the next slog, the most bizarre thing happened. Clough just sat there, rooted to his seat. While Venables rabbited away, no doubt tactically rearranging his tactical plan, Clough sat there motionless. God knows what his players thought. Actually, probably everyone knows what his players thought. Just when you started to suspect that he couldn't get up, up he got and went to talk to a young policeman standing nearby. Then he went back to his seat, ignoring his players.

The final card of the 1991 final was dealt to Des Walker. It's late and everyone's tired. They want to go home; well, everyone except the manic Keane. Still Spurs attack. A cross comes over and it's looking at Mabbutt's head. If he gets near it, it's in, no question. Crossley's lost. Then Walker intercepts, just as he's done a million times before, but his header isn't as strong as it should be. It's down. It goes in the net. He scores an own goal, and he looks shot.

'That's one of the only things I wish I could change. Obviously I know Des well; I've played with him lots of times for England and he's a very nice bloke. If it had been Mabbsy that would have been even better but it was a shame for Dessie. I remember at the final whistle there was a moment of euphoria and then I thought, "Well, I'd better go and pat Des on the head and commiserate a bit." You've got to feel for someone in that situation. It was rough on him. Obviously you'd sooner win with an own goal from Des Walker than lose, but it would have been nice another way.'

Game, set and match. Forest weren't going to come back. They'd barely attacked since Pearce's goal and now they were beaten. Spurs had won. The club was saved. Everyone was happy. Meanwhile, at a hospital not a million miles away, the surgeons were operating.

Epilogue

A player like Gary Lineker at a time in his career like that; is he just a gun for hire, a sharp-shooting mercenary? Or does he really buy into it, become a Spurs player? Is there a defining moment, something that happens that turns the footballer into a Spurs player?

'When you play for a club, you do get a feeling for it – we're not totally cynical. I think that happens pretty quickly. I suppose that sounds strange from someone like myself who's played for four or five top clubs. It is weird, but after you've been at that club for a couple of weeks, it feels like you've been part of that club all your life. It means more to you than any other club you've ever played for. My club's always been Leicester and it still is Leicester; but as soon as you get to play for a club, suddenly that means more to you than the club you supported as a boy. That might change when you finish playing, but at the time it's true, it's not bullshit. Amazingly, you become part of it. You immediately get that "anti" feeling against the rivals. At Everton, I was only there a year, but you get into that culture straightaway. The average fan would probably find that hard to believe, that a club can mean as much to the player as it does to the supporter, but I think it does.

'I think of Spurs as one of the stylish clubs. I was coming back from Barcelona and I'd had a few offers from abroad but none of them was quite right. There was Monaco, which was huge money but which would have been like playing Sunday League. I didn't fancy that. Fiorentina and Genoa in Italy were interested and they're lovely places, but they're teams that were always going to be struggling in the Italian league. I think that if you go to Italy, you've got to play with the top teams or you've got no chance as a striker. So I thought, unless someone like Milan came in . . . I nearly went to Inter, but they bought Klinsmann instead – Barcelona wouldn't sell me. I thought unless it was a club like that, I'd be better off, with it being a year before the World Cup, if I was back playing in the centre. I'd been playing on the wing in Barcelona, and I wanted to make sure I was in the team for the Italy World Cup. Also, one of the main reasons I signed for Spurs was because of Chris Waddle, and we had to sell Chris Waddle two weeks after I'd signed, because of money. I'm telling you, I wasn't a happy boy when I found out.'

They must have known when they signed you that they were going to sell him?

'No, they didn't; not according to them. It's something I'll never know. I was very disappointed and depressed for a while.

'I just fancied London, having lived in Barcelona. Also, having broken the news to Michelle that we weren't going to live in Florence, I thought I'd get away with London, but I wasn't sure about anywhere else. I would have gone to Arsenal or Spurs. So I suppose I'm giving it away that I didn't have any strong feelings about one or the other – I'd never supported them. The big advantage with Spurs was that I knew Terry Venables and how he likes his teams to play. And also, there was the fact that Arsenal weren't interested. I don't think that they were interested in breaking the wage structure then.

'I nearly went to Spurs when I was playing for Leicester although I didn't know it at the time. Apparently Spurs offered £900,000 and Leicester stuck out for £1 million, and it was never paid. Leicester, having promised to tell me about bids from any of the bigger clubs, didn't. It came out at the tribunal when they were trying to up the bid from Everton, and they said, "Well, we've received a £900,000 bid before from Spurs," and I was like, "Oh really?" So that was interesting. That was 1985 and Glenn Hoddle was there then. I would've fancied that.'

14

REACH FOR THE SKY

Jürgen Klinsmann

Klinsmann in the flesh was a completely new phenomenon. A footballer who was bright, witty, articulate, intelligent and good looking; blond and slim, too. It was, frankly, baffling to all concerned. It was as if a new animal had been discovered. People just looked, the press gawped as Jürgen, with all the skill of a streetwise card-sharp, performed the most complete of personal makeovers.

'Jeremy, what do you think of that German footballer? That's your team, isn't it?'

When Spurs signed Jürgen Klinsmann, my mother commented on it. My mother, a woman who – no disrespect – wouldn't know one end of a football pitch from the other, commented on Klinsmann signing for Spurs. Quite how this happened is worth a book in itself, but let's have a go.

It's a moot philosophical point, I suppose, whether the person is on the inside or the outside, whether their public image is a true reflection of the self or a facade designed for a specific purpose. Take, for example, Margaret Thatcher. Prior to taking over the chairmanship of what we now know as OffBrit plc, she looked like a hectoring, blue-rinse harridan draped in the dowdy clothes of a provincial schoolteacher. Post-election and after a visit to Tim Bell's poodle parlour, she looked like a hectoring, blue-rinse harridan draped in the smart clothes of a provincial schoolteacher. Still, it fooled everyone for a few years.

While it's true that we all manipulate our own image to suit the persona that we would like to present to the outside world, nothing quite compares to the way that the media does it for others; to help us understand them, obviously. Take the case of Jürgen Klinsmann. Consider, for a moment, the word German, how it isn't in italics, how it isn't in inverted commas, how it isn't distinguished from the words around it at all. Yet it carries with it a connotation that goes far beyond that of simply stating a nationality. Merely seeing the word can inspire the sanest of *Guardian*-reading vegans to a peculiar form of madness. 'The ball did cross the bloody line and anyway, who won the War?'

Jürgen wasn't just German. He was tall, handsome, slim and blond. There was a time in the early 1990s when Jürgen Klinsmann came to symbolise an all-round horridness that curiously transcended football. Where it all came from is easy to see – the 1990 World Cup. England were doing okay, but they were always going to get beaten; and if they were always going to get beaten, they were always going to get beaten by the Germans. England against Germany, the international Spurs against Arsenal. It is a classic confrontation that spiritually dates back to before the dawn of history: good against bad, the inspired against the relentless, the human against the mechanical. So we lost and, natch, Spurs' most inspired human – Chris Waddle – was held responsible. Germany went on to win the tournament and, in a wonderful piece of surreal irony, England walked off with the Fair Play trophy. Peter Cook couldn't have written a better ending. As the trophy was being awarded, it gave the chance for Big Ron Atkinson, in his guise as TV analyst, to come out with his classic: 'Terry Butcher's shaking Jürgen Klinsmann's hand . . . it's a wonder the German hasn't fallen over.'

By the time that the 1994 World Cup came around, football was merely Klinsmann's theatre; he had long left its back-page parochialism and had been elevated to the level of international celebrity. His pre-competition status had been cemented by a televised European Cup match, playing for Monaco against AC Milan. Challenged by Milan's Costacurta, Klinsmann went down with such alacrity that the crowd feared he'd had a coronary. In one of Germany's opening World Cup matches against Spain, he fell so expertly that ITV's Alan Parry was moved to observe that Klinsmann 'went down as if a sniper in row E had caught him'. He became an icon, a *Spitting Image* figure. *The Guardian* printed an article entitled 'Why I Hate Jürgen Klinsmann'. It was a joke, of course, but to have a headline like that (and an article that reflects it) and to be assured that readers will know it's a joke, that relies on a very high level of celebrity.

Meanwhile, at White Hart Lane a whole different story had unfolded. It's a story for another time, another place and another set of lawyers, but briefly, this is what happened. The Spurs manager, Terry Venables, and the Spurs chairman, Alan Sugar, had a bit of a barney. Venables, a former Spurs player and a perceived 'football man' left and Sugar, boss of Amstrad computers and perceived to be a man who'd talk Hoovers with my mother if you questioned him on the merits of the sweeper system, was left as top cat, the leader of the gang. Was Sugar popular at White Hart Lane? No. He was called many things, but popular wasn't one of them. He brought in Ossie Ardiles, another ex-Spur, to replace Venables and this placated the fans, but only marginally; like the difference between being Michael Howard and John Major.

Ardiles, hugely popular as a player but now stigmatised as being 'Sugar's man', knew the best way for a beleaguered Spurs boss to win over the fans. So off he went to the funny-looking, curiously exotic World Cup star shop and bought Romanian Ilie Dumitrescu. 'There,' he thought, 'that'll do for me. Now, let's see. Ilie's knees are going . . . wobbly?' said Ardiles to no one in particular. 'No, not wobbly. Trembly. Yes, trembly. Ilie's knees are going trembly.' He smiled a contented smile and sat back and waited for the 1994–95 season.

The 1994–95 season was, even by Spurs's standards, a drama. If regular life at the Lane was the stuff of soap, the 1994–95 season was a Bafta-winning Christmas special. Again, it's a story for another time and another place. It's the same set of lawyers, but we still can't afford them. Take your mind back to the season before. Think, for a moment, of Terry Venables and Alan Sugar as two heavenly bodies, two stars that were on a collision course, briefly dazzling with their combined light, but doomed from the first. When the inevitable happened, the fall-out was monumental. Everywhere you looked, there were white dwarves.

While Sugar and Venables were busy ensuring that their lawyers' children went to good schools, Sugar let slip the word 'bung' – and the walls came tumbling down. It emerged that a series of alleged financial dealings from the 1980s Scholar era were found to have some alleged irregularities and the powers that be came down on Spurs like a ton of bricks. A court ruling on 14 June 1994 left the club in turmoil – a £600,000 fine, barred from the FA Cup, 12 points deducted before the season had even started.

It got better: on appeal, Sugar got the 12-point penalty halved – albeit at a cost of £150,000 per point. And then it got worse: Ardiles bought a bunch of seemingly sub-standard players. And it got even worse: players started to leave. Then it got better. Dumitrescu. And into the middle of this madness stepped Jürgen the German. It seems that Sugar was at a party in St Tropez and started chatting to a man who just happened to be Klinsmann's lawyer. As you do . . .

Newspaper profiles, articles, stories, hard-bitten media men were lining up to be played like a sunburst Les Paul. *The Guardian* ran an article headlined 'Why I Love Jürgen Klinsmann' (such a witty bunch at *The Guardian*). Slowly the new truth emerged. A man of untold wealth, he drove a Volkswagen Beetle, the original people's car and the ultimate anti-materialistic symbol. He was a Friend of the Earth, he gave to Greenpeace, on Wednesday afternoons after training he saved whales, he was a vegetarian, he was a vegan, he wouldn't even boil a vegetable. In the age of the iffy agent and the bung, Jürgen negotiated his own contracts, he was his own man. And all the time, Jürgen clocked up the PR brownie points. The truth of any of this is, and was, irrelevant, just as it was to his previous media incarnation as Herr Dive Bomber. The net result was that you didn't just want Jürgen in your team, you wanted him in your family. If Tim Bell had done as good a job on Margaret as Jürgen did on Jürgen, she'd have made him a deity.

He came complete with a sense of humour that was swathed in a self-deprecatory charm that just couldn't fail to beguile. Later in the year he was discussing Ossie Ardiles's short reign as Spurs manager. Questioned as to what he thought Ossie did wrong, he said: 'I liked Ossie and his style, it was just that we made individual mistakes. But maybe there was a problem that he changed the back four after every game.' Perfect. He starts off liking Ossie, then volunteers to take his fair share of the blame before sliding the knife in.

Perhaps the thing about Jürgen (we can call him Jürgen now) is that it was real. When I was making my initial approaches to players for this book, different players responded differently. Jürgen replied with a handwritten letter saying that, yes, he'd consider it a privilege to be included. This is a man whose team, Bayern Munich, were just about to play in the final of the UEFA Cup. This is a man who is about to lead Germany into the European Championship. This is a busy man, a man with things on his mind. Yet he still found time to write me a letter. It sounds small, but it's the small things that count.

'That's the measure of the man,' said Steve Perryman when I mentioned it to him. 'He's proper, you know? At Spurs, Klinsmann was fantastic. First class – 100 per cent. The smallest of small little warm-up exercises with a ball, he was absolutely 100 per cent, whereas the normal superstar response would have been, "What are we doing this for?"

'I know a lot of things about Klinsmann behind the scenes, people he befriended. There's a fella who used to help him out, drive him about, and his wife used to answer his mail and things. Klinsmann and his girlfriend used to go round to their flat on a council estate in Edmonton on a Sunday afternoon and sit there on the floor playing with the kids and the dog. That went along with everything we knew about him as a player, and the effort he put into his training. Of course he could have been a bighead if he wanted to. I'm sure if he went on holiday he didn't go to Southend, he went somewhere exotic; but most of the time, in front of you, he was really . . . you wanted him to succeed. Sometimes when people get a lot of fame and success, there is jealousy and you're not too unhappy to see them fall on their face, but this fella, you were desperate for him to succeed. Absolutely proper. He did it right, all the time. Very professional. Wouldn't just smile at you and tell you it was all right if it wasn't. If it was wrong you knew all about it.'

That's Steve Perryman and, in the land of Steve Perryman, 'absolutely proper' and 'very professional' is as good as you get.

In retrospect, the only truly surprising thing about the whole episode was the ease with which Jürgen manipulated the situation. It took four incidents for him to change everything. At his first press conference after signing for Spurs, he asked the assembled lizards if they knew of any diving schools in north London. Fifteen love. In his first few matches for the Spurs, he couldn't stop scoring. Thirty love. Then, in a match he knew was being televised, he celebrated his first goal for the club in a competitive match by running over to the supporters and diving on the ground. Forty love. Lastly, in the post-match, players-in-the-tunnel, talk-us-through-your-goal-then *Match of the Day* interview, the question was asked, and the camera settled back waiting for the obligatory 'Stevie knocked it through to Stevie and the ball came over and I see the keeper off his line . . .' Instead, a curious thing happened. Flanked by adoring team-mates, Jürgen hit the camera with syllables and intonation, with logic and perception. Game, set and season. The boy done great.

Quite why Jürgen the German decided to come to Spurs was

a mystery. Foreigners in the English League weren't unusual, but they were usually polyfilla Scandinavians or thrill-seeking East Europeans. Klinsmann was one of the few true stars of the international game. He could have gone anywhere, chosen any club. From Stuttgart to Inter Milan to AC Monaco via the World Cup to Tottenham seemed an odd choice. What made the great man move from Monte Carlo to N17?

'If you spend two years in Monaco, it's a great life and I enjoyed those two years there but I missed the public, the fans singing during the game. We had an average crowd during the Championship of 5,000 people – it's not a lot of atmosphere. We had a great year, qualified for the European Cup, and the Champions League was always sold out; but these games were exceptions. I needed something to happen. I needed something new. What I needed was full stadiums again.

'I didn't know a lot about the club, to be honest. I knew about the tradition of the club. I said that if I came over to England, I wanted to come to London because London is a cosmopolitan place. It is a city where it would be very interesting to live. I came over and made myself a mental picture of Tottenham Hotspur. I think that was the right way, because, if not, you can have certain expectations and be a little bit disappointed. But I was not disappointed at all. In fact on the contrary, I was impressed by the amount of supporters the club had.

'It was similar to Bayern Munich. Wherever Bayern play, thousands of supporters follow them. I was impressed that the same thing happened at Tottenham. You know, wherever we played, it didn't matter if I was in Newcastle or in Manchester, there were always thousands of Spurs supporters. I didn't know that there were so many. I mean, the first friendly was in Dublin against a Third Division team; the stadium was sold out with 12,000 people and 11,000 were Spurs fans, in Ireland. I said, "But we are not in London." And the players said to me, "Jürgen, you'll see wherever we play, we have our fans there." That was impressive for me because I didn't know it.'

In many ways, Klinsmann and Spurs were made for each other. Just as he was more than a mere footballer, Spurs, as we've seen, are as much a prime-time soap as a football club. Under the unlikely regime of Alan Sugar and 'the dapper little Argentinian', White Hart Lane once again was transformed. And who did they credit?

'From the moment he came, there has been a change in

everything,' said Ardiles. 'From being no-hopers who couldn't sign anybody, we have suddenly become the place to be.' More pertinently, as news of his signing broke, Spurs shares rose 21 per cent.

Paparazzi were everywhere. Interest was immense. There were so many cameras at Spurs' training ground, it was like open house at Di's. And every time the flash went 'snap', there was that blond smile giving it everything; and there the next day was the by now familiar marzipan profile, headlined something like 'This Charming Man'; 1–0 to Germany. It really was that easy.

Just as Jürgen was charming them off the pitch, Ardiles's Spurs were charming them on it. And just as Jürgen was a novel kind of footballer, so Ossie came up with a novel kind of team formation: crap defence, no midfield, all-star attack. It was like watching a display by the Red Devils where all the planes are manned by kamikaze pilots – huge entertainment, but doomed to glorious failure. You watched the exhibition and you were entranced by the audacity of it all, but at the same time you waited for the implosion. If you went to a Spurs game during this period, you'd never leave to go to the loo. By the time you got back to your seat, anything could have happened. Headed by the Famous Five – Sheringham, Anderton, Dumitrescu, Klinsmann and Barmby – Spurs suddenly became the team that everyone wanted to see. As an idea, it was brilliant. As a concept, as a notion, it was a masterstroke. As a practical consideration, it soon became apparent why no one had used the formation before.

In the first game they won 4–3 at Sheffield Wednesday. I remember watching the game on Teletext, laughing at the sheer Tottenhamosity of it all. 1–0, 0–0 . . . leave those scores to the Highbury mob; 4–3 away – that's a Spurs score. It was all a celebration, a carnival.

In the Sheffield Wednesday game, his first goal was like a calling card. The cross came in and Klinsmann moved his body as if to move forward. His marker, the redoubtable Des Walker, obsessively stuck to his man. He too moved forward. But then a curious thing happened. Looking as if he was going forward, Klinsmann actually moved back, thus creating a yard of space between himself and his marker. By the time Walker had realised he'd been duped, the cross had come in and the by now unmarked Klinsmann had knocked the ball into the net. That was the goal. The celebration was even more newsworthy. Followed by his gleeful team-mates, Jürgen ran over to the touchline and flung himself head-first on to the ground. He celebrated his goal by diving. It was a huge mickey-take and very, very funny; Teddy Sheringham's idea, apparently.

In the next match, his first home league game against Everton, he did it again.

'When we did the second dive it was because Teddy's little boy, Charlie, had this wish; if he scored another one, please do the dive again. It was a nice goal to score and it was nice that the whole team came over and we did the dive again, and it was nice that even Ian Walker went 80 yards out of his goal area to do it, too.' More seriously, he scored another two goals. David Lacey in *The Guardian* wrote: 'There is an inevitability about Klinsmann's goals which will depress many a Premiership defence this year.'

But then it all began to go horribly, Tottenhamously wrong. A victory over Ipswich, but that barely counted, and then we lost at home to Southampton. When you start to get beaten by the likes of Southampton, well, questions are going to be asked.

Klinsmann: 'I was also convinced that it would work out with Ossie because the mistakes we made were individual mistakes. I mean, we lost games because of individual mistakes. We conceded goals not because the technique was wrong or because the organisation was wrong, but because somebody kicked over the ball and left it in front of the striker and he kicked it in. Any confidence problems we had were not because it didn't work out, because in some ways it was working and we won some good games but then we lost to Notts County. Yup, that was a bad experience.'

That was the last straw. Spurs were still 'out' of the FA Cup; and the League Cup was the only real hope of glory. To go out of the Cup, that's one thing; to get beaten 3–0 by Notts County . . .

Was it difficult when Ossie got sacked?

'It was difficult because I didn't know what was coming up. I didn't know how it continues, because I knew Ossie and how he treated the players and about his philosophy of football. But once the decision came that he was sacked, there was a moment – an insecure moment. You never know who's coming next, and everyone was worried about who would take over. I'd had a few managers where I realised that we're not getting along perfectly – which is normal because it's impossible that it always fits together. But when Gerry came, after the first few training sessions, I knew it was going to work out because he was similar to Ossie and he treated the players with a lot of respect. There was a good feeling from the first moment.

'The change was that Gerry decided on not playing with five attacking players. He sacrificed Dumitrescu for a second defensive midfielder and it was an important move, especially for the defence, because they were better covered and also because Ilie was not the kind of player who liked to work for the team. If you have that attitude, it doesn't work if you play with five attacking players. Another reason it changed was that Gerry said: "Okay, I have my back four now and they are playing." He gave them a couple of chances in a couple of games and that was important for their self-confidence. Take the case of Colin Calderwood. He needed to have the trust of the manager that he can also make mistakes. Ossie, he changed the back four after each game and got mixed up.'

It must have been a huge personal pressure for Klinsmann; the only one of the three European superstars left, playing in a team that had undergone a radical change in a very short time, living in a goldfish bowl, new manager, new playing system . . . Talk about trembly knees . . .

'What pressure? I don't know – pressure is relative. I think it was difficult for the team to handle the situation because no one knew how it would continue. Were we still banned from the FA Cup? What about the six-point reduction? It was just a strange situation, and we didn't know how it would end. It was not good for the whole environment. But once it was decided – once Sugar got us back in the FA Cup and got us back the six points – it was a real boost. It was a boost for the whole club, for the fans, for the team. You believed a lot more in the club. The whole battle against the FA went on for a long time, and there were so many speculations that no one knew how to look at the situation. Once it was resolved, it helped the club, also Alan Sugar as the president – his own position and business reputation it had an incredible result. You could see that in the faces of the fans.

'That was when I started to learn about the meaning of the FA Cup. In Germany, the German Cup has an importance and a lot of tradition, but that's when I realised that the FA Cup is more important than the European Cup – for the football fans. I mean for the players it's probably equal, but it showed me that it is so important. In Italy for example, the Italian Cup, until you're playing the final game, no one is interested. The final tells you if you're going to Europe or not. But for the rest, they don't care that much.'

For the players, and this is as true for the experienced pros like Sheringham as for the young hot-shots like Barmby and Anderton, having a Jürgen Klinsmann around must have been a blessing. Someone so experienced, so travelled, so world weary. Did they, I wondered, see him as a bit of a father figure?

'No, for sure not as a father figure. Maybe in the very beginning they looked up to me, because they didn't know what kind of person I was. But after a couple of days, after a couple of weeks, I don't think they looked up at me. They thought, "Okay, he's played in a couple of countries, he has a certain experience. What can I learn from this guy?" That's what they tried then. And the attention on me also got them a certain recognition for their daily work.

'Players from Tottenham were called up for the national team. You know, there were suddenly four players from Tottenham in the English side, and this was also a recognition for my work. I said, "That means we're doing a good job," and I was very happy. The best moment for me was, for example, when Colin Calderwood was called for the first time for the Scottish team because he was very insecure at the beginning of the season. I could see month by month he improved, and then for him a dream came true when he got called to play for Scotland. I remember that day, you know. When I came to the training ground and I knew that Colin was playing for Scotland, I was so proud of him. Everyone was so happy for him. That gives you such a great feeling, saying, "Hey, all this work you did these last months, this guy, he's made it now." That makes you happy, when your team-mate makes it. We were very good friends, and that's another reason I was so pleased. I liked him very much and I liked his attitude – he really worked hard, and he's got great charm.'

That's another potential problem for the international superstar, mercenary footballer: making friends. You fly in on your private jet with your Gucci shoes and tax-exile lawyer, your favourite food isn't steak and chips, and maybe the first thing you do with your first pay packet isn't to buy a mock Tudor pile in the country. But somehow, you just know that making friends wouldn't really be a problem for our Jürgen.

'It was easy because they made it easy for me. They accepted me from the first day and you just felt one of them. It made it easier, too, because I already spoke English. When I went down to Italy and I had to learn the language, it takes you half a year or even longer. Dumitrescu had this problem at Spurs. He couldn't communicate with the other players and that makes it tough for you. I could speak to them even if I had some problems with the dialect. I mean, Colin especially was tough for me to understand.'

Klinsmann came and went in the twinkle of an eye. In less than a year he made an impact that most players couldn't achieve in two lifetimes. One minute he was a hated German, the next he was charming and urbane, the very next, after being voted the Footballer of the Year and having the seemingly inevitable row with Alan Sugar, he was gone. And he was the one who lasted. Ardiles and his sidekick, Steve Perryman, had gone to Japan, land of the rising pay packet. Ilie Dumitrescu had gone to the reserves, to Seville and, finally, to West Ham. Gica Popescu, the third member of Spurs' jet-set contingent, had gone to Barcelona. Nick Barmby went too, to Middlesbrough via a career-threatening haircut. By the time the next season started, with Anderton out injured, only Sugar and Sheringham remained. It was a bizarre irony that it was these two who were left. Sugar, the non-football pragmatist, and Sheringham, whose iffy transfer to Spurs from Nottingham Forest had first given the high court the nod about Spurs' finances.

Even by Spurs' extraordinary standards, it had been an extraordinary season. Asking Jürgen Klinsmann to pick one match seems a touch churlish.

Liverpool 1 (Fowler)
Tottenham Hotspur 2 (Sheringham, Klinsmann)

FA Cup quarter-final
11 March 1995

Liverpool: James, Jones, Scales, Ruddock, Babb, McManaman, Redknapp, Barnes, Walters, Rush, Fowler.
Tottenham Hotspur: Walker, Austin, Edinburgh, Howells, Calderwood, Mabbutt, Anderton, Barmby, Rosenthal, Sheringham, Klinsmann.
Attendance: 39,592

It had to be the FA Cup really. A tournament that Spurs weren't even in when Klinsmann first signed. Football fans, even the odd sane one, are a curious lot. People who'd go out of their way to walk under a ladder will say, with complete seriousness, 'Well, you see, it's the Mongolian year of the cat and there's a nine in the year. Orient will win the Cup. Their name's written on it.' It's a perverse logic that my mother, a woman who spends her life throwing salt over her right shoulder, would throw out of the window (unless it was a full moon, of course). The FA Cup: Spurs were banned from it, then they were back in it. Their year, obviously.

'There are a couple of games that stand out, particularly the FA Cup quarter-final in Liverpool when I scored in the last minute. In the Championship we'd played in Liverpool before, but in the League, it doesn't matter if you win or you lose. It is important, but there's always another game the next week. In the Cup we knew that if we won or lost there would be a cut-off. Spurs had never won an FA Cup match in Liverpool before and it made it very special towards the end, very special for the fans.'

As a situation, it was a classic double-edged sword. Spurs can stay in the FA Cup, but first they must go to Anfield and survive . . .

How did the atmosphere at Anfield compare to somewhere like the San Siro?

'It's difficult to say. I mean, the San Siro is a beautiful stadium, too, and the atmosphere there is great. I think that Anfield has its special past because of the history of Anfield Road and the reputation of Liverpool as a club team in Europe, especially in the 1970s. But the atmosphere in the stadium, when people stood up and gave us a standing ovation and we were the away team – for me, that was a very special situation because I never experienced anything like that before; the fair play of the Liverpool fans saying, "Okay, they were the better team" or "They won that game, so we give them our compliments." And the fact that we won . . . I mean, the atmosphere in the locker room was almost like we'd won the FA Cup.'

It was, said Liverpool manager Roy Evans, 'a cracking game of football'. Robbie Fowler put Liverpool ahead after a jinking run by Mark Walters had left the Spurs defence behind. Rather than timidly folding into pretty shapes, the new Spurs, inspired by David Howells, fought back. Under Ardiles, Howells, a perfectly solid English kind of defensive midfielder, had been left languishing in the reserves. A defensive midfielder was not very glam, not very 'beautiful game'. Who needs a defensive midfielder when you've got 15 superstar attackers?

When Gerry Francis took over, Howells returned; a classic, unsung but essential hero. On the stroke of half-time, Klinsmann got the ball, had a look around and planted it into the path of Sheringham, who swung a perfect side-footed shot into the far corner; a superb, curling strike.

The second half was tighter, both sides predictably frightened of errors. Then, with two minutes left, Sheringham returned the compliment. He flicked the ball in to Klinsmann, who finished less spectacularly than Sheringham, but no less clinically: 2–1, game over.

'The way the season started, with the six points deducted and we were not in the FA Cup and then suddenly we were back in the FA Cup, and we found ourselves in the quarter-final against Liverpool at Anfield Road. So we tried to make this dream of getting to Wembley come true. In the end it didn't work out but these moments in Liverpool I won't forget, for sure.'

Epilogue

Were you surprised by the initial hostility of the British media?

'I wouldn't say surprised. When you come from another country you have to learn about the country, you have to learn about their media situation, and I knew that in every country it is different. I had no expectations. That's what I did when I went to Italy and to France, and I learnt then to adapt myself.'

And what about the diving stories? Were you aware of any of that before you came to England?

'No, I wasn't aware of that at all. I just saw myself in a situation and really didn't know what to do. I thought, "What's going on here?" And the German media took it over too, you know; "What are they going to do with our player?" I was just lucky that I had a few people who taught me about the English media and how they try to test you. I had a friend who had lived in London for five or six years and he said, "You only have one chance – you have to make a joke out of it. You have to put another joke on the top of the joke they make with you." So I made this joke about the diving school at my presentation at the press conference and that kind of calmed the situation down. Doing the dive was Teddy's idea before the game at Sheffield. Before the first game, he came over and said, "Hey, you score the goal, I'll do the dive." I said, "That's a funny idea," but I was thinking, "I hope he scores one" because you don't know before the game if you will get the opportunity. It just worked out perfectly. And I think that turned around a lot of things regarding the fans, the people, also the supporters from the other team. They looked at you in a totally different way then and they saw that you could handle the irony of the English media.'

Is the media very different here to, say, Germany?

'Yes, I would say it's a few steps higher than in Germany and you have the competition between the papers. If you take London, you've got eight or nine tabloids, and in Germany you have in certain cities, maybe three or four tabloids and then one tabloid over the whole country. And so the situation is different and is a lot more extreme than in Germany. I had to learn that too. I mean, there were photographers following me during the first six to eight weeks; when I went to the bakery, when I went to the grocery store. I mean, I saw them, it was not that they were so good at hiding that you could not see them. I have no problem seeing 30 yards ahead, it's not so far. They were standing there and shooting at you and you think, "What are they shooting? What kind of rolls you buy?" They were going into shops and getting information on what I was buying, what I was doing. I just said to one owner of a shop, when they next come in, tell them that if they want to save a lot of money in the next year, they can stop doing that shit because I'm a professional and I know exactly what I should and shouldn't do. That's when they stopped. They got my message and, suddenly, from the next day on, they were gone. It was also a good lesson for me.'

As a parting shot, I told Klinsmann what Steve Perryman had said about him working with the locals.

'I think it's different for a foreign player compared to a player who lives or grows up in a country. When I went to Italy and in France, I tried to get in touch with the people, so I can learn their mentality and about their lifestyle. You can't expect them to get in touch with you; you can't go into a new country and say, "Well I'm a well-known soccer player and people will have to come over to me and talk to me." Maybe this is the problem with a lot of players going into a foreign country; that they expect the people to get in touch with them, and then after some months they realise that it's not working out. You have to show the people that you want to work in their place; you are a guest there.'

CAREER HISTORIES

RON HENRY

Year	League		FA Cup		League Cup		Europe		Total	
	App	Gls	App	Gls	App	Gls	App	Gls	App	Gls
54–55	1								1	
55–56	1								1	
56–57	11									
57–58	15								15	
58–59	8								8	
59–60	25		4						29	
60–61	42		7						49	
61–62	41		7				8		56	
62–63	42	1					7		50	
63–64	29						2		31	
64–65	41	1	4						45	1
65–66	1								1	
Total	247	1	23				17		287	1

Other Matches: 1962 – FA Charity Shield v England X1 (3–2)
1963 – FA Charity Shield v Ipswich (5–1)

Where they are now?

Runs a garden nursery specialising in potted plants. Still coaches the kids at Spurs.

DAVE MACKAY

Year	League		FA Cup		League Cup		Europe		Total	
	App	Gls	App	Gls	App	Gls	App	Gls	App	Gls
58–59	4								4	
59–60	38	11	3						41	11
60–61	37	4	7	2					44	6
61–62	26	8	7				7	2	40	10
62–63	37	6	1				6	2	44	8
63–64	17	3					2	1	19	4
64–65						NO APPEARANCES				
65–66	41	6	2	2					43	8
66–67	39	3	8						47	3
67–68	29	1	5				2		36	3
Total	268	42	33	4			17	5	318	51

Other matches: 1962 – FA Charity Shield v England X1 (3–2)
1963 – FA Charity Shield v Ipswich (5–1)
1968 – FA Charity Shield v Manchester United (3–3)

Where they are now?

Coach of the under-17 national team in Qatar.

CLIFF JONES

Year	League		FA Cup		League Cup		Europe		Total	
	App	Gls	App	Gls	App	Gls	App	Gls	App	Gls
57–58	10	1							10	1
58–59	22	5	4	2					26	7
59–60	38	20	4	5					42	25
60–61	29	15	6	4					35	19
61–62	38	16	7	4			8	4	53	24
62–63	37	20	1				6	2	44	22
63–64	39	14	2				2		43	14
64–65	39	13	4						43	13
65–66	9	8	2						11	8
66–67	20	6	5						25	6
67–68	30	12	4	1			3	1	37	14
68–69	7	5			2	1			9	6
Total	318	135	39	16	2	1	19	7	378	159

Other matches: 1962 – FA Charity Shield v England XI (3–2)
1963 – FA Charity Shield v Ipswich (5–1)

Where they are now?

Teaches part-time in Islington, north London. Relaxes with his family and his two dogs.

RALPH COATES

Year	League		FA Cup		League Cup		Europe		Total	
	App	Gls	App	Gls	App	Gls	App	Gls	App	Gls
71–72	32	2	4		5		9	2	50	4
72–73	32	2	3		7	1	7	3	49	3
73–74	36	3			1		10	4	47	1
74–75	30	1	2		1				33	6
75–76	24	2	2		6				32	7
76–77	31	3	1		2				34	1
77–78	3								3	1
Total	188	13	12		22	1	26	9	248	23

Other matches: 1972 – Anglo-Italian League Cup (2 apps)

Where they are now?

After finishing with professional football, joined Barnet Council as their sports co-ordinator. In 1987, joined GEC as their sports facilities manager. 'It's not just football, though we have four football teams. The first team has won the championship this year which is very pleasing.'

STEVE PERRYMAN

Year	League		FA Cup		League Cup		Europe		Total	
	App	Gls	App	Gls	App	Gls	App	Gls	App	Gls
69–70	23	1	4						27	1
70–71	42	3	5		6	1			53	4
71–72	39	1	5		6	1	12	3	62	5
72–73	41	2	3		10	1	10		64	3
73–74	39	1	1		1		12		53	1
74–75	42	6	2		1				45	6
75–76	40	6	2	1	6				48	7
76–77	42	1	1		2				45	1
77–78	42	1	2		2				46	1
78–79	42	1	7	1	2				51	2
79–80	40	1	6		2				48	1
80–81	42	2	9		6				57	2
81–82	42	1	7		8		8		65	1
82–83	33	1	3		2		3		41	1
83–84	41	1	4		3		11		59	1
84–85	42	1	3		5		8		58	1
85–86	23	1	5		4				32	1
Total	655	31	69	2	66	3	64	3	854	39

Other matches: 1970 – Texaco Cup (3 apps)
1972 – Anglo Italian Cup (2 apps)
1981 – FA Charity Shield v Aston Villa 2–2
1982 – FA Charity Shield v Liverpool 0–1
1986 – Screen Sport Super Cup (5 apps)

Where they are now?

Assistant manager to Ossie Ardiles at Shimitzu-S-Pulse in Japan.

JOHN DUNCAN

Year	League		FA Cup		League Cup		Europe		Total	
	App	Gls	App	Gls	App	Gls	App	Gls	App	Gls
74–75	28	12	2						30	12
75–76	37	20	2	1	7	4			46	25
76–77	9	4	1						10	4
77–78	27	16	2	1	1	3			30	20
78–79	2	1			2				4	1
Total	103	53	7	2	10	7			120	62

Where they are now?

Manager of Chesterfield FC.

PAT JENNINGS

Year	League		FA Cup		League Cup		Europe		Total	
	App	Gls	App	Gls	App	Gls	App	Gls	App	Gls
64–65	23								23	
65–66	22		3						25	
66–67	41		8		1				50	
67–68	42		5				4		51	
68–69	42		4		6				52	
69–70	41		4		1				46	
70–71	40		5		6				51	
71–72	41		5		7		12		65	
72–73	40		3		10		10		63	
73–74	36		1				10		47	
74–75	41		2		1				44	
75–76	40		2		6				48	
76–77	23		1		1				25	
Total	449		43		39		36		590	

Other matches: 1967 – FA Charity Shield v Manchester United 3–3 (Jennings scored direct from goalkick)
1970 – Texaco Cup
1972 – Anglo-Italian League Cup Winners Cup
1986 – Screen Sport Super Cup

Where they are now?

Coaches at Spurs, does a bit of 'entertaining' and PR at Spurs, plays golf with Keith Burkinshaw.

GARTH CROOKS

Year	League		FA Cup		League Cup		Europe		Total	
	App	Gls	App	Gls	App	Gls	App	Gls	App	Gls
80–81	40	16	9	4	6	2			55	22
81–82	27	13	7	3	7		5	2	46	18
82–83	26	8	2	1	4	3	4	3	36	15
83–84	10	1			1		1	1	12	2
84–85	22	10	3	1	2	4	6	3	33	18
Total	125	48	21	9	20	9	16	9	182	75

Other matches: 1982 – FA Charity Shield v Liverpool 0–1

Where they are now?

Broadcaster. Co-presents Greater London Radio's sports show. Hosts 'Black London', a chat show. Involved in BBC TV sports coverage.

'I've recently been offered a post at a football club which I find quite extraordinary. I never ever thought I'd be asked to join someone else's football club. It's as a coach, I suppose. Maybe it would lead to being manager. I'm not going to do it. It's attractive – or at least it's very attractive to my ego, but it's not what I really want to do.'

GLENN HODDLE

Year	League		FA Cup		League Cup		Europe		Total	
	App	Gls	App	Gls	App	Gls	App	Gls	App	Gls
75–76	7	1							7	1
76–77	39	4	1		2	1			42	5
77–78	41	12	2	1	2				45	13
78–79	35	7	5	1	2	1			42	9
79–80	41	19	6	2	2	1			49	22
80–81	38	12	9	2	6	1			53	15
81–82	34	10	7	3	8	1	8	1	57	15
82–83	24	1	1		3		1		29	1
83–84	24	4	3		3	1	6		36	5
84–85	28	8	3		3		6		40	8
85–86	31	7	5	1	5				41	8
86–87	35	3	6	1	8	4			49	8
Total	377	88	48	11	44	10	21	1	490	110

Other matches: 1981 – FA Charity Shield v Aston Villa 2–2
1982 – FA Charity Shield v Liverpool 0–1
1986 – Screen Sport Super Cup (2 apps)

Where they are now?

Manager of the England team.

GARY MABBUTT

Year	League		FA Cup		League Cup		Europe		Total	
	App	Gls	App	Gls	App	Gls	App	Gls	App	Gls
82–83	38	10	3		5		4	1	50	11
83–84	21	2	2		2		9	2	34	4
84–85	25	2	2		4		4		35	2
85–86	32	3	5		5	1			42	4
86–87	37	1	6	3	8				51	4
87–88	37	2	2		3				42	2
88–89	38	1	1		5				44	1
89–90	36		1		7	1			44	1
90–91	35	2	6	1	6				47	3
91–92	40	2	2		6		8	1	56	3
92–93	29	2	5		2				36	2
93–94	29				3				32	
94–95	36		6	1	2				44	1
95–96	32		6		3				41	
Total	465	27	47	5	61	2	25	4	598	38

Other matches: 1982 – FA Charity Shield v Liverpool 0–1
1986 – Screen Sport Super Cup (6 apps)
1991 – FA Charity Shield v the Arsenal 0–0

Where they are now?

Fighting the good fight.

GARY LINEKER

Year	League		FA Cup		League Cup		Europe		Total	
	App	Gls	App	Gls	App	Gls	App	Gls	App	Gls
89–90	38	24	1		6	2			45	26
90–91	32	15	6	3	5	1			43	19
91–92	35	28	2		5	5	8	2	50	35
Total	105	67	9	3	16	8	8	2	138	80

Other matches: 1991 – FA Charity Shield v the Arsenal 0–0

Where they are now?

Everywhere you look.

JÜRGEN KLINSMANN

Year	League		FA Cup		League Cup		Europe		Total	
	App	Gls	App	Gls	App	Gls	App	Gls	App	Gls
94–95	41	20	6	5	3	4			50	29
Total	41	20	6	5	3	4			50	29

Where they are now?

Playing for Bayern Munich (or Chelsea or back at Spurs or considering the player/manager job at the Orient, depending on which paper you read). Captain of the German national team, winners of Euro '96.